LIBRARY OF HEBREW BIBLE/ OLD TESTAMENT STUDIES

429

Formerly Journal for the Study of the Old Testament Supplement Series

(PER)MUTATIONS OF QOHELET

Reading the Body in the Book

Jennifer L. Koosed

t&t clark

NEW YORK • LONDON

T & T Clark International, 80 Maiden Lane, New York, NY 10038

T & T Clark International, The Tower Building, 11 York Road, London SE1 7NX

T & T Clark International is a Continuum imprint.

Library of Congress Cataloging-in-Publication Data
Koosed, Jennifer L.
(Per)mutations of Qohelet: Reading the Body in the Book / Jennifer L. Koosed.
   p. cm. — (Library of Hebrew Bible/Old Testament Studies, 429)
   Includes bibliographical references (p.) and index.
   ISBN 0-567-02632-9 (hardcover)
   1. Bible. O.T. Ecclesiastes--Criticism, interpretation, etc. 2. Body,
Human—Religious aspects. 3. Identity (Psychology) I. Title.
II. Series.
BS1475.52.K66 2006
223'.806—dc22
                                         2005026039

Printed in the United States of America

06 07 08 09 10   10 9 8 7 6 5 4 3 2 1

CONTENTS

ACKNOWLEDGMENTS

This book is a revision of my doctoral dissertation, completed at Vanderbilt University. I would first like to thank my dissertation committee, and especially my first reader, Renita J. Weems. The other members were Douglas A. Knight, Jack Sasson, Amy-Jill Levine, and Idit Dobbs-Weinstein. Thank you all for your time, insight, and critique. The students at both the Divinity School and the Graduate Department of Religion generate an atmosphere of camaraderie, intellectual stimulation, and emotional support. I could not ask for a better group of colleagues. I am especially grateful to Darla Schumm, Alice Hunt, Herb Marbury, Teresa Hornsby, Deborah Appler, Emily Askew, Steve Cook, and Chris Dungan. Joel Beaupré, who joined us from the philosophy department, also deserves a heartfelt thank you.

I would also like to extend a special thanks to Melissa Stewart, my long-suffering partner in writing. One winter, we devised a plan that came to be called the "Dissertation Tour USA." During the summer of 2001, we put all of our belongings in storage and loaded up my red sports-like car with laptops, books, and camping gear. Four months and fifteen states later, I had the 100-page skeleton of my dissertation, which then became this book. Financially solvent, home-owning friends sponsored us, and I would like to thank each one: Ellen Roberds and Jarad Bingham (Divinity School alumni), Jennifer Hensel and Jeremy Richmond, Susie and David Long, and Tim and Becky Eberhart (also Divinity School alumni).

The process of transforming my dissertation into the book it is today could not have been accomplished without the exacting reading of Robert Paul Seesengood. Thank you for all the conversations and for seeing possibilities in my work that I had not seen. The comments and encouragement from series editor Claudia Camp have also been essential to the final form of this project. Thank you for making this publication of my first book seem so effortless by being such a wonderful editor. Thanks also to the people who worked with me on the final preparation of the page proofs: Henry Carrigan (Continuum) and Duncan Burns (Forthcoming Publications).

Finally, I dedicate this book to the three women who taught me to read: my mother, Sharyn Koosed-Boyce; my high school English teacher, Mary Sawan; and Amy-Jill Levine, who introduced me biblical studies when I was nineteen and searching for a new major.

ABBREVIATIONS

BDB	Francis Brown, S.R. Driver, and Charles A. Briggs. *A Hebrew and English Lexicon of the Old Testament*. Oxford: Clarendon, 1907
BHS	*Biblia hebraica stuttgartensia*
Bib	*Biblica*
CBQ	*Catholic Biblical Quarterly*
ETL	*Ephemerides theologicae lovanieneses*
ExpTim	*Expository Times*
HAR	*Hebrew Annual Review*
HS	*Hebrew Studies*
HUCA	*Hebrew Union College Annual*
ICC	International Critical Commentary
ITC	International Theological Commentary
ITQ	*Irish Theological Quarterly*
JBL	*Journal of Biblical Literature*
JBR	*Journal of Bible and Religion*
JQR	*Jewish Quarterly Review*
JPSV	Jewish Publication Society Version
JSOT	*Journal for the Study of the Old Testament*
JSOTSup	*Journal for the Study of the Old Testament*, Supplement Series
JSPSup	*Journal for the Study of the Pseudepigrapha*, Supplement Series
JTS	*Journal of Theological Studies*
LXX	Septuagint
MT	Masoretic text
NIV	New International Version
NRSV	New Revised Standard Version
OTL	Old Testament Library
RSV	Revised Standard Version
StudBib	*Studia Biblica*
TZ	*Theologische Zeitschrift*
VTSup	*Vetus Testamentum*, Supplements Series
WBC	Word Biblical Commentary
ZAW	*Zeitschrift für die alttestamentliche Wissenschaft*

Chapter 1

INTRODUCING QOHELET

CRITIC: A. *Scribere* (Latin): to scratch, to write, to incise, to scribble, to circumscribe, to inscribe, to prescribe, to proscribe, to describe, script, scribe, scripture, manuscript, scriptorium. B. *(Dis)crimen* (Latin): judgment, crime, recrimination, distinction, discrimination. C. *Sker* and variant *kar* (Indo-European), caro (Latin): flesh, carnal, carnage, carnival, charnel, incarnate, carrion.[1]

Who is Qohelet?

Because the book of Qohelet is a knot of contradictions, this question has proven to be both troubling and irresistible to readers. Although it is a part of the Hebrew Bible's Wisdom corpus, it is ambivalent even about this core theme: "And I gave my heart to know wisdom and to know madness and folly. And I knew that also this is chasing after wind" (1:17);[2] and yet "I saw that there is more advantage in wisdom than in folly as there is more advantage in light than in darkness" (2:13). Consider whether one should pursue pleasure rather than wisdom: "Behold this which I saw to be good: it is beautiful to eat and to drink and to see goodness in all of one's toil which one toils under the sun . . ." (5:17 [Eng 5:18]); or perhaps pleasure is ultimately absurd too: "I said in my heart, 'Come now, I will make a test of pleasure and see good.' But behold, also this is *hebel*" (2:1). And consider further what may be the most disturbing contradiction in a work of sacred scripture: "Fear God and keep his commandments; for this is all of humanity. For all deeds God will bring into judgment including every concealed thing, whether good or evil" (12:13–14); and, "To all the same fate comes, to the righteous and to the wicked, to the good, and to the clean and to the unclean, to those who sacrifice and to those who do not sacrifice; as are the good, so are the sinners; those who swear are as those who fear an oath" (9:2). Is there no justice? What is a reader to do?

These contradictions have worried commentators since the beginnings of Qohelet interpretation. The first recorded conversation about this difficult book centered on its inconsistencies: "R. Judah b. R. Samuel B. Shilath said in Rav's name: The sages sought to withdraw the book of Qohelet because its words are mutually contradictory. Why then did they not withdraw it? Because it begins

---

1.   The Indo-European root word of "critic" and some of its variants, culled from a list assembled by Vincent Leitch, *Deconstructive Criticism: An Advanced Introduction* (New York: Columbia University Press, 1983), 265.

2.   All biblical quotations are my own translations unless otherwise noted.

with words of Torah and it ends with words of Torah."[3] What worried the rabbis has continued to worry modern scholars, thereby prompting James Crenshaw to declare that the essential issue in the study of Qohelet in the twentieth century has been the question of integrity.[4] How does one explain the contradictions in the text—multiple authors, a pious redactor, or disputation dialogue?

The history of research regarding the contradictions and therefore the authorship of the text has been guided largely by historical-critical questions with some forays into literary-critical methods. All of these theories of authorship relate directly to the commentator's assumptions concerning the consistency of identity. However, beginning with the linguistic theories of Saussure, translated into psychoanalysis by Lacan, and furthered in philosophy and literary criticism by Barthes and Derrida, the stability of language and identity has been undermined. Postmodern theories have revised both our notions of the self and of the text. Both can be incoherent, fragmented, lacking a stable center, contingent. This describes the text of Qohelet, and insofar as the text creates a speaker, the identity of the speaker as well.[5]

But neither texts nor identities are disembodied. Both are material objects. Language is an organ of the body, and this physicality manifests itself in writing. The body is embedded in the text through the naming of body parts (eye, hand, heart). And this same body is encoded in form, structure, and syntax, so that the text becomes a body with organs, systems, and even a life of its own.[6] I propose to ask the following questions of Qohelet: What is the relationship between texts and bodies? And how do both relate to questions of identity? In other words, I will examine the body in the text, the body of the text, and how these relate to the body of the reader. This book argues that the language of the body is not incidental to meaning, and that the body manifests itself on both the level of content and the level of form. The physical body and the textual body are intertwined, and reading the body in the book opens up new meanings in and interpretations of the book of Qohelet.

Who is Qohelet? This is Qohelet. We pick up Qohelet's body every time we pick up the text, we read the body, turn its pages, touch its body with our own. The tendency in scholarship has been to see through the text to the author(s) behind it. But the text is not a transparency; rather, it is a body—it has weight,

3.   *B. Shab.* 30b, as quoted in Michael V. Fox, *A Time to Tear Down and a Time to Build Up: A Rereading of Ecclesiastes* (Grand Rapids: Eerdmans, 1999), 1. It is difficult to date rabbinic literature precisely. The Mishnah was compiled in approximately 200 CE. See also M. J. Broyde, "Defilement of the Hands, Canonization of the Bible, and the Special Status of Esther, Ecclesiastes, and Song of Songs," *Judaism* 44 (1995): 66–78.

4.   James Crenshaw, "Qoheleth in Current Research," *HAR* 7 (1984): 41–56.

5.   Although there has never been a sustained postmodern reading of Qohelet, this aspect of the book has been noted by Roland Murphy and Elizabeth Huwiler, *Proverbs, Ecclesiastes, Song of Songs* (Peabody, Mass.: Hendrickson, 1999); Choon-Leong Seow, *Ecclesiastes* (AB 18C; New York: Doubleday, 1997); Fox, *Qohelet and His Contradictions* (JSOTSup 71; Sheffield: Almond Press, 1989); and idem, *A Time to Tear Down*.

6.   Martin J. Gliserman, *Psychoanalysis, Language, and the Body of the Text* (Gainesville: University Press of Florida, 1996).

substance, skin. It lives and moves through history and time, multiplying, proliferating, living on apart from the body that birthed it. The book is a body, and the book speaks of bodies. It speaks of the body's organs and senses; it concerns itself with the pleasures and pains of the body. In the book of Qohelet, a picture of the speaker is formed through the language of selfhood and autobiography ("I" language), and also through the construction of Qohelet's body. There is no voice without this body in and of the text. Who is Qohelet? This is Qohelet—the body of the book and the body in the book.

The Body in the Book

The biblical books are full of bodies. God creates a variety of bodies in the first few chapters—astronomical, zoological, botanical, geological, and anthropological (Gen 1–3). Although the human bodies in creation's drama take center stage, other bodies play key roles too. Animals and plants actually get the story rolling when the snake initiates a conversation with the woman about a piece of fruit (Gen 3:1–7). The interaction between these three—and then four when the man joins in—inaugurates a perpetual discord between human, animal, vegetable, and mineral bodies (the soil which is fated to resist the toil of the man). They all then leave Eden to embark on various adventures, conflicts, and couplings.

The biblical books are full of bodies; yet, viewing the Bible through the lens of "body" is an emerging mode of inquiry in biblical studies. Biblical scholars are not immune to the attractions of sex and violence. Consequently, the biblical bodies that have garnered the most attention have been the sexy bodies in the Song of Songs,[7] the bloody body of Jesus hanging on the cross,[8] and the variously violated bodies in the book of Revelation.[9] Paul's ideological, theological, and ethical struggles with the human body have also drawn scholars into analysis and interpretation.[10] Stephen Moore's most recent contribution to the

---

7. For two recent examples, see Fiona C. Black, "What is My Beloved? On Erotic Reading and the Song of Songs," in *The Labour of Reading: Desire, Alienation, and Biblical Interpretation* (ed. Fiona C. Black, Roland Boer, and Erin Runions; Atlanta: Society of Biblical Literature, 1999), 35–52, and Carey Ellen Walsh, *Exquisite Desire: Religion, the Erotic, and the Song of Songs* (Minneapolis: Fortress, 2000).

8. E.g. Stephen D. Moore, *God's Gym: Divine Male Bodies of the Bible* (New York: Routledge, 1996). Moore's book also addresses the (in)corporeality of God in the Hebrew Bible, rabbinic literature, and Jewish mystical texts. Other writings on the subject of the body of God include Howard Eilberg-Schwartz, *The Savage in Judaism: An Anthropology of Israelite Religion and Ancient Judaism* (Bloomington: Indiana University Press, 1990); idem, "The Problem of the Body for the People of the Book," in *People of the Body: Jews and Judaism from an Embodied Perspective* (ed. Howard Eilberg-Schwartz; Albany: State University of New York Press, 1992), 17–46; and idem, *God's Phallus and Other Problems for Men and Monotheism* (Boston: Beacon, 1994); David Biale, *Eros and the Jews: From Biblical Israel to Contemporary America* (Berkeley: University of California Press, 1997); and Daniel Boyarin, *Carnal Israel: Reading Sex in Talmudic Culture* (Berkeley: University of California Press, 1993).

9. E.g. Tina Pippin, *Apocalyptic Bodies: The Biblical End of the World in Text and Image* (New York: Routledge, 1999).

10. E.g. Dale B. Martin, *The Corinthian Body* (New Haven: Yale University Press, 1999).

field has a chapter on each of these bodies—Song of Songs, Jesus, Paul, and Revelation.[11] Compared to such titillating topics, the body of and in Qohelet fades to invisibility.

Although readers have largely neglected Qohelet's body, readers have felt a strong sense of individual personality in the book. Almost every commentary on Qohelet articulates the character of the speaker and links this speaker to the author. Michael Fox argues that Qohelet focuses on the "organizing conscious-ness of the sage" so that his personality is a prominent feature of the text.[12] Martin Hengel notes the "marked 'individuality' of authorship" in Qohelet.[13] Shannon Burkes states that "Although the word 'Qoheleth' is a pseudonym, his personality is fully present. . . ."[14] E. S. Christianson bases a portion of his nar-rative argument on the reader's experience of "sensing a self"[15] when reading Qohelet. M. Sneed calls Qohelet a "filthy rich intellectual" and assesses his words accordingly.[16] William Brown characterizes Qohelet as one who "shares his personal discoveries and bares his soul."[17]

Whether or not a text accurately represents the personality of its author, without a certain literary artistry a reader would never feel strongly about that personality.[18] Therefore, I begin my inquiry into Qohelet with the following question: How do words create a personality so vivid that the history of scholar-ship has been dominated by a conflation of this personality with the author(s) of the text, and this author(s) passionately pursued?

Elaine Scarry opens *Dreaming by the Book* with a similar question: How is it possible that verbal art produces images so vivid that they "acquire the vivacity of perceptual objects"?[19] Verbal art, she notes,

> is almost bereft of any sensuous content. Its visual features, as has often been observed, consist of monotonous small black marks on a white page. It has *no* acoustical features. Its tactile features are limited to the weight of its pages, their smooth surfaces, and their exquisitely thin edges. The attributes it has that are directly apprehensible by perception are, then, meager in number.[20]

---

11. Stephen D. Moore, *God's Beauty Parlor: And Other Queer Spaces in and around the Bible* (Stanford, Calif.: Stanford University Press, 2001).

12. Fox, *Qohelet and His Contradictions*, 159.

13. Martin Hengel, *Judaism and Hellenism: Studies in their Encounter in Palestine during the Early Hellenistic Period* (Philadelphia: Fortress, 1981), 116.

14. Shannon Burkes, *Death in Qoheleth and Egyptian Biographies of the Late Period* (Atlanta: Society of Biblical Literature, 1999), 112.

15. Eric S. Christianson, *A Time to Tell: Narrative Strategies in Ecclesiastes* (JSOTSup 280; Sheffield: Sheffield Academic Press, 1998), 177.

16. M. Sneed, "The Social Location of the Book of Qoheleth," *HS* 39 (1998): 41–51.

17. William Brown, *Ecclesiastes* (Interpretation; Louisville, Ky.: John Knox, 2000), 121.

18. Older texts which highlight Qohelet's personality include J. Paterson, "The Intimate Journal of an Old-Time Humanist," *RL* 19, no. 2 (1950): 245–54; and Elizabeth Stone, "Old Man Koheleth," *JBR* 10 (1942): 98–102.

19. Elaine Scarry, *Dreaming by the Book* (Princeton: Princeton University Press, 1999), 5.

20. Ibid.

And yet, these words produce images so vivid that they can be compared to the perceptions evoked by paintings, sculptures, and other forms of visual art. Through a close analysis of how novels and poems cause us to make and move pictures in our heads, Scarry explores how worlds are created by texts. She rightly claims and then demonstrates that "Reading entails an immense labor of imaginative construction."[21]

Though Scarry meticulously documents how readers are compelled to create images of wind-swept heaths, the flight of spears during the Trojan War, or Levin skating across a glacine pond, she never addresses the question of how the reader comes up with Catherine and Healthcliff, Achilles and Hector, or Levin and Kitty, in the first place.[22] How do words construct people—in both body and soul, their physicality and their personality? How is it possible for a reader to have such a clear picture of Qohelet? The identification with Qohelet that many scholars feel is so intense that Gerhard von Rad cites this identification as one of the most dangerous pitfalls for scholars seeking the meaning of the biblical book.[23] For von Rad, scholarly neutrality and objectivity are necessary and these are woefully lacking in studies of Qohelet. Identification with the speaker in the text slides almost imperceptibly into pronouncements about the author behind the text, and this then becomes the primary though unacknowledged rubric through which scholars make their source-critical decisions. We feel with Qohelet the pain of toil and the joy of pleasure. We hear when Qohelet speaks, and we hear when a different voice intrudes. We know Qohelet.

The bulk of Qohelet scholarship has been committed to uncovering the author(s), and the literature is replete with unexamined assumptions about how authors relate to their texts. Meanwhile, the study of other biblical books has shifted away from such projects through attention to developments in literary criticism and critical theory.[24] In literary criticism, the twentieth century has been characterized by the displacement of the author as the interpretive key to the text.

New Criticism, which emerged in the 1920s and 1930s, sought to remove literary criticism from the "extraneous" concerns of sources, author's background, politics, social history, and especially the author's intentions in his or her work. Rather, the focus became close readings of texts with the historical questions

21. Ibid., 37.
22. Scarry does mention this phenomenon in her book *The Body in Pain: The Making and Unmaking of the World* (New York: Oxford University Press, 1985), 305: "What is . . . peculiar about the charge of 'pathetic fallacy' is that it is only invoked by a literary commentator if the artist has made a tree speak, but is not invoked in the more extreme and (for an artist) habitual act of making a nonexistent presence (Catherine, Tess, Anna) speak, and speak with such complexity and palpable sentience."
23. Gerhard von Rad, *Wisdom in Israel* (Nashville: Abingdon, 1972), 232. I will return to von Rad's position in Chapter 7.
24. In biblical studies, the break with historical criticism came with James Muilenberg's address to the Society of Biblical Literature in 1968, subsequently published as "Form Criticism and Beyond," *JBL* 88 (1969): 1–18. His students, Phyllis Trible in particular, further defined rhetorical criticism, which then became the basis for all literary-critical inquiries into the Hebrew Bible.

bracketed out of the interpretation. The intention of the author has no more authority over the meaning of the text than any other person's ideas about what the text means.[25]

Further displacement (even death and dismemberment) of the author came from post-structuralist theorists. Roland Barthes, a prominent French post-structuralist, wrote an influential article entitled "The Death of the Author." Although writing after New Criticism's shuttling of the author, Barthes finds the idea of the author so pervasive that this figure still holds sway over interpretation:

> The image of literature to be found in ordinary culture is tyrannically centred on the author, his person, his life, his tastes, his passions. . . . The *explanation* of a work is always sought in the man or woman who produced it, as if it were always in the end, through the more or less transparent allegory of the fiction, the voice of a single person, the *author* "confiding" in us.[26]

The idea of an author limits interpretation. It makes the author the final word and closes the text. A text is not, however, the production of a single creative mind. Rather, "a text is made of multiple writings, drawn from many cultures and entering into mutual relations of dialogue, parody, contestation. . . ."[27] Writing is always quotation, intertext.[28] All of these fragments come together not in the author, but in the reader: "The reader is the space on which all the quotations that make up a writing are inscribed without any of them being lost; a text's unity lies not in its origin but in its destination."[29]

According to Barthes, both the text and the reader are nexuses in the mesh of language. Neither one is a single entity, coherent, contained. By focusing on the interaction of and interconnection between texts and readers, he highlights the physicality of language and its effects on the reader's body. For Barthes, the body can be as difficult to grasp as the self(s) it contains and the language it speaks, writes, and reads. As Barthes says in his autobiography, "Which body? I have several."[30]

Body Definition

In pursuit of my query about how the book of Qohelet creates such a strong sense of the speaker that this speaker has been conflated with an author, theories that examine the connections between language and the body will be employed.

---

25.   See Vincent B. Leitch, *American Literary Criticism from the 30s to the 80s* (New York: Columbia University Press, 1988), 24–59, for a history of the movement.

26.   Roland Barthes, "The Death of the Author," in his *Image–Music–Text* (trans. Stephen Heath; New York: Hill & Wang, 1977), 142–48 (143). The article was originally published as "La mort de l'auteur," *Mantéia* V (1968).

27.   Ibid., 148.

28.   Barthes is one of the primary theorists of "intertextuality." For a history of the development of this idea and its use in literary theory, see Graham Allen, *Intertextuality* (New York: Routledge, 2000). For its uses in biblical studies, see Danna Nolan Fewell, ed., *Reading Between Texts: Intertextuality and the Hebrew Bible* (Louisville, Ky.: John Knox, 1992).

29.   Barthes, "The Death of the Author," 148.

30.   Barthes, *Roland Barthes by Roland Barthes* (New York: Hill & Wang, 1977), 60–61.

Even though the body has become a site of study in various fields of knowledge, the conceptualization of the body tends to fall into one of two mutually exclusive categories: biologism and sociologism. Donn Welton explains these terms at the beginning of his edited volume *Body and Flesh*:

> Biologism thinks of the bio-physical composition and causal chains of the body as sufficient to explain everything that we might attribute to conscious life. Sociologism takes the body as consisting of bio-physical materials that either are then shaped into units of behavior that correlate to variables (first variation), or are organized by acts of interpretation that employ socially stable, semantic oppositions that reflect the socio-political codes of a given society, which are then internalized by its members through processes of symbolic interaction (second variation).[31]

However, as Welton goes on to point out, both biologism and sociologism treat the body as an object and hence share a core objectivism. Postmodern body philosophy can be characterized as an approach to the body that challenges "the underlying assumption of objectivism."[32] Postmodern body philosophy seeks to deconstruct the binary opposition of biologism/sociologism, also known as essentialism/constructivism.

Even at the simple level of definition, the body confounds easy classification. Writing on religion and the body, Sarah Coakley underlines this problem:

> The notable explosion of thought and literature on the subject of the "body" in the last decades has begged a question of definition which is not so easily grasped, let alone answered. It is as if we are clear about an agreed cultural obsession—the "body"—but far from assured about its referent. . . . But why, then, are "bodies" simultaneously so ubiquitous and yet so hard to get our "hands" around?[33]

Sarah Coakley is not the only one who has noticed this difficulty. Welton concludes the introduction to his edited volume with the following statement: "it [human embodiment], the most obvious of things, is one of the most perplexing."[34] And Judith Butler confesses at the opening of *Bodies that Matter*:

> I began writing this book by trying to consider the materiality of the body only to find that the thought of materiality invariably moved me into other domains. I tried to discipline myself to stay on the subject, but found that I could not fix bodies as simple objects of thought. Not only did bodies tend to indicate a world beyond themselves, but this movement beyond their own boundaries, a movement of boundary itself, appeared to be quite central to what bodies "are." I kept losing track of the subject. I proved resistant to discipline. Inevitably, I began to consider that perhaps this resistance to fixing the subject was essential to the matter at hand.[35]

The body is caught between a quite obvious materiality and a complex of historical, theological, philosophical, sociological, psychological, biological,

---

31. Donn Welton, ed., *Body and Flesh: A Philosophical Reader* (Malden, Mass.: Blackwell, 1998), 2.

32. Ibid.

33. Sarah Coakley, ed., *Religion and the Body* (New York: Cambridge University Press, 1997), 2–3.

34. Welton, *Body and Flesh*, 8.

35. Judith Butler, *Bodies that Matter: On the Discursive Limits of "Sex"* (New York: Routledge, 1993), ix.

and various other cultural discourses. Therefore, it proves impossible simply to think "the body."

Judith Butler's work on the body emerges out of these tensions between discourse and materiality. Her book *Bodies that Matter* begins by outlining the arguments for and against constructivism (or, to use her term, "linguistical monism," i.e. everything is language). The standard constructivist argument, notes Butler, produces both the refutation and the confirmation of its own enterprise. Constructivists always have to concede something physical, material.[36] There is a body with certain features, reproductive organs, hormones, etc. On the other hand, essentialists always have to concede something constructed.[37] After all, there has to be some imported marking in order to differentiate what will be included and excluded from the definition of "sex" and "gender," for example. Both terms contain the other within.[38]

This observation allows Butler to open up body theories and even the body itself to deconstruction.[39] The very terms (or referents) "materiality" and "language" do not signify apart from one another:

> The materiality of language, indeed, of the very sign that attempts to denote "materiality," suggests that it is not the case that everything, including materiality, is always already language. On the contrary, the materiality of the signifier (a "materiality" that comprises both signs and their significatory efficacy) implies that there can be no reference to a pure materiality except via materiality. Hence, it is not that one cannot get outside of language in order to grasp materiality in and of itself; rather, every effort to refer to materiality takes place through a signifying process which, in its phenomenality, is always already material. In this sense, then, language and materiality are not opposed, for language both is and refers to that which is material, and what is material never fully escapes from the process by which it is signified.[40]

At the same time, materiality and language cannot be simply reduced to one another:

> Language and materiality are fully embedded in each other, chiasmic in their interdependency, but never fully collapsed into one another, i.e., reduced to one another, and yet neither fully ever exceeds the other. Always already implicated in each other, always already exceeding one another, language and materiality are never fully identical nor fully different.[41]

In this way, postmodern body philosophy concerns itself with the materiality of both the body and language in conjunction with the power of discourse and linguistic constructivism.

In her next book, *Excitable Speech*, Butler looks at another phenomenon that brings language and body together: hate speech. In order to answer the questions

---

36. Ibid., 10.

37. Ibid., 11.

38. See also Diana Fuss, *Essentially Speaking: Feminism, Nature, and Difference* (New York: Routledge, 1989).

39. Butler, *Bodies that Matter*, 8. Welton also cites the "crucial transformation effected by Jacques Derrida and deconstruction" in body theory. Welton, *Body and Flesh*, 4.

40. Butler, *Bodies that Matter*, 68.

41. Ibid., 69.

of how and why words wound and what should be done legislatively about it, Butler employs the language theories of Shoshana Feldman among others.[42] Although the specific problem of Butler's book is not a focus for the present study, the power of words to wound and the emergence of Qohelet as a "palpable sentience" rely on the same principles: both straddle the simultaneous "incongruity" and "inseparability"[43] of speech and body. Feldman in particular "reminds us that the relation between speech and the body is a scandalous one, 'a relation consisting at once of incongruity and of inseparability. . . .' "[44]

Language can wound us because we are "in some sense, linguistic beings, beings who require language in order to be."[45] Language and the body are not only inseparable because our bodies are linguistically constituted, but also because the body is the instrument of language. Language is materially constituted.

The body is the instrument of language, but the speaking body is neither in full control of its speech, nor is the speaking body reducible to its speech.

> Feldman thus suggests that the speech act, as the act of a speaking body, is always to some extent unknowing about what it performs, that it always says something that it does not intend, and that it is not the emblem of mastery or control that it sometimes purports to be. She calls attention to the way in which a speaking body signifies in ways that are not reducible to what such a body "says". . . . The speech act says more, or says differently, than it means to say.[46]

Butler continues with a description of the historicity of language. This historicity extends into the past and into the future. Any word is dependent upon its history of meaning and can recall all of its other acts and contexts, and it only endures through the possibility of its future repetition.[47] For these reasons, a word can never be completely mastered by the individual that speaks at any given time. But rather than this signaling a split between language and body, the act, which is "an enigmatic and problematic production of the *speaking body*, destroys from its inception the metaphysical dichotomy between the domain of the 'mental' and the domain of the 'physical,' breaks down the opposition between body and spirit, between matter and language."[48] Philosophy and the flesh "remain incongruously interrelated."[49]

---

42. Butler's philosophical foundation for *Excitable Speech* is far ranging and includes Nietzsche, Louis Althusser, Pierre Bourdieu, Toni Morrison, Paul de Mann, J. L. Austin, and Jacques Derrida.

43. Judith Butler, *Excitable Speech: A Politics of the Performative* (New York: Routledge, 1997), 10. Butler is citing Shoshana Feldman, *The Literary Speech Act: Don Juan with J. L. Austin, or Seduction in Two Languages* (trans. Catherine Porter; Ithaca, N.Y.: Cornell University Press, 1983), 96.

44. Ibid.

45. Ibid., 1–2.

46. Ibid., 10.

47. Ibid., 20.

48. Ibid., 11.

49. Ibid.

In *Excitable Speech*, Butler concentrates upon the spoken word, but her proposals have application to the written word as well. Butler states that the word, the thing, and the act cannot be easily unraveled,[50] which suggests that a book is not simply a transparent conduit between author and reader. The book itself is a thing that acts through the reading process.

The question raised earlier in reference to Elaine Scarry's work on the power of words to effect sense-perceptions is answered in another way by Judith Butler.[51] The reason words can create characters is the same reason words can wound. We are vulnerable to language[52] because we are linguistically consti-tuted. Therefore, language can create people in texts who effect us just like certain words can hurt us. Language is produced, spoken, heard, written, read by our bodies, and it is a physical phenomenon itself. Qohelet is the written effect of its author(s) that exceeds any and all intentions of its author(s) not only because of the historicity of all language but particularly because of the historic-ity of texts. To read Qohelet is to enter into relationship with (and become vul-nerable to) both Qohelet's thought and Qohelet's body—and both are embedded in the book, both are the book.

Although there has been a shift in recent years in the reading of the contra-dictions of the text, none of these scholars can resist the lure of historical criticism. Carol Newsom points out that it is "striking that scholarly work on Ecclesiastes has remained, with very few exceptions, the province of traditional historical criticism."[53] Newsom suggests that fixing authorship and structure is an attempt to control the meaning of this disconcerting biblical book. My book challenges the very way we read and assign meaning, the very way we think of integrity and unity of meaning. The real question is what is at stake in the schol-arly controversies about integrity.

In addition to the fact that historical criticism still dominates Qohelet scholar-ship, there has also never been a sustained focus on the body in the book. Even studies such as Antoon Schoors's on repeated words fail to discuss the repeated body words.[54] Schoors does discuss the verbs related to seeing but immediately

---

50   Butler's connecting word, thing, and act is reminiscent of the multiple meanings of the Hebrew word *dābār*, which can signify "word," "thing," and "event." And is, perhaps, a testimony to her own Hebrew school training.

51.   By placing Elaine Scarry and Judith Butler together I am not suggesting that either their projects or their methods are the same. I do, however, believe that both fit within the parameters of my project. I will explicate my reasoning at the end of this first chapter.

52.   Ibid., 26.

53.   Carol Newsom, "Job and Ecclesiastes," in *Old Testament Interpretation: Past, Present, and Future* (ed. James Luther Mays, David L. Petersen, and Kent Harold Richards; Nashville: Abingdon, 1995), 177–94 (184). See also I. J. J. Spangenberg, "A Century of Wrestling with Qohelet: The Research History of the Book Illustrated with a Discussion of Qoh 4,17–5,6," in *Qohelet in the Context of Wisdom* (ed. Antoon Schoors; Leuven: Leuven University Press, 1998), 61–92; and Craig Bartholomew, *Reading Ecclesiastes: Old Testament Exegesis and Hermeneutical Theory* (Rome: Editrice Pontificio Istituto Biblico, 1998), 173–205, for their review of the postmodern methods in Qohelet scholarship.

54.   Antoon Schoors, "Words Typical of Qohelet," in Schoors, ed., *Qohelet in the Context of Wisdom*, 17–39.

moves from physicality to abstract notions of understanding. And, though he notes that "heart" (*lēb*) is one of the most repeated words in Qohelet, he does not offer any interpretation of this, only that it is a word for further study. Historical criticism regards the text as a diaphanous web of disembodied words through which one can peer at the author or the author's time period. An examination of the body of the text and in the text reveals a different Qohelet—a Qohelet in one's hands, physically present in the book and as the book.

Summary of Order

The second chapter of this book examines the language of autobiography in Qohelet (the persistent first-person singular pronoun) and the genre designations that have emerged from this marker. Despite the fact that Qohelet was written long before modern notions of authorship emerged, such notions can still shape understandings of Qohelet. As the sampling of scholarly work above amply demonstrates, when Qohelet is read, the author is heard, confiding in us. But names, authors, and autobiographies are not as transparent as is generally assumed. Examining contemporary literary theories of autobiography, which have been shaped by the ideas of identity promulgated by Lacan, as well as the ideas of language disseminated by Derrida, I deconstruct such scholarship. The "author" read in Qohelet is only an effect of the text and its interactions with the reader. It is not its origin or final cause.

The book of Qohelet forms a picture of the speaker not only through language of selfhood and autobiography, but also through the construction of Qohelet's body. The third chapter will begin the probing of the body of the speaker by looking at the two body parts that are repeatedly named in the book: the heart and the eye. The word *lēb* is used in the MT of Qohelet 40 times. In fact, "heart" appears more frequently than *hebel*, the word that exemplifies one of the primary themes of the book. Second in frequency are words related to the eye and seeing. These sections will address the semantic range of the words in Qohelet as well as explore the syntactical function of the words in the text. The naming of body parts constructs a body through the text, and embeds the body in the text. The body parts, then, act as points of reference for the reader, connecting body to body.

This focus on the body continues through an examination of the pain and the pleasure experienced throughout the body of Qohelet. Commentators from Talmudic rabbis to contemporary critics have wrestled with the contradictions in the text. Chapter 4 argues that the vacillation between pleasures (injunctions to eat and drink, the pursuit of the comforts of the flesh in Qoh 2) and pain (toil, labor, despair) produces desire. Qohelet, much like the Song of Songs, creates desire in the reader through ambiguity of meaning and interpretation.

The fifth chapter will look at how the gendered body is made manifest in Qohelet. This will entail a focus on Qoh 7, specifically 7:26, "And I found more bitter than death the woman. She is a snare and her heart is nets, her hands are fetters." There will also be reference to how the female body is represented in the discourses on pleasure in other parts of the book (9:9). Despite the obvious misogyny in this verse, the gendered body in Qohelet is neither coherent nor stable.

Chapter 6 will examine the decay and death of the body. The structure of Qohelet has always been a problem for interpreters. Many have proposed solutions, but each proposal must suppress some aspect of the text in order to make a fit. Rather than proposing another idea for the structure, this chapter argues that the structure is in a state of decay, which enacts the decaying of the aging and dying body. Death in Qohelet entails two themes: the loss of memory and the flattening of differences. At the level of the physical body, no one is remembered after death, and there is no differentiation made in death between the wise and the foolish, or even between the human and the animal. Death comes for all. Qohelet then enacts this inevitable decay of the body through a decay of the text. The physical body and the body of the book are intertwined. At the level of the textual body, meaning requires both repeatability and differentiation (Derrida's concept of "iterability"), two things extinguished by death. Therefore, Qohelet's meditation on death examined in both content and form becomes an exploration of the limits of signification.

The last chapter will address the epilogue in Qoh 12. This is the part of Qohelet most likely to be attributed to another hand. There is a change in the speaking voice and an espousal of traditional piety which contradicts the general tenor of the book. However, neither of these features is absent from the rest of the text. There are shifts in the speaking voice throughout, and general piety (even the phrase 'fear of God') is interwoven throughout the book. If the end of Qoh 12 is to be removed on these accounts, the entire book unravels. The history of interpretation of this section will again be relevant to the analysis. The argument is not that one author or many wrote the book we now have—for these are historical-critical questions. Rather, the argument advanced is that the commentators' assumptions about coherent identities and unified texts shape their interpretations. Even in this chapter, a focus on the body is helpful. The emphasis is on the keeping of the commandments (12:13). This is an espousal of ritual or right action rather than right theology.

Postmodern theory, feminist theory, and deconstruction inform my reading of Qohelet. Each of these approaches is distinct; each has its own history of development, and its own questions and concerns. However, they do intersect and interact. Postmodernism, feminism, and deconstruction have been in conversation and in conflict. And it is not only their points of intersection that serve this study, but also the tensions among these approaches, for the tensions foster creative engagement and open up the "dynamic . . . possibilities of risk and relationships."[55]

---

55.   David Jobling, Tina Pippin, and Ronald Schleifer, eds., *The Postmodern Bible Reader* (Malden, Mass.: Blackwell, 2001), ix. Jobling, Pippin, and Schleifer are referring to their own project of reading the Bible together with various "postmodern" theories.

A caveat: all three of these terms—"postmodernism," "feminism," and "deconstruction"—defy easy definition because all three challenge the very idea of easy definition. And all three encompass a broad range of philosophies, approaches, theorists, and disciplines. However, I will attempt a few words of definition for each of the theories that inform my reading.

Hans Bertens opens his history of postmodernism with the conundrum of the term: "Postmodernism is an exasperating term, and so are postmodern, postmodernist, postmodernity, and whatever else one might come across in the way of derivation. . . . Postmodernism, then, is several things at once."[56] And although the term was coined by Jean-François Lyotard in his book *The Postmodern Condition* (first published in 1979 and translated into English in 1984), the ideas that coalesced around the term had older and deeper roots.[57] However, for my purposes, Lyotard's definition is a sufficient starting point: "Simplifying to the extreme, I define *postmodern* as incredulity towards metanarratives."[58] Although Lyotard is critical towards all "grand narratives of legitimation," he is leveling a critique particularly against the foundational principles of the Enlightenment as expressed throughout the history of modernity. Postmodernity calls into question the idea that there are transcendent and universal truths which can and do serve as the foundational principles of Western intellectual and cultural traditions. Rather, as Nancy Fraser and Linda J. Nicholson point out, "in the postmodern era legitimation becomes plural, local, and immanent. In this era, there will necessarily be many discourses of legitimation dispersed among the plurality of first-order discursive practices."[59] Postmodernity, then, becomes a critical stance that decries totalities of any kind and espouses multiplicity, particularity, fragmentation, and difference.

"Feminism" too entails a critique of metanarratives and it began its critique of certain sources of legitimation long before the coining of the term "postmodern." Specifically, feminism is a critique of male domination and all aspects of civilization that serve to support such domination. It insists on the centrality of gender analysis in every context. Consequently, its political commitments are the source of its philosophical critique, not vice versa as it is with postmodernism.[60] Despite the different directions of the approach, both feminism and postmodernism share a suspicion of claims to objectivity, reason, and universality.

In the analysis of Fraser and Nicholson, feminism and postmodernism are two "political-cultural currents"[61] that can correct each other's weaknesses. The danger of postmodernism is its tendency to relativism and its potential to

56. Hans Bertens, *The Idea of the Postmodern: A History* (New York: Routledge, 1995), 3.

57. Bertens's *The Idea of the Postmodern* does not discuss Lyotard's work until p. 122.

58. Jean François Lyotard, *The Postmodern Condition: A Report on Knowledge* (Minneapolis: University of Minnesota Press, 1984), xxiv.

59. Nancy Fraser and Linda J. Nicholson, "Social Criticism without Philosophy: An Encounter between Feminism and Postmodernism," in *Feminism/Postmodernism* (ed. Linda J. Nicholson; New York: Routledge, 1990), 19–38 (23).

60. Ibid., 19–20.

61. Ibid., 19.

undermine powerful political tools through its philosophical critiques. Feminism, however, is prone to the creation of other metanarratives in its critique of androcentric ones, and therefore is vulnerable to a universalizing of its own. Combining the two results in a postmodern-feminist theory that

> would tailor its methods and categories to the specific task at hand, using multiple categories when appropriate and forswearing the metaphysical comfort of a single feminist method or feminist epistemology. In short, this theory would look more like a tapestry composed of threads of many different hues than one woven in a single color.[62]

"Deconstruction" is associated with but not identical to postmodernism. Whereas postmodernism can be descriptive of an almost infinite variety of practices and viewpoints, deconstruction is "primarily a complex, close exegesis of texts."[63] To deconstruct is not a destructive act violently perpetrated on an unarmed text. Although popular use of the term emphasizes the "destruction" executed when ideas, texts, and ideologies are relentlessly critiqued, deconstruction has a more precise definition:

> Deconstruction involves analyzing the operations of difference in texts, the ways in which meanings are made to work. The method consists of two related steps: the reversal and displacement of binary oppositions. This double process reveals the interdependence of seemingly dichotomous terms and their meaning relative to a particular history. It shows them to be not natural but constructed oppositions, constructed for particular purposes in particular contexts.[64]

Within (de)construction is both destruction and construction, and these two activities are held in tension.

The theorists I include in my book do not speak with one voice, nor do they all fit comfortably within the three approaches I explicate above. Elaine Scarry, for example, is a literary critic who avoids such labeling. Yet, she is included in the recent *Postmodern Bible Reader*, and I include her here in my work. The editors justify their decision by noting that her interpretations, especially of biblical texts, examine "the implications of certain binary oppositions—between verbal and material, visible and invisible, creation and deconstruction, justice and injustice."[65] It is precisely her concern with the verbal and the material that draws her into my project as well. Scarry, Foucault, Butler, Barthes, Derrida are not threads of a single color. Rather, they help me create a "tapestry composed of threads of many different hues."[66]

---

62. Ibid., 35.

63. David W. Odell-Scott, "Deconstruction," in *Handbook of Postmodern Biblical Interpretation* (ed. A. K. M. Adam; St. Louis: Chalice, 2000), 55–61 (56).

64. Joan W. Scott, "Deconstructing Equality–Versus–Difference: Or, the Uses of Poststructuralist Theory for Feminism," in *Conflicts in Feminism* (ed. Marianne Hirsch and Evelyn Fox Keller; New York: Routledge, 1990), 134–48 (137). For another concise definition, see also John D. Caputo, *Deconstruction in a Nutshell: A Conversation with Jacques Derrida* (New York: Fordham University Press, 1997), 31–36.

65. Jobling, Pippin, and Schleifer, *The Postmodern Bible Reader*, 274.

66. Fraser and Nicholson, "Social Criticism without Philosophy," 35.

At the close of her study on Hosea—a study which reads Hos 1–3 through semiotics, deconstruction, feminist theory, and finally through feminist deconstruction, Yvonne Sherwood writes that by using these "new-er" criticisms she has

> been able to bring to the center of analysis observations that have long been repressed in margins and footnotes. The text's disjunctive style and its capacity to subvert itself are no longer seen as negative features outside the critical language but as features that can be accounted for within the critical language. Difficulties in the text are no longer seen negatively, but creatively, and tensions can be interpreted not as the frustration of meaning but as a way of suggesting different meanings.[67]

If the reader can cease to regard tensions as problems that need to be solved, contradictions as differences that need to elided, then a general sensitivity to and respect for complexity will be cultivated. Although Sherwood does not state this explicitly, such an approach to texts can have consequences in the world outside of the text, particularly if the interrelationship between text and reader and world is already a part of the interpretive framework. In terms of the present study, the interrelationship is highlighted through the focus on the body.

This type of reading is significant for religious texts because religious texts powerfully influence the ways we regard one another and the ways we treat one another. "Disjunctive styles" are not quandaries for meaning. They do not necessitate the imposition of theories of coherence, theories that serve to obliterate the disjunction. Rather, disjunction and difference are the very moments that promote creativity and the proliferation of meaning in our texts, in our selves, and in our world.

Who is Qohelet? The question will always continue to be answered in a myriad of ways. Any one theory excludes the others, and these others clamor at the edges, destabilizing the coherency of the promulgated theory. Who is Qohelet? Every time we try to define Qohelet, Qohelet changes before our very eyes. What follows is one more deviation, aberration, alteration, modification, variation, innovation, transformation, transmogrification, transubstantiation, transmutation, permutation, mutation. . . . Keep your eye on the body, if you can.

---

67.   Yvonne Sherwood, *The Prostitute and the Prophet: Hosea's Marriage in Literary-Theoretical Perspective* (JSOTSup 212; Sheffield: Sheffield Academic Press, 1996), 328.

Chapter 2

CALLING QOHELET NAMES*

And what if one were to compile all the names that one has ever been called?
Would they not present a quandary for identity?

—*Judith Butler*[1]

The genre designation of "fictional autobiography" for the book of Qohelet is
not new. It has been recommended by Tremper Longman, Leo Perdue, Choon-
Leong Seow, William Brown, and E. S. Christianson, most recently.[2] However,
since Qohelet scholarship is deeply embedded within historical criticism, the task
of the interpreter has remained to remove the fictional dross in order to uncover
the pure autobiography below. Commentators quickly move to determine the
historical "I" and then read accordingly. I propose to read Qohelet as a fictional
autobiography but not in a manner that (ab)uses the text to get to the author
behind it. By naming Qohelet a "fictional autobiography" this chapter serves
both to highlight the uneasy relationship between fact and fiction in any text,
and to open up Qohelet to analysis through literary theories on the relationship
between identity and language, selves and texts. Employing Jacques Derrida's

* A version of this chapter was originally presented at the Southeastern Regional Meeting of
the Society of Biblical Literature in Atlanta, Georgia, March 2002.

1. Butler, *Excitable Speech*, 30.

2. Tremper Longman III, *The Book of Ecclesiastes* (Grand Rapids: Eerdmans, 1998), 15–20.
See also his *Fictional Akkadian Autobiography: A Generic and Comparative Study* (Winona Lake,
Ind.: Eisenbrauns, 1991), 120–23 (Longman finds Qohelet most similar to the Cuthaean Legend of
Naram-Sin); Leo G. Perdue, *Wisdom and Creation: The Theology of Wisdom Literature* (Nashville:
Abingdon, 1994), 194–202 (Perdue concludes that Qohelet closely resembles grave biographies and
royal testaments); Choon-Leong Seow, "Qohelet's Autobiography," in *Fortunate the Eyes that See*
(Fs. D. N. Freedman; ed. A. Beck et al.; Grand Rapids: Eerdmans, 1995), 257–82 (Seow believes
that Qohelet's strongest parallels are West Semitic and Akkadian royal inscriptions); Brown,
Ecclesiastes, 7–8 (Brown demurs that he is not as confident of the designation as Longman but
agrees that there is preponderance of autobiographical material in the book, while in his *Character
in Crisis: A Fresh Approach to the Wisdom Literature of the Old Testament* [Grand Rapids: Eerdmans, 1996], 5, Brown calls Qohelet "a series of confessions," and thus underlines the autobiographical nature of the book according to his analysis); Christianson, *A Time to Tell*, 33–42, 128–72
(whereas most commentators label the Solomonic guise as the fictional element in the autobiography
and limit this guise to the first two chapters, Christianson argues that the Solomonic guise continues
throughout the book through various allusions to kingship).

analysis of the proper name and the law of genre, as well as literary-critical theories of autobiography, this chapter will examine the language of selfhood in Qohelet. Its "I" is elusive, its genre unstable, its name not quite proper.

What's in a Name?

Qohelet tells us who he is.[3] The opening lines of the book of identify the speaker of the text: *dibrê qōheleṭ ben-dāwid melek bîrûšālāyim* ("The words of Qohelet, son of David, king in Jerusalem," Qoh 1:1). And later in the chapter, the speaker himself declares *ʾănî qōheleṭ hāyîtî melek ʿal-yiśrāʾēl bîrûšālāyim* ("I, Qohelet, have been king over Israel in Jerusalem," 1:12). But I do not believe him.

What kind of name is Qohelet? The word obstinately refuses to yield its meaning.[4] Hebrew is a consonantal language, which builds up its words on the foundations of trilateral roots. "Qohelet" is a form of the verbal root *qhl* meaning, in *nipʿal*, "to be gathered together, congregate"; and in *hipʿil*, "to convoke an assembly." With the notable exception of the lexicon by Brown, Driver, and Briggs (BDB), most commentators identify the form here as a feminine *qal* participle, which is otherwise unattested in the Hebrew Bible. BDB, though admitting feminine form of the word (*tāw*-ending), names it a masculine noun,[5] presumably based upon the masculinity of the speaker in the book of Qohelet. The speaker's masculinity is determined by his identification as "son" and "king" in v. 1. BDB further suggests the translation "great collector (of sentences)" based upon an Arabic construction in which feminine endings are used to intensify meaning, thus "realizing the idea in its completeness."[6]

Even the ancient sources are uncertain of the meaning of this name, and in their translations there is interpretation. In the LXX, the word for "Qohelet" is *Ekklesiastēs* (from *ekklēsia*) meaning broadly a member of a citizens' assembly, and therefore could be translated "citizen."[7] The readers of the Gospel of Matthew forged a more narrow meaning for *ekklēsia*—"church." Gregory of Thaumaturgos's third-century commentaries and Jerome's fourth-century Vulgate assume some sort of cultic leadership for *ekklesiastēs*, which eventually leads to Martin Luther's influential (though anachronistic) proposal of "der Prediger" ("Preacher"). The English name "Ecclesiastes" is derived from the Latin transliteration of the Greek word.

The rabbis in the Midrash *Qohelet Rabbah* cite 1 Kgs 8:1—"Solomon assembled (*yaqhēl*) the elders of Israel"[8]—and translate "Qohelet" accordingly as "assembler." Many contemporary scholars follow some form of this identification

---

3. The word "Qohelet" appears seven times: 1:1, 2, 12; 7:27; 12:8, 9, 10.
4. For a survey of the proposals about form and meaning, see Seow, *Ecclesiastes*, 95–97.
5. BDB, 875.
6. Ibid.
7. Henry George Liddell, *An Intermediate Greek–English Lexicon* (New York: American Book Company, 1888), 239, defines *ekklēsiastēs* as "a member of the *ekklēsia*" and *ekklēsia* as "an assembly of the citizens regularly summoned."
8. *Qoh. Rab.* 1:1, 2, as cited in Seow, *Ecclesiastes*, 95.

by noting Solomon's activity of "assembling" wisdom, wealth, and women
(1 Kgs 3–11).[9]

Is Qohelet a proper name, a title, or a job description? There is some evidence
from the Persian period that feminine-ending nouns denote the title of an office.
Ezra 2:55 and Neh 7:57 both speak of a *sōperet*, and Ezra 2:57 and Neh 7:59 of
a *pōkeret haṣbāyîm*. These may be feminine nouns used as the titles of cultic
offices, though this is not certain, and the NRSV simply transliterates these words
as if they were proper names. If one follows this pattern, "Qohelet" is then the
title of a cultic office as well. After all, out of the seven times this word appears
in the book, at least one instance includes the definite article (*ha-*).[10]

The lack of a single, reliable translation of this name has led to a few creative
propositions. Drawing a parallel from Jewish writings later than Qohelet, E.
Renan proposed that the consonants *qhlt* be read as a cryptogram, similar to the
name Rashi for Rabbi Shelomo Yizkhaki.[11] This type of abbreviation is quite
common in Judaism; many great scholars and mystics are more generally known
by their anagram than their given name. Other examples include Rambam for
Rabbi Moshe Ben Maimon (or Maimonides), and the Besht for the Baal Shem
Tov ("Master of the Good Name"), the founder of Hasidism. But there is no
evidence for such constructions during any of the possible times of Qohelet's
writing. Renan refrained from deciphering the cryptogram that he proposed.

Frank Zimmermann makes a similar argument, though he does offer a translation.[12] According to Zimmermann, *qhlt* is a mistranslation of the Aramaic
knšh, which means "gatherer." The sages who translated Qohelet chose to translate the proper name rather than transliterate it. The numerical value of *knšh* is
375, which corresponds to the numerical value of the name Solomon in Hebrew.
Zimmermann argues that *knšh*, as a neurotic man, would have understood this
coincidence to be of great import, perhaps believing that he was even the
"reincarnation" of Solomon.[13] Is "Qohelet" an undecipherable cryptogram, acro-
nym, or a mistranslation of an Aramaic word with the same numerical value as
Solomon?

Michael Fox offers a single dissenting opinion in the designation of the form
of the word. He does not think that it is necessary to posit a *qal* participle that is
not attested anywhere else. Rather, basing his conclusion on a word study by B.
Kedar-Kopfstein,[14] he understands "Qohelet" to be a noun derived from a noun.
Examples of this type of word formation include *bôqēr* ("cowherd") from *bāqār*

9. Seow, *Ecclesiastes*, 97; James Crenshaw, *Ecclesiastes* (OTL; Philadelphia: Westminster, 1987), 33–34.

10. Qoh 12:8, and possibly 7:27, if the text is emended.

11. E. Renan, *L'Ecclesiaste traduit de l'Hébreu avec une étude sur l'age et le caractère du livre* (Paris: Levy, 1882), 13–15. See also Seow, *Ecclesiastes*, 96.

12. Frank Zimmermann, "The Aramaic Provenance of Qohelet," *JQR* 36 (1945–46): 17–45 (43–44), and *The Inner World of Qohelet* (New York: Ktav, 1973), 85–87.

13. Zimmermann, *The Inner World of Qohelet*, 86.

14. Benjamin Kedar-Kopfstein, "Semantic Aspects of the Pattern *qôtel*," *HAR* 1 (1977): 155–76, as cited in Fox, *A Time to Tear Down*, 161.

("cattle") and *kōrēm* ("vinter") from *kerem* ("vineyard").[15] While it is probable that the word Qohelet is related in meaning to the noun *qāhāl* and thus means something like "assembler," one should note that the meanings of some noun-derived nouns have a tenuous connection to their parent noun. One example of this is *ḥōbēl* ("sailor") from *ḥebel* ("rope"). As Fox points out, "most nouns in this category are, loosely, doer nouns or occupation-nouns, but their meaning cannot be simply projected from the *qal*."[16] Therefore, the obvious connection between the roots of "Qohelet" and *qāhāl* may not tell us anything about meaning.

"Teacher" (NRSV), "Preacher" (Luther), "Citizen" (LXX), "Gatherer" (Seow), "Collector" (Crenshaw), "Assembler" (*Qohelet Rabbah*), proper name, crypto-gram, or title . . . any translation out of the Hebrew forecloses on too many other possible meanings and thereby suppresses the word's ambiguity. We have barely begun our reading of this book, and already we are struggling with simple signi-fication. Is Qohelet just a particularly opaque word? Or is our struggle emblem-atic of a deeper aporia? What is a proper name,[17] and what is its relationship to systems of language to texts? Why does every study of Qohelet, including this one, begin with the quest for the meaning of the name?

To approach these questions concerning the proper name we must examine the very nature of language. In the early part of the twentieth century, Ferdinand de Saussure proposed a theory of language and birthed the field of *semiology*, or the study of signs.[18] A sign is comprised of two parts: the signifier and the signified. The signifier is the form or sound; the signified is the concept or that to which the sound refers. For example, the signifier "tree," composed of four phonemes, refers to the plant that generally grows quite tall and is characterized by a trunk and branches of bark with green leaves at the tips—the signified. Further, signifiers are chains of arbitrary sounds, bearing only an arbitrary rela-tionship to what they signify. In other words, language is not an absolute system inextricably bound to an external reality. The connection between the signifier (the word or sound) and the signified (the concept or object) is a matter of con-vention. With nothing to guarantee the link between the two component parts of any sign, all signs are inherently unstable. There is always a gap between the signifier and the signified.

Language, then, is a system of differences. It is only possible to know the meaning of a word through other words. I indicated the signified of the signifier "tree" through a series of other signifiers, each which could be endlessly multi-plied through other words (e.g. "plant" refers to a living organism that produces

15.   Fox, *A Time to Tear Down*, 161.

16.   Ibid.

17.   Even if it could be demonstrated conclusively that "Qohelet" was originally a title, Qohelet sill functions as a proper name—both the proper name of the book and the proper name of the speaker in the book.

18.   There are many good explications of Saussurian linguistics and its consequences. See, for example, Leitch, *Deconstructive Criticism*, 7–10, 24–29. See also Sherwood, *The Prostitute and the Prophet*, 93–98.

its energy from the sun through the process of photosynthesis; "living" is an adjective that describes anything that can adapt to its environment and reproduce itself; *ad nauseam* . . .). Words have meanings only insofar as they are different from other words; they do not carry within them any meaning in and of themselves but always are referencing another word, moving further along on a chain of signification. Any arrival at the thing-in-itself is permanently delayed, differed, supplemented, supplanted by this series of differences without end and without origin.

Yet, a name appears to operate outside of this system of difference. It refers directly to that which it names without the mediation of translation or definition. A "tree" may be inextricably entangled in a web of signifiers, but I am Jennifer Koosed. In his Superscript to Derrida's autobiography, Geoffrey Bennington calls the ideal of proper nomination "the very prototype of language" and "the keystone of logocentrism."[19] With the proper name, there is no deferral of meaning, or, to use a term coined by Derrida, there is no *différance*.[20]

A name appears to operate outside of this system of difference, but only at first glance. A promise of referentiality is withdrawn as soon as it is given. The name functions on the presupposition of an almost organic connection between the signifier and the signified. The hope behind the painstaking attempts to pin down the meaning of "Qohelet" is that the translation will tell us something essential about who (or what) Qohelet is. But this hope cannot withstand examination. Bennington continues: "there is no proper name."[21] Proper names, like common nouns, must operate within a system of difference, must designate one individual and not another, and are thus marked by traces of these others. Like any other sign, there is a gap between the signifier and the signified, and this space leaves the sign open to difference/*différance*. There are two features of the proper name that underscore its place within a system of difference: iterability and the inscription of death.

The phenomenon that Derrida calls "iterability" refers to more than just the proper name. Iterability is "the impossible union of a singular occurrence and a general law."[22] In order to be meaningful, the name must be as unique (singular) as the person who bears it, and yet, in order to function, it must be repeatable

---

19. Geoffrey Bennington and Jacques Derrida, *Jacques Derrida* (Chicago: University of Chicago Press, 1993), 104–5.

20. *Différance* is a mis-spelling of the French word *différence*, a mis-spelling that can only be seen in writing but not heard in speech. Derrida uses this word as a way of indicating three interrelated notions. As summarized by Leitch: "(1) 'to differ'—to be unlike or dissimilar in nature, quality, or form; (2) 'differre' (Latin)—to scatter, disperse; and (3) 'to defer'—to delay, postpone" (Leitch, *Deconstructive Criticism*, 41). Derrida's own work is permeated by the "neither word nor concept" of *différance*. They include *Of Grammatology* (trans. Gayatri Chakravorty Spivak; Baltimore: The Johns Hopkins University Press, 1976); "Difference," in *Margins of Philosophy* (trans. Alan Bass; Chicago: University of Chicago Press, 1982), 1–27; and *Speech and Phenomena and Other Essays on Husserl's Theory of Signs* (trans. David B. Allison; Evanston, Ill.: Northwestern University Press, 1973), 129–60.

21. Bennington and Derrida, *Jacques Derrida*, 105.

22. Derek Attridge, "Introduction: Derrida and the Question of Literature," in *Acts of Literature* (ed. Derek Attridge; New York: Routledge, 1992), 1–29 (17–18).

(conform to a general law). It must be able to be used in a variety of contexts, repeated and understood as a proper name, functioning in the absence of its bearer.

Derrida arrives at his analysis of iterability through a critique of J. L. Austin's speech–act theory.[23] Austin defines two ways in which speech effects change: illocutionary and perlocutionary force. However, as Derrida points out, Austin has failed to take into account "the structure of *locution* (thus before any illocutory or perlocutory determination),"[24] and therefore his rigorous distinctions are blurred by the problems inherent in the common root. Austin assumes a link between the intention of the speaking subject and the consequences of the speech whereas Derrida questions the very ability of communication to, well, communicate. Though Austin does acknowledge that communication can fail, rather than see this as the possible risk of any locution, he defines failure in terms of the particular circumstances of the total speech act and consequently insists that failure is abnormal. Derrida positions this possibility of failure in the very law of communication itself.[25]

All language, particularly language that has either illocutionary or perlocutionary force, functions as a form of citation:

> Could a performative utterance succeed if its formulation did not repeat a "coded" or iterable utterance, or in other words, if the formula I pronounce in order to open a meeting, launch a ship or a marriage were not identifiable as *conforming* with an iterable model, if it were not then identifiable in some way as a "citation"?[26]

And once it is a citation it is not a pure singularity. It is this repeatability that opens language up to context, circumstance, and therefore change:

> Internal division of the trait, impurity, corruption, contamination, decomposition, perversion, deformation, even cancerisation, generous proliferation or degenerescence. All these disruptive "anomalies" are engendered—and this is their common law, the lot or site they share—by *repetition*.[27]

The proper name is an instance of this iterability.

As a dependent upon the two contradictory principles of singularity and repeatability, the proper name is caught in a double bind. In speaking of the play "Romeo and Juliet," Derrida illustrates the double bind:

> "O Romeo, Romeo, wherefore art thou Romeo?" She does not say to him: why are you called Romeo, why do you bear this name (like an article of clothing, an ornament, a detachable sign)? She says to him: why *are you* Romeo? She knows it: detachable, aphoristic though it be, his name is his essence.[28]

23. J. L. Austin, *How to Do Things with Words* (Cambridge, Mass.: Harvard University Press, 1962).

24. Jacques Derrida, "Signature Event Context," in his *Limited Inc.* (Evanston, Ill.: Northwestern University Press, 1988), 1–23 (14).

25. Ibid., 15.

26. Ibid., 18.

27. Jacques Derrida, "The Law of Genre," *Glyph* 7 (1980): 202–29 (204), as quoted in Robert Smith, *Derrida and Autobiography* (Cambridge: Cambridge University Press, 1995), 100.

28. Derrida, *Acts of Literature*, 426.

Yet, it is only in abandoning the name that Romeo can live his love, and therefore live truly as himself. "Romeo is Romeo, and Romeo is not Romeo. He is himself only in abandoning his name, he is himself only in his name."[29] This is not just a meditation on the specific situation involved in this tragic story of star-crossed lovers. Rather, it illustrates the precise is/is not of all proper names.[30] In this scene, Juliet expresses "the fatal truth of the name."[31] The proper name is not (im)possible.

Romeo and Juliet can only end the tragedy of the name with their own deaths. This leads us to the second aspect of the proper name: inscribed in any proper name is the death of the person to whom it refers. The proper name exists in order to refer to someone in his or her absence, to stand alone and to stand in for, without the presence of its bearer.[32] Death is simply a more permanent absence: "The name is made to do without the life of the bearer, and is therefore always somewhat the name of someone dead."[33] The name lives on and substitutes for the life of its bearer; paradoxically, the signifier has a longer existence than its signified—it is the more permanent aspect of the sign.

In the end, the proper name is a sign like any other. As such, there is a gap between the signifier and the signified. This gap fractures the name and opens it up to interpretation, instability, (mis)reading, error. And at its center is absence, nothingness, death. There is space between my name and me, and into this space others can enter. And, as my name wanders in and out of other contexts, standing in for me, it can be changed and shaped and misshaped by these contexts. Rather than telling us something essential about who (or what) Qohelet is, the inevitable meditation on his name only serves to reinforce our inability to collapse the signifier with the signified, and only underscores Qohelet's elusiveness. I have brought his name into my (con)text and have thus further separated it from its origin, perhaps even altering it beyond reckoning.

Further examination of Qohelet's self-identification yields only additional confusion. I am suspicious of his claims of ancestry. He gives us these clues in 1:1 and 1:12: "son of David," "king in Jerusalem," "over Israel." To state the obvious, according to the biblical record, David never had a son named Qohelet. Qohelet identifies himself as a "king over Israel in Jerusalem" (1:12), which could only refer to the united monarchy. Since Saul never really ruled in Jerusalem, the phrase could only refer to David or Solomon. And since David cannot be his own son, this only leaves Solomon. Although *ben* does not necessarily refer to a literal son but can also mean someone of a particular lineage, when the

---

    29.   Ibid., 427.
    30.   As Derrida himself notes (*Acts of Literature*, 65) in an interview about this essay: "And what only goes for one work, one proper name, evidently goes for any work, in other words for any singularity and any proper name."
    31.   Ibid., 427.
    32.   In "Signature Event Context," Derrida argues that the purpose of all signifiers is to function in the absence of the signified. The proper name then becomes a particular case of this general rule. See pp. 3–12.
    33.   Jacques Derrida, *The Post Card: From Socrates to Freud and Beyond* (trans. Alan Bass; Chicago: University of Chicago Press, 1987), 39.

text speaks of "son of David," a son is always a son. In Samuel and Chronicles, the phrase "son of David" always refers to Solomon, except for three occasions when the phrase indicates another one of David's many sons (2 Sam 13:1 [twice] and 2 Chr 11:18).

Despite this evidence, the equation of Qohelet with Solomon is still an interpreter's assumption. Never does the speaker in the text call himself Solomon, though presumably it would have been easy to do so. Other texts which claim Solomonic authorship, such as Song of Songs, Proverbs, Wisdom of Solomon, and the Odes of Solomon, all explicitly name Solomon in the title or superscription. The speaker in our text certainly alludes to such Solomonic authorship, but stops short of naming it explicitly. Why? Was Solomon using an alias?

But this explanation does not work either, for the language of the book clearly points to a much later date than any reckoning of Solomon's reign could yield.[34] The scholarly consensus places Qohelet within the Persian or Hellenistic period. Within these boundaries, dates vary but tend toward the third and fourth centuries B.C.E. The primary evidence for these dates is the peculiar language of the book. Most telling are the two Persian loan words: *pardēsîm* ("parks," 2:5), and *pitgām* ("sentence," 8:11). In addition to Qohelet, Persian words are found only in Chronicles, Ezra, Nehemiah, Esther, and Daniel. Based upon their content, there is clear evidence that these books were written during the post-exilic period. Therefore, it is likely that Qohelet was as well. There are also many Aramaisms—loanwords and syntactic features. The Aramaisms have prompted a few scholars to argue for an Aramaic original.[35] Although there is the occasional Aramaism in texts commonly thought to be pre-exilic, the high concentration in Qohelet again points to a post-exilic date.

Later developments in Hebrew are also present in Qohelet. The particle *še-* is used 68 times. For the singular first-person pronoun ("I"), *°ănî* rather than *°ănōkî* is used exclusively.[36] The particle *°et* is used not only to mark the direct

---

34.   Hugo Grotius was the first to notice the post-exilic language of Qohelet in 1644. In the words of Franz Delitzsch, "If the Book of Koheleth were of old Solomonic origin, then there is no history of the Hebrew language"; see Franz Delitzsch, *Commentary on the Song of Songs and Ecclesiastes* (trans. M. G. Easton; Edinburgh: T&T Clark, 1877; repr., Grand Rapids: Eerdmans, 1982), 190. See Seow, *Ecclesiastes*, 11–21, for a concise summary of the issues and interpretations involved with the language and dating of Qohelet.

35.   The theory of an Aramaic original is first proposed by F. C. Burkitt, "Is Ecclesiastes a Translation?" *JTS* 23 (1921–22): 22–28. This is followed by Zimmermann, perhaps its most vociferous champion: Zimmermann, "The Aramaic Provenance of Qohelet"; idem, "The Question of Hebrew in Qohelet," *JQR* 40 (1949–50): 79–102. See also C. C. Torrey, "The Question of the Original Language of Qohelet," *JQR* 39 (1948–49): 151–60; and H. L. Ginsberg, *Studies in Kohelet* (New York: Jewish Theological Seminary of America, 1950), 1–40. Robert Gordis refutes this position in the following works: "The Original Language of Qohelet," *JQR* 37 (1946–47): 67–84; idem, "The Translation Theory of Qohelet Re-examined," *JQR* 40 (1949–50): 103–16; idem, "Koheleth—Hebrew or Aramaic?" *JBL* 71 (1952): 93–109; idem, *Koheleth: The Man and His World* (New York: Schocken, 1951), 60–62; the later edition *Koheleth: The Man and His World* (New York: Schocken, 1955), 399–400 (Supplementary Note A: The Theory of an Aramaic Origin of Koheleth).

36.   Bo Isaksson suggests that this may be a characteristic of the Northern Hebrew dialect rather than a mark of Late Biblical Hebrew, though taken with the other evidence it is difficult to support

definite object but also to mark indefinite direct objects, which is a characteristic of Late Biblical Hebrew. The feminine demonstrative pronoun is always *zōh* and not *zōt*. Qohelet is written in the post-exilic period, not during the monarchial era, far away from Solomon or any Davidic king in Jerusalem.[37] Is Qohelet a forgery? Since the proper name functions in the absence of its bearer, who is to guarantee its meaning? Who can guard it from being wielded by someone else altogether, someone by another name?[38]

I can only conclude that Qohelet, whoever he is, is lying to me.

The author and Solomon cannot be easily equated. My quest for the meaning of the name has only led to a proliferation of etymologies behind the name and a proliferation of translations in front of the name. I have demonstrated with "Qohelet" J. Hillis Miller's observation about the strategy of etymology in criticism: "the effect of etymological retracing is not to ground the word solidly but to render it unstable, equivocal, wavering, abysmal. All etymology is false etymology. . . ."[39] As my analysis of the root of the word has led to instability rather than fixity, each new naming—"Teacher," "Preacher," "Collector," "Gatherer"—has removed us from the origin and instead has substituted for that origin. The substitution both adds to and supplants Qohelet; in other words, each name is a supplement.[40] But each new name can be a supplement only because the name itself is a supplement—a substitute that adds to and supplants the person to whom it refers. Again quoting Miller, "Each word inheres in a labyrinth of branching interverbal relationships going back not to a referential source but to something already, at the beginning a figurative transfer. . . ."[41]

To summarize, the author is using a persona who is writing under a pseudonym whose meaning we do not understand. Qohelet multiplies the usual gaps that always already occur between the signifier and the signified through a series of supplements. The speaker is hidden by the use of the proper name "Qohelet." "Qohelet" obfuscates rather than illuminates identity.

Genre Games

Since the question "Who is Qohelet?" has not resulted in any clear meaning, perhaps the question "What is Qohelet?" will be a more productive avenue of inquiry. Perhaps answering the question "What is Qohelet?" will also answer the

his thesis. See Bo Isaksson, *Studies in the Language of Qoheleth: With Special Emphasis on the Verbal System* (Stockholm: Almqvist & Wiksell, 1987), 142.

37. For a concise summary of the argument for a post-exilic date, see Choon-Leong Seow, "Linguistic Evidence and the Dating of Qohelet," *JBL* 115, no. 4 (1996): 643–66. In this article, Seow argues quite convincingly for a Persian period date.

38. In his essay on the proper name and signature, Derrida points out that his signature at the end is a counterfeit. See "Signature Event Context," 21.

39. J. Hillis Miller, "Ariadne's Thread: Repetition and the Narrative Line," *Critical Inquiry* 3 (1976): 55–77 (70).

40. Derrida develops the idea of the supplement particularly in his reading of Rousseau in *Of Grammatology*. See also Leitch, *Deconstructive Criticism*, 169–78.

41. Miller, "Ariadne's Thread," 70.

question "Who is Qohelet?" For many commentators, genre analysis is necessary because correct genre identification is entwined with the questions of the
meaning of the text, the setting, and the literary relationship with other texts.[42]
However, as will be demonstrated, the project of naming the genre and then
deriving meaning from that name is fraught with as much uncertainty and
ambiguity as the project of the proper name of Qohelet.

The identification of genre is one of our expectations as readers. We all come
to a text with our assumptions of a certain set of conventions. As Derrida asserts,
we place the text before the law of genre. Derrida explicates three foundational
presuppositions in our system of conventions.

"The first axiomatic belief is our recognition that the text I have just read has
its own identity, singularity and unity."[43] Included in this belief is the existence
of clear boundaries for the text (beginning and end) and the belief in an original
version, in this case in Hebrew. This last point is particularly important for it
allows the text to participate in our laws of authorship and copyright. Although
our modern notions of copyright laws are not relevant for the production of
Qohelet, they are relevant to our reception of Qohelet, if only unconsciously.
Secondly, we presuppose that the text has an author.[44] Even though this convention is quite recent in history, it has still left an indelible stamp on biblical
scholarship. The first rumblings of modern critical consciousness concerning the
Bible circled around the proposition that Moses wrote (or did not write) the Pen-
tateuch. Consequently, modern biblical criticism traces its genealogy back to its
founding father—source criticism. Sometimes there is the displacement of an
author with a school, but both are conceived as functioning in the same way.
Qohelet was churned through source criticism early on, and there is not a book
on the text that does not begin with some foray into the critical method.

"Our third axiom or presupposition is that in this text . . . events are related,
and the relation belongs to what we call literature."[45] This axiom begs the questions of who decides, who judges, and according to what criteria is this literature
named.[46] What kind of literature is it? The law of genre demands purity, com-
monality in singularity, and specific marks of identification. Genres are not to be
mixed: "as soon as genre announces itself, one must respect a norm, one must
not cross a line of demarcation, one must not risk impurity, anomaly or mon-
strosity."[47] Genre immediately denotes boundaries, laws, and conventions. After
Derrida lays out these presuppositions of reading, he challenges them, he plays

---

42.   For example, Fox (*A Time to Tear Down*, 5) states, "To understand the source and significance of Qohelet's ideas we must set them within the context of his intellectual background. For
this we look primarily (but not exclusively) to didactic Wisdom Literature, because the book of
Qohelet is closest to this genre in form, subject matter, and, to a large extent, ideology." See also
Perdue, *Wisdom and Creation*, 194.

43.   Derrida, *Acts of Literature*, 184. The following is dependent upon two essays by Derrida:
"Before the Law," and "The Law of Genre."

44.   Ibid., 185.

45.   Ibid., 186.

46.   Ibid., 187.

47.   Ibid., 224–25.

with the limits of genre and the laws of its convention and demonstrates them permeable, unstable, open. Like the proper name, pursued because of the hope it will tell us something essential about who Qohelet is, genre names too are open to difference, iterability, the gap within and between the signs. As we will see, naming the genre brings us no closer to Qohelet.

The proposals about the genre of this strange little book have been varied. There is no consensus, but they tend to fall into two main camps: (1) sayings collection, and (2) first-person narrative.[48] Regarding the first, there are clear connections between Qohelet and such classic sayings collections as Proverbs, Ben Sirach, and *Pirke Avot*—hence its inclusion in the broad genre category of Wisdom Literature. But the trait of the book that distinguishes it from almost every other text is its consistent first-person narrative. Consequently a whole series of genre designations based upon this second trait have emerged. "I" (*ʾănî*) is the primary mark of this genre.

The word "I" appears 29 times in the book of Qohelet.[49] The majority of these instances (19) occur with first person singular verbal forms. In Classical Biblical Hebrew the personal pronoun is only used before the verb in order to emphasize the subject. Qohelet's usage is unusual because the pronoun appears after the verb, and thus has no (typical) emphatic meaning.[50] Whereas some have argued that this is a feature of Late Hebrew or Mishnaic Hebrew, Schoors notes that there are no "convincing parallels" in the texts that represent these time periods. The use of *ʾănî* "rather appears to be a peculiarity of Qohelet's style."[51]

In another major recent work on Qohelet's language, Bo Isaksson goes further: "the feature of the added pronoun gives the sentence an enhanced weight, which may emphasize an emotional expression, an important conclusion, or the introduction of a new line of thought."[52] Isaksson then quotes another scholar— Takamitsu Muraoka—approvingly: he asserts that Muraoka's conclusion is "indisputable": "the recurring 'I' is, as it were, an expression of the philosophical meditating ego of Qoheleth, as he observes and meditates upon the world around him and human life in it."[53] Isaksson notes that there is an "autobiographical thread" throughout Qohelet connected not only to the use of *ʾănî* but also to the verbal system, specifically the use of the perfect. Translations of the verbs fail to convey the dynamic nature of the perfect—it is not to be equated with an English simple past. Rather, he reads the verbs as conveying "the impression of the author being present in the text."[54] For Isaksson, there is a clear link between the speaker in the text and the author behind the text.

48. Perdue, *Wisdom and Creation*, 194.
49. Qoh 1:12, 16 (twice); 2:1, 11, 12, 13, 14, 15 (thrice), 18 (twice), 20, 24; 3:17, 18; 4:1, 2, 4, 7, 8; 5:17; 7:25, 26; 8:2, 12, 15; 9:16.
50. Antoon Schoors, *The Preacher Sought to Find Pleasing Words: A Study of the Language of Qoheleth* (Leuven: Peeters, 1992), 160.
51. Ibid.
52. Isaksson, *Studies*, 166–67; cf. Schoors, *The Preacher*, 161.
53. Takamitsu Muraoka, *Emphatic Words and Structures in Biblical Hebrew* (Jerusalem: Magnes/Hebrew University, 1985), 49, as quoted in Isaksson, *Studies*, 167.
54. Isaksson, *Studies*, 46.

Isaksson is not alone. Once the "I" is specified as the primary mark of genre in Qohelet, Qohelet is identified as some sort of autobiography—royal testament,[55] reflection,[56] journal.[57] Then the interpreter reads accordingly by assuming certain continuities between the speaker in the text and the historical author or authors who wrote the text. R. N. Whybray offers a series of questions that exemplify the parameters within which most Qohelet scholars operate:

> Is the book a straightforward literary work written by Qoheleth, like a modern theological or philosophical treatise? Or, since Qoheleth was a teacher, is it possible that it is a transcript of lectures which he had previously delivered orally? Or is it, perhaps, an adaptation of those lectures for more literary purposes? Did he compile it from a series of written notes which he had previously made? Or was it compiled by an editor, or even by a succession of editors? Did such editors, if such there were, simply arrange and transcribe the material available to them, or did they add new material of their own? If so, were such additions merely minor ones? Or were they substantial additions intended in some way to modify Qoheleth's original teaching?[58]

For Whybray, the existence of a man, a teacher, behind the text is assumed. The question is only to what extent do we have his original teachings. He cites the use of the first person singular verb and pronoun as evidence of the individual thinker who employs the pen-name Qohelet: the "'I' is clearly the author himself."[59] But autobiography is not as easy to read as Whybray's assumptions may indicate.

The problems with the genre of autobiography begin at its origin. While the term "autobiography" first appeared in 1786 in the preface to Ann Yearsley's *Poems*,[60] this does not answer the question of who wrote the first autobiography.[61] Nor does it answer the more pressing question of what constitutes an autobiography, and what its defining features, characteristics, and structures are. And even more troubling and significant, what are the issues of truth and history, design and selfhood involved in writing and reading lives? With the

---

55. Von Rad, *Wisdom in Israel*, 226; and Crenshaw, *Ecclesiastes*, 29. Crenshaw sees Qohelet as a conglomeration of genres that include instructions, truth-statements, and rhetorical questions along with the royal testament.

56. Roland Murphy, *Ecclesiastes* (WBC 23A; Dallas: Word, 1992), xxxi.

57. Kathleen Farmer, *Who Knows What is Good? A Commentary on the Books of Proverbs and Ecclesiastes* (ITC; Grand Rapids: Eerdmans, 1991), 149.

58. R. N. Whybray, *Ecclesiastes* (Old Testament Guides; Sheffield: Sheffield Academic Press, 1989), 22–23.

59. Ibid., 38.

60. Jeffrey L. Staley, "Autobiography," in Adam, ed., *Handbook of Postmodern Biblical Interpretation*, 14–19 (14). But the questions begin already. According to the *Oxford English Dictionary*, Southey coined the term in 1809. I could find no consensus in the literature concerning the originator of the term.

61. And does the author have to name his or her text an "autobiography" for it to be an autobiography? The genealogy of origins is complicated by the fact that the first book published explicitly as an "autobiography"—W. P. Scargill's *The Autobiography of a Dissenting Minister* in 1834—is generally classified as a "romance." See James Olney, "Autobiography and the Cultural Moment: A Thematic, Historical, and Bibliographical Introduction," in *Autobiography: Essays Theoretical and Critical* (ed. James Olney; Princeton: Princeton University Press, 1980), 3–27 (5–6).

emergence of critical commentary on autobiography in the mid-twentieth century, the literary-critical community has been embroiled in these issues.[62]

The very word "autobiography" structures the three-front attack on the genre's
integrity.[63] First, the "bio" came into question, undermining the "rather naïve"
assumption that a person could narrate his or her life in a manner approaching
history, and that that life progressed on a contained linear course.[64] Rather, a life
has no harmonious coherency except for that imposed upon it through a
meaning-making narrative. Secondly, the "auto" came under scrutiny: were
there "no agonizing questions of identity, self-definition, self-existence, or self-
deception"[65] to which the reader need attend? Attending to the issues involved in
self-representation brings issues of the fictive construction of the self and truth
to the fore. The "I" in "auto" is not a neutral and transparent voice. As Timothy
Adams declares at the beginning of his recent study, "All Autobiographers are
unreliable narrators, all humans are liars. . . ."[66]

Finally, "an emphasis on the death of the unified self has led to a concern for
the rhetorical, linguistic function of 'selves' and 'readers.'"[67] Operating under
the influence of the psychoanalytical theories of Lacan and their simultaneous
appropriation and deconstruction by Derrida and other poststructuralists,[68]
concentration has shifted to the "graphy" of autobiography, the process of
writing and inscribing a self within a text. The primary mark of autobiography is
the "I." The "I" links the author to the text and provides a unifying principle
within the text and between the text and life. Yet it is precisely in the "I" that the
primary instabilities of the genre lay. Like all signs, there is no guaranteed
connection between the word and that to whom it refers. The self itself lacks a
stable center. The very subject who is supposed to guarantee the unity and stability of the text is neither coherent nor constant.[69]

Qohelet scholars who classify the book as some sort of autobiography seem to
be unfamiliar with the controversies in autobiographical studies over whether any
ancient text can even be spoken of as "autobiography." There is no consensus

---

62. It is widely stated that the modern era in autobiographical theory began with Roy Pascal's
study *Design and Truth in Autobiography* (London: Routledge & Paul, 1960). But other candidates
include Georges Gusdorf's "Conditions et limites de l'autobiographie," in *Formen der Selbstdarstellung: Analekten zu einer Geschichte des literarishen Selbstportraits* (ed. Günter Reichenkron;
Berlin: Duncker & Humblot, 1956), 105–23. Who coined the term, who wrote the first one, and who
wrote the first criticism remain irresolvable questions.

63. Staley, "Autobiography," 15.

64. Olney, *Autobiography*, 20.

65. Ibid.

66. Timothy Adams, *Telling Lies in Modern American Autobiography* (Chapel Hill: University
of North Carolina Press, 1990), ix.

67. Staley, "Autobiography," 16.

68. Derrida first spoke of Lacan in an interview in 1971, published in English as "Positions,"
in *Diacritics* 2 (1972): 35–43, and *Diacritics* 3 (1973): 33–46. He further developed his critique in
"The Purveyor of Truth," *Yale French Studies* 52 (1975): 31–113.

69. Leigh Gilmore, "The Mark of Autobiography: Postmodernism, Autobiography, and Genre,"
in *Autobiography and Postmodernism* (ed. Kathleen Ashley, Leigh Gilmore, and Gerald Peters;
Amherst: University of Massachusetts Press, 1995), 3–20 (6).

concerning the origin of the genre, but there is a dominant argument that situates its emergence within the modern concept of individuality; thus autobiography is made a product of European civilization: Augustine[70] begat Rousseau begat Henry Adams, and so on.[71] It is only during the Enlightenment that a concept of an individual and unique subject emerges, a necessary idea for the formation of autobiography.

Defining autobiography as a product of the Enlightenment would seem categorically to exclude the texts of the ancient Near East. But neither scholars of literary history nor scholars of the ancient world can agree if biography or autobiography as a genre existed in antiquity.[72] The lack of consensus is illustrated most strikingly in two articles both within Jack Sasson's edited volume, *Civilizations of the Ancient Near East*. First, Olivier Perdu, writing an article on "Ancient Egyptian Autobiographies," states: "The genre of biography was not known in pharonic Egypt. Autobiographies, however, are well attested. . . ."[73] On the other hand, an article on "Autobiographies in Ancient Western Asia" by Edward L. Greenstein claims: "There is no autobiography as such in the ancient world. . . . "[74] Greenstein then follows with a discussion of "autobiographical texts" that do exist but are distinguished from "autobiography," which does not. Pulled out of context, the sentences above seem to be stating diametrically opposed positions. However, both authors caution against confusing ancient Near Eastern autobiographies with modern Western autobiographies, which suggests that their differences lie more in how they employ the terms than in the content of their positions.

In all of these descriptions there is confusion about the differences among "biography," "autobiography," "biographical," and "autobiographical" that indicates an underlying confusion between literature and history, fiction and fact. The term may remain the same while the definition of the term shifts. Even when scholars speak of such texts as Egyptian mortuary texts, this confusion appears. Since the "I" of these texts is dead, they are clearly biographical and not autobiographical by definition—unless the Egyptians had powers lost to us now, the dead do not come back from beyond the grave to speak of their lives. But even the "biography" breaks down when the person enters the afterworld and begins to describe his or her experience in the afterlife. Needless to say, the biographer in question would have no way of knowing whether or not the biography after death was accurate.

The slippages in definitions infiltrate discussion of Qohelet's genre, because in order to put it in a category it must be compared with other texts also in said

---

70. But already the genealogy shakes at its foundations, for this "modern European" genre began with an African man in late antiquity.

71. Gilmore, *Autobiography and Postmodernism*, 5.

72. The following discussion is indebted to Burkes, *Death in Qoheleth*, 171–76.

73. Olivier Perdu, "Ancient Egyptian Autobiographies," in *Civilizations of the Ancient Near East* (ed. Jack Sasson; New York: Scribner, 1995), 2243–54 (2243).

74. Edward L. Greenstein, "Autobiographies in Ancient Western Asia," in Sasson, ed., *Civilizations of the Ancient Near East*, 2421–32 (2421).

category. That is the definition of genre analysis. William Brown is an example
of a recent commentator who analyzes Qohelet's genre under the influence of
definitional confusion. He notes that the autobiographical style is parallel to
other ancient Near Eastern texts, especially Egyptian texts, and as such Qohelet
is an obituary, "indeed the obituary of life itself."[75] In the discussion of autobiography that follows, Brown first puts autobiography in quotes and compares
it to Egyptian grave "biographies," but then deletes the quotes around autobiography and compares Qohelet to Augustine's *Confessions*. The first is clearly
fictional, the second is clearly not. Which one is Qohelet?

The recent discussions in autobiographical criticism mirror both modern
scholarship's project and problem of establishing Qohelet's genre. Commentators compare Qohelet to other ancient Near Eastern texts that also speak in the
first person. Once Qohelet connects to other works, the genre boundaries are
drawn, and interpretation can commence. For example, Burkes argues that
Qohelet most closely resembles Egyptian mortuary texts of the Late Period. This
identification then becomes the foundation of her thesis concerning a "paradigm
shift which is taking place across the ancient Near East in this period [Judah's
"Second Temple Period" and Egypt's "Late Period"], and is manifested analo-
gously in both cultures."[76] Seow believes that Qohelet most closely resembles
Akkadian royal inscriptions. The implications of identifying Qohelet's genre
thus are to highlight irony in the book. Qohelet adopts the propagandist rhetoric
of royal inscriptions in order to demonstrate the exact opposite of what the royal
inscriptions assume: the permanency of mighty deeds.[77]

Both Longman[78] and Perdue[79] devote significant portions of their books to
detailed comparisons between Qohelet and other texts from the ancient Near
East—*The Dispute between a Man and his Ba*, *The Gilgamesh Epic*, *The Com-
plaints of Khakheperre-Sonb*, *The Dialogue of Pessimism*, *The Cuthaean Legend
of Naram-Sin*, the Akkadian poem "I Will Praise the Lord of Wisdom." The list
goes on. Genre classification is supposed to denote boundaries, laws, and conventions. It is supposed to provide a stable foundation upon which interpretations may be built. Yet, when one investigates the literature of the ancient Near
East, the intertextual web continues to spin out (of control). Like the proper
name, naming the genre brings us no closer to Qohelet. The genre cannot remain
pure, the fiction be separated from the fact, the identity of the speaker explored
in this text when genre in general, and the very mark of autobiography in
particular, even those in which the historicity of the speaker can be confirmed, is
fundamentally unstable.[80]

75. Brown, *Ecclesiastes*, 7.
76. Burkes, *Death in Qohelet*, 6.
77. Seow, "Qohelet's Autobiography," 284.
78. Longman, *Fictional Akkadian Autobiography*.
79. Perdue, *Wisdom and Creation*.
80. The instability of identity even includes gender. In French, "genre" and "gender" are the
same word: "the masculine gender [*genre*] is thus affected by the affirmation through a random drift
that could always render it other. . . . The genders/genres pass into each other" (Derrida, *Acts of
Literature*, 245). Qohelet's "gender/genre trouble" will be further explicated in Chapter 5.

Courting Scandal

Ann Jefferson has noted that "the conjunction of autobiography and fiction in actual writing practice is still apt to be felt as something of a scandal."[81] But scandal touches more than just a few renegade works that play fast and loose with the truth. It goes to the very heart of the genre. Autobiography is caught between the primary division within literature: fiction and history. It is insufficiently objective, since the eyewitness narrator is too embedded in the account and his/her subjectivity infuses the entire narration. On the other hand, it is insufficiently subjective, since it is too constrained by fact to be art.[82] Autobiography proves to destabilize both categories, neither purely one nor the other.

The focus of early autobiographical criticism had been the separating out of truth from fiction (the design of the narrative) and then concentrating on the presentation of the truth; in other words, weeding out the lies and the license to find out what really happened. But, as autobiographical critics have begun to acknowledge, this separation is not always clear or easy, and often the "lies" are just as significant, sometimes even more significant, than the "truth."[83] Rather than remaining pure, fiction invades autobiography through its unstable boundaries. In turn, autobiography invades fiction. And when dealing with the text of Qohelet, with no possible way of verifying the historical truth of the claims of the speaker, the problems and possibilities endlessly multiply.

"There is perhaps no other book in the Hebrew Bible that has such relentless individualism," states E. S. Christianson in his study on Qohelet and narrative. Consequently, numerous works purporting to explore Qohelet's personality have emerged.[84] Acting like the early autobiographical critics in literary studies, most scholars who employ some version of the tag "fictional autobiography" for Qohelet confine the fictional elements to the Solomonic guise. Once the Solomonic disguise is discredited, the rest of the text is simply "autobiography." In the representative words of Whybray: "Even though in the first part of the book he uses the device of pretending to be King Solomon . . . there is no doubt that throughout the book this 'I' is a real and not a fictitious 'I.'"[85]

I do not want to misrepresent the literature, thereby making it into a coherent whole against which to brandish my foil.[86] Some scholars of Qohelet certainly

---

81. Ann Jefferson, "Autobiography as Intertext: Barthes, Sarraute, Robbe-Grillet," in *Intertextuality* (ed. Michael Worton and Judith Still; New York: Manchester University Press, 1990), 108–29 (108). The vitriolic critical and public responses of such boundary-crossing works as Gertrude Stein's *The Autobiography of Alice B. Toklas* and Mary McCarthy's *Memories of a Catholic Girlhood* demonstrate this. See the chronicle of these works reception in Adams, *Telling Lies*.

82. Gilmore, *Autobiography and Postmodernism*, 6; Olney, *Autobiography*, 3–5.

83. This is Timothy Adams's thesis.

84. Christianson cites studies from E. H. Plumptre, "The Author of Ecclesiastes," *ExpTim* 2 (1880): 401–30, to Stone, "Old Man Koheleth," to Zimmermann, *The Inner World of Qohelet*, all of which focus on Qohelet's personality.

85. R. N. Whybray, *Two Jewish Theologies: Job and Ecclesiastes* (Hull: University of Hull, 1980), 6; as quoted in Bartholomew, *Reading Ecclesiastes*, 153.

86. For a perceptive analysis of the literature on this point, see Bartholomew, *Reading Ecclesiastes*, 146–57.

acknowledge a bit of trepidation about an easy conflation of the speaker and the author. Longman expresses his concern in a footnote.[87] Fox calls Qohelet the persona employed by the author.[88] Christianson distances himself from a whole-sale conflation of the speaker with an historical author.[89] But even when caution about conflating the "I" of the text with the author is expressed, this caution is designed to make the construction of the author more historically accurate, not to call the very connection between texts and authors into question, nor to signal the wholesale death of the author. But the author of Qohelet is, indeed, dead.

Texts survive the deaths of their author:

> Death reveals the power of the name to the very extent that the name continues to name or to call what we call the bearer of the name, and who can no longer answer to or answer in and for his name. And since the possibility of this situation is revealed at death, we can infer that it does not wait for death. Or that in *it* death does not wait for death.[90]

Autobiography, a text more intimately attached to the proper name of its author than any other, is infused with death. It leaves those who penned it behind, slaying them so it can stand alone, continuing to live long after they are cold in their graves. Qohelet has survived the death of its author(s) over two millennia ago. Derrida writes, in language evocative of Qohelet himself:

> At the very least, to be dead means that no profit or deficit, no good or evil, whether calculated or not, can *ever return again* to the bearer of the name. Only the name can inherit, and this is why the name, to be distinguished from the bearer, is always and *a priori* a dead man's name, a name of death. What returns to the name never returns to the living.[91]

"Only the name can inherit"—all of our searches for the author(s) behind Qohelet are literary constructions in front of the text, endlessly multiplying "Qohelet," creating him/her/them over and over again, not discovering or uncovering an author behind the name. Instead, the author is only the name.[92]

Who is Qohelet? This is Qohelet. The repetition of the "I" asserts an identity in the text, provides a skeleton, which is fleshed out by the words used for bodies, and by the imagination of the reader. The textual identity is unified only

87.   Longman, *The Book of Ecclesiastes*, 21 n. 75.

88.   Fox (*A Time to Tear Down*, 371) writes: "Since there is an implied author mediating Qohelet's words, we cannot simply identify Qohelet with the author. Qohelet is a character created in the work who may be a close expression of the author's attitudes, but whose words cannot be assumed to be inseparable from the ideas of his creator."

89.   Christianson also remarks upon the device of implied author in *A Time to Tell*, 161.

90.   Jacques Derrida, *Mémoires: For Paul de Man* (trans. Cecile Lindsay et al.; New York: Columbia University Press, 1989), 63. As Yvonne Sherwood points out in her entry on "Derrida" in Adam, ed., *Handbook of Postmodern Biblical Interpretation*, 69–75 (69): "you could say that being Derrida gives Derrida rather extreme insight into the absence or deferral of the writing subject, the way in which 'one's mortality, infinitude, is inscribed in everything one inscribe[s]' . . . for, as he mused in an interview in one of the many recent conferences 'on' him, to be constantly named/ quoted/abstracted as 'Derrida' is 'like being dead without being dead.'"

91.   Derrida, *The Ear of the Other*, 7, as quoted in Smith, *Derrida and Autobiography*, 73.

92.   Leitch, *Deconstructive Criticism*, 177.

because it is bound up in one body of words (not one body of an historical author). Even though the content is contradictory, the words unstable (needing textual emendation from time to time), perhaps written by one perhaps more (perhaps none), the readers feel a presence, not because we are experiencing the sage, but because we are experiencing the words on the page, wrapped around the "I" like skin on bones.

With Qohelet we are reading the "autobiography" of an author who is writing using a persona who is writing under a pseudonym whose meaning we do not understand, a text whose authorial, spatial, and temporal origins are hidden in the past. If there are problems with making historical pronouncements on auto-biographies that we can date, for which we have other sources for the biography of the author, then biblical commentators reading Qohelet as some kind of autobiography are hopelessly naive. As Craig Bartholomew points out, "the comparison of Ecclesiastes with fictional autobiography confirms what literary studies of autobiography alert us to; the 'I' of autobiography can be very elu-sive."[93] The reader does not know who Qohelet is beyond the words on the page. And one can only watch as even this "I" eludes, resisting efforts to pin it down, define it, make it into a stable referent that can be simply read. I can call Qohelet names, but those names refer only to my own anxiety about identities that cannot be contained by analysis.

93. Bartholomew, *Reading Ecclesiastes*, 153.

Chapter 3

FRAGMENTS OF QOHELET'S BODY

> To write by fragments: the fragments are then so many stones on the perimeter of a circle: I spread myself around: my whole little universe in crumbs; at the center, what?
>
> —*Roland Barthes*[1]

The concerns with authorship, integrity, and genre all stem from the historical-critical presuppositions that the text is best understood in terms of its origins, the intentions of the people who penned it, and the historical forces that shaped its composition. With these concerns in mind, readers see *through* Qohelet. But Qohelet is an opaque, material object. What do we see when we shift our vision, refocus our eyes, and look *at* Qohelet? We see a multifaceted body, several bodies, fragments of bodies in and of the book.

Qohelet begins and ends with words of weariness. In the opening poem (Qoh 1:2–11) the world is displayed as a series of repetitions: generations come and go, the sun rises and sets, the winds blow north and south, the streams flow down and around—there is constant movement but no linear progress or completion. No matter how many streams flow into the sea, it will never be full (1:7).

As the earth, so the body: "All words are wearisome (*yĕgē'îm*); no one is able to speak. The eye is not sated (*tiśba'*) with seeing; the ear is not full (*timmālē'*) with hearing" (1:8). Our senses are full of the world; yet they never cease their work. There is constant activity but no final resting place. And there is an intimate connection between words and bodies. Words are wearisome, *yĕgē'îm*, a word (either adjective or stative participle) associated with toil, fatigue, exertion, endurance.[2] Eyes are not sated, satisfied, satiated—a verb (*śb'*) that connotes physical satisfaction, the satisfaction of the appetites.[3] And ears are not full of hearing—a verb (*ml'*) that can connote physicality as well.[4]

There is also an allusion to the epilogue in 1:8—as mentioned, the book begins and ends with weariness. Qohelet 12:12 warns: "And more than this, my son, beware; in the making of many books there is no end, and much study is

---

1. Barthes, *Roland Barthes by Roland Barthes*, 92.
2. BDB, 388. BDB also suggests "the toil-worn."
3. Ibid., 959–60. In its verb, noun, and adjective form, *śb'* is most frequently used to indicate the satisfaction of one's appetites, specifically having enough to eat and drink.
4. Ibid., 569–71. The root *ml'* is used in more contexts than the root *śb'*, so it is not as frequently linked to a physical fullness or satisfaction.

wearying to the flesh." Intellectual activity is a bodily toil. In the Hebrew Bible, speech is figured through the organs of speech. Hans Walter Wolff writes:

> there is no other part of the human body of which so many different activities are predicated as the human mouth, with its lips, tongue, palate and throat, in so far as these are organs of speech. . . . The capacity of language provides the essential condition for the humanity of man.[5]

Language is both part of the body and expressed through the body.

The book of Qohelet forms a picture of the speaker not only through language of selfhood and autobiography but also through the construction of Qohelet's body. Following Toni Morrison and Shoshana Feldman, Judith Butler attributes the force of the speech-act to the relation between speech and body. Butler notes that the presence of the body is different in speech than in writing, though neither "makes the body immediately present."[6] According to Butler, the difference between speech and writing lies in the fact that the body in speech is obviously present, hence contributing to the overall rhetorical effect. However, the presence of the body in the book "can remain permanently unclear."[7] The distinction can be over-emphasized and I think Butler underestimates the force of the written word. Whereas it is true that the body in the book is not "immediately present" and can remain "permanently unclear," it is not absent. The power of the written body lies precisely in its lack of clarity, its indecidability.

Books are material objects, and bodies are embedded in books. Martin Gliserman begins his book on psychoanalysis, language, and the body by stating his thesis: "the vital, deep-structural presence of the body is a core phenomenon of language, sometimes exquisitely represented in the novel—and it is that body in the novel to which we respond; it is to be connected to that body that motivates our reading."[8] He draws on the linguistic work of Noam Chomsky as support. Chomsky writes: "We may regard the language capacity virtually as we would a physical organ of the body and can investigate the principles of its organization, function and development in the individual and the species."[9] Gliserman extends Chomsky's linguistic theories "by suggesting that language is an organ, an organ about organs, and an organ that writes itself into its communications. And it replicates itself where and when it can. We will be able to see how the body makes its appearance in different layers or facets of (the structure of) language."[10] Gliserman charts three levels in which the body is manifest in texts.

First, the body and its parts are explicitly named in the text. This is the most basic manifestation of the body in the book. Second, the body is presented symbolically through spatial descriptions of interiors, the environment, objects. Third, the body is encoded in the syntax of the sentence—the movement and

---

5. Hans Walter Wolff, *Anthropology of the Old Testament* (Philadelphia: Fortress, 1974), 78.
6. Butler, *Excitable Speech*, 152.
7. Ibid.
8. Gliserman, *Psychoanalysis*, 1–2.
9. Noam Chomsky, *Rules and Representations* (New York: Columbia University Press, 1980), 185, as quoted in Gliserman, *Psychoanalysis*, 2.
10. Gliserman, *Psychoanalysis*, 2.

tension and shape of its structure enacts the body in the text.[11] Together, repeated words and multiple levels

> form semantic webs. Words have at least a double life—they generate and fulfill our narrative lust, but they also live in another (deconstructed, synchronic, slipped) universe of discourse. When we focus on the semantic webs of the body, untangling them from the narrative, we see how embedded the body is in the text and that it articulates its concerns.[12]

The intricate interconnections between the body and language, spoken and written, demonstrate that the mind/body dualism dominant in much of the history of Western culture cannot be sustained. The body "laces" itself into narrative, not just as a metaphorical figure of speech, but in a way that undermines the very distinctions between them.

As noted above, Roland Barthes, when writing about his body asks, "Which body? I have several."[13] The following chapters will probe six manifestations of the body in the book of Qohelet. The present chapter will examine the eye and the seeing body, the heart and the thinking/feeling body. The next chapter will explore the pain of the toiling body, and the pleasure experienced by the sensing body. Chapter 5 considers the gendered body. And Chapter 6 probes the decaying and dying body. The body has been an infrequently examined facet of the book of Qohelet. By reading the body as it is manifested in the book at different levels—content, symbol, form—Qohelet emerges in various permutations.

Creatures of Earth

The body of Qohelet begins to form. The first level of bodily inscription is at the surface level of naming. Qohelet names the human being ʾādām in the third verse of the text in a question that asks what is the profit of a human's toil. The body is introduced as a toiling body. The word ʾādām is part of Qohelet's distinctive vocabulary. It is used 49 times, more frequently than any other word in the text. In contrast, the more particular word for "man" (ʾîš), is employed only 10 times.[14] The use of this word underscores Qohelet's main interest—"human existence in general."[15] Therefore, ʾādām has a universalistic meaning, even when the definitive article is found in front of it.[16]

---

11. Ibid., 30.
12. Ibid., 8. Even though I am indebted to Gliserman's basic framework for how bodies embed in texts, my work differs quite significantly from his. After establishing his interpretive frame, Gliserman moves on to psychoanalyze the authors of various books based upon the ways in which they write the body into their texts. In direct contradiction to my project, he uses the body in the book to reconstruct the body (and psyche) of the author.
13. Barthes, *Roland Barthes on Roland Barthes*, 60–61.
14. Qoh 1:8; 4:4; 6:2 (twice), 3; 7:5; 9:14, 15 (twice); and 12:3.
15. Robert Gordis, "Was Kohelet a Phoenician? Some Observations on Methods of Research," *JBL* 74 (1995): 103–14. As his title indicates, Gordis was writing against Dahood who argued that Qohelet's distinctive use of ʾādām was indicative of the "Phoenician branch of Northwest Semitic" in his "Canaanite-Phoenician Influence in Qoheleth," *Bib* 33 (1952): 3–52, 191–221. See also Antoon Schoors, "Words Typical of Qohelet," in *Qohelet in the Context of Wisdom*, 17–39 (17).
16. Schoors argues this point in "Words Typical of Qohelet," 17–20.

As the general human referent, *ʾādām* can include women as well. But just like the use of the "universal" term "man" in English, this universal is still weighted toward the masculine body. Ambiguity in the usage of *ʾādām* is seen throughout the Hebrew Bible, beginning in the beginning, the creation stories. God first creates *ʾādām*, an undifferentiated earth creature (Gen 2:7). Out of *ʾādām*, *ʾiššâ* ("woman") is formed (Gen 2:22). Yet the noun *ʾādām* is still used to refer to the male creature in contrast to the female creature after the sexual differentiation takes place (e.g. Gen 2.22; 3.8, 12).[17] Qohelet's text is addressed to a male audience and his *ʾādām* is ambiguous, though primarily male. In one instance he even contrasts *ʾādām* with *ʾiššâ* (Qoh 7:28).

But *ʾādām* is more than just the more general term for humankind. It is also a word that plays on the word for "earth," *ʾǎdāmâ*. While this play is explicitly cited in relation to the creation stories in Gen 2–3, it is rarely mentioned again in modern scholarship. However, the dirt clings to *ʾādām* wherever it goes. Thus, more than just being a universal indicator, it always also references the earthy flesh of the human being, creature of the humus, earthling.

In this *ʾādām* there are hearts and eyes. In Qohelet, the two organs repeated most frequently throughout the text are the heart and the eye. The word *lēb* is used in Qohelet 42 times. Also high in frequency are words related to the eye and seeing (9 and 47 occurrences, respectively). The following sections of this chapter will address the semantic range of heart and eyes in Qohelet, as well as explore the symbolic and syntactical function of the words in the text. How does the naming of body parts construct a body through the text or embed a body in the text? How does the body in the text interact with the reader's body?

The repeated naming of body parts creates a picture of the speaker that is physical, thus adding to the autobiographical features that constitute the construction of the speaker in the mind of the reader. "For subjectivity is not, after all, an out-of-body experience."[18] The skin is the boundary of the body as the cover of the book is the boundary of the body of the text, and "certainly discursive capillaries circulate one's 'flesh and blood' through the textual body. . . ."[19] The body of Qohelet begins to form in the blink of an eye and the beat of a heart.

Story of the Eye

Reading is not just a mental activity. It is an activity of the hand and an activity of the eye.[20] The hands cradle the book, fingers feeling the edges of the page,

---

17.   That *ʾādām* in this context is an undifferentiated earth creature has been argued most convincingly by Phyllis Trible, *God and the Rhetoric of Sexuality* (Philadelphia: Fortress, 1978), 80. See also Mieke Bal, *Lethal Love: Feminist Literary Readings of Biblical Love Stories* (Bloomington: Indiana University Press, 1987), 112–14.

18.   Sidonie Smith, "Identity's Body," in Ashley, Gilmore, and Peters, eds., *Autobiography and Postmodernism*, 266–92 (266).

19.   Ibid.

20.   The following section of this study assumes visual perception. For people who cannot see, reading becomes an experience of only the hands (if reading through the language of Braille) or an experience of the ears (if reading through recordings). Having been a reader for a visually impaired

perhaps stroking them or ruffling them as the eye moves across the page, in English from left to right and back again, in Hebrew from right to left. It is true that this physicality is minimal since it is geared to engage and trigger the imagination and the intellect. It is minimal but it is not absent. It cannot be completely taken for granted. Bodily positions for reading are also important. Generally, one seeks to have the body at rest, comfortable and relaxed, either sitting or reclining; thereby minimizing physical stimulus, stress, and movement, yet maximizing the sensations of comfort and relaxation. Different books lend themselves to different physical positions. A novel almost requires recline, whereas a textbook may be better comprehended if the reader is sitting up, mirroring the attention needed in the mind by a certain attention/tension in the body.[21]

This is our entry into the eye of the text. How are you sitting now?

The word ʿáyin ("eye") is used in the book of Qohelet 9 times,[22] and verbs for seeing (rʾh, "to see") are used 47 times.[23] Whereas "eye" in Qohelet has not met with any scholarly inquiry, "to see" has been scrutinized. Following the noun ʾādām ("man" or "human") and the verb hyh ("to be"), rʾh ("to see") is the most frequently used word in Qohelet. Studies on this word focus particularly upon its first person usage—where the speaker claims to have seen this or that for a total of 21 times.[24] One should include in this list Qoh 1:16 where Qohelet's heart sees, and 2:12 where Qohelet turns to see, making a total of 23 times. However, neither translators nor commentators have remained content with the simple literal meaning of "to see" for rʾh.

The suggestions vary. George A. Barton translates the verb as "to experience," and Robert Gordis follows his lead.[25] Barton notes in particular that rʾh includes the entire range of experiences and not just pleasurable ones. Antoon Schoors cautions that Barton's stress on the range of experiences should not obscure the connotation of pleasure that still emerges in certain verses. Schoors cites two examples in which "seeing" is equated with enjoyment: "and he let his soul enjoy pleasure (herʾâ ṭôb, "cause to see good" [2:24]) and "enjoy (rěʾēh "see") life with a woman" (9.9). Other verses where rʾh could be translated as "to enjoy" include 5:17 and 6.6.

Loader stresses observation not in the physical but in the intellectual sense, and he uses rʾh as his genre-mark. He then labels these passages in Qohelet

woman for many years, I am aware of the difference in sensation and perception in each of the ways of reading. But I will await her article on the subject, and not address that difference here. Qohelet presupposes a sighted reader.

21. Of course, this is up to the individual reader. I have a friend who read for her PhD qualifying exams primarily while in the bathtub.

22. Qoh 1:8; 2:10, 14; 4:8; 5:10; 6:9; 8:16; 11:7, 9.

23. Qoh 1:8, 10, 14, 16; 2:1, 3, 12, 13, 24 (twice); 3:10, 13, 16, 18, 22 (twice); 4:1, 3, 4, 7, 15; 5:7, 12, 17 (twice); 6:1, 5, 6; 7:11, 13, 14, 15, 27, 29; 8:9, 10, 16 (twice), 17; 9:9, 11, 13; 10:5, 7; 11:4, 7; 12:3.

24. The first person singular of the perfect tense appears 18 times: Qoh 1:14; 2:13, 24; 3:10, 16, 22; 4:4, 15; 5:12, 17; 6:1; 7:15; 8:9, 10, 17; 9:13; 10:5, 7. The first person singular of the imperfect tense appears three times: 4:1, 7; 9:11.

25. George A. Barton, *A Critical and Exegetical Commentary on the Book of Ecclesiastes* (ICC; Edinburgh: T&T Clark, 1908), 88; and Gordis, *Koholeth*, 204.

"observations."[26] Concentrating on the first person use of the verb, Michel reads *rā'îtî* as "I consider" or "I examine."[27] For him, in certain cases, the empirical act of literally seeing is clearly not the meaning of the word. Here he cites Qoh 2:24, though he does not translate *r'h* as "enjoy" as Schoors does above. Michael Fox reads *rā'îtî* in a similar way as "I realize."[28] Schoors concurs particularly with Fox's argument and cites the difficult verse 5:17 where he translates *r'h* as "to discover": "Behold, that which I have discovered (*rā'îtî*) is good, that it is becoming to eat and drink. . . ."[29] Qohelet "discovers" or "realizes" based upon his experiences and his reflections.

Schoors takes the reader through the different verses that use the verb *r'h*, and he explores the different translation possibilities as suggested by scholars such as Gordis, Michel, Fox, Loader, Barton, and Ginsburg. By so doing, Schoors demonstrates that *r'h* is a word with a range of meanings:

> In sum, in Qohelet the form *rā'îtî* has not the fixed meaning as suggested by Loader (observation) or Michel (examination), but depending on the object and the context, it can mean either of them and also realization or conclusion.[30]

Contrary to these interpreters, there is one case where Qohelet may mean simply "to see": "I saw (*rā'îtî*) all of the living who walk about under the sun . . ." (4:15a).

Scholars go to great lengths to determine the precise meaning of *r'h*, particularly when Qohelet himself is the subject of the verb, and they have done us all a great service in exploring the metaphorical and figurative range of *r'h*. These inquiries and others like them are not wrong. Just like the English verb "to see," the Hebrew verb has a semantic range that runs the gamut from literal to various metaphorical meanings. But this type of inquiry begs the question: Why the eye and why "to see" and not another Hebrew word that means "think" or "believe" or some other word that foregrounds abstract mental reasoning?[31] And then: Why do scholars find it necessary to argue against any simple, plain, and literal reading in favor of the figurative and metaphorical in all cases? When Schoors suggests that *r'h* means physical seeing in 4:15, he must argue the point:

> The literal meaning, the physical sense-act of seeing, is not only relevant in Qoh 4.15. The repetition of the verb as well as the repetition of the organ (the eye) has an effect in the text. In the words of Phyllis Trible, the "psychic" and the "physical" connect.[32] By using words of seeing, the text is taking the reader through the process of observing and understanding the world in the reader's body. The seeing of Qohelet is also

---

26.   J. A. Loader, *Polar Structures in the Book of Qohelet* (New York: de Gruyter, 1979), 25.

27.   Diethelm Michel, *Untersuchungen zur Eigenart des Buches Qohelet* (New York: de Gruyter, 1989), 35.

28.   Fox, *Qohelet and his Contradictions*, 188–90.

29.   Schoors' translation, "Words Typical of Qohelet," 29; cf. idem, *The Preacher Sought*, 139.

30.   Schoors, "Words Typical of Qohelet," 32.

31.   For example, the verb *ḥšb* ("to think"). Qohelet does use this word in its noun form—*ḥešbôn*, "reckoning" or "account." The noun is unique to Qohelet and appears in Qoh 7:25, 27; 9:10.

32.   Trible here is discussing the implications of the metaphor of the "womb" to speak of God's compassion. But her general argument that the physical meanings of the words are not incidental but integral to the metaphorical meanings corresponds with my argument about the bodily words in Qohelet. They are not "just" metaphors. See Trible, *God and the Rhetoric*, 51.

occasionally linked to a verb of motion: "I turned to see" (Qoh 2:12). Not only is the speaker seeing and turning to see, and having his heart see, but the speaker is then commanding the reader to see—an imperative to mark a conclusion (for example, Qoh 7:27). In effect, the speaker is saying that he has seen; now he wants the reader to see too. Turn and look at this. The reader's body is being moved along.

Whether or not a particular instance of *r³h* means to observe, enjoy, consider, realize, it also always means "to see" in every instance, and this baseline meaning does not disappear in the abstraction of mental activity—"to see" adheres to *r³h*, the eye moves and takes in light, information, experience. Nor is it necessary to pin down the meaning(s) of *r³h*, since they all are at play every time the word is used. There would be no seeing (whether realizing, or considering, or examining) without seeing, for the primary way that information enters the body is through the eye, particularly when that body is reading its information.

Elaine Scarry links the movement of the reader's eye across the page with the ability of the imagination to move pictures across the mind:

> The eyes, meanwhile, are also in motion, rolling from left to right and back again, skating down the page, darting back to a detail missed, then forward again. Their actual motion is incorporated into the motion of fictional persons so that our somatic mimesis of what is happening in the book works to substantiate and vivify motions on the mental retina that are wholly imaginary.[33]

By using the verb "to see," Qohelet is creating a mimetic experience—it is as if the speaker is saying, "as I moved through life observing and realizing through the use of my eye, you, the reader, are observing and realizing too through the use of your eye moving across this page." The mimetic experience induced by the words for seeing contribute to the strong identification readers feel with the speaker. They both use their eyes to see.

Hans Walter Wolff, in his otherwise comprehensive examination of the anthropology of the Hebrew Bible, ascribes little importance to the eye. Seeing is only discussed in conjunction with hearing, as both "are necessary in order to perceive the acts of Yahweh. . . ."[34] "But," continues Wolff, "the opening of the eye comes through the word."[35] In other words, hearing is primary. Certainly in an oral culture, hearing words would be a more common experience than seeing them on a page. But without exception these biblical words, which are "heard," appear in a text that is read and therefore seen. In ancient times, as in modern times, the Bible is publicly read aloud, and hearing is thereby an important part of the experience of scripture.[36] But it is *read* aloud and therefore always mediated by a seeing eye before reaching a hearing ear.[37]

33. Scarry, *Dreaming By the Book*, 148.
34. Wolff, *Anthropology of the Old Testament*, 75.
35. Ibid.
36. The book of Qohelet is read in its entirety during the Jewish holiday of Sukkot. The only passage in Qohelet that is read during Christian services is 3:1–9. It is the alternative lectionary reading for January 1.
37. In the book *Body Symbolism in the Bible*, Thomas Staubli and Silvia Schroer attribute Wolff's striking omission of the eye to his "word-centered theology of hearing" and the Protestant "hostility to images"; see Thomas Staubli and Sylvia Schroer, *Body Symbolism in the Bible* (trans.

Edouard Dhorme ascribes more importance to the eye than Wolff does.[38] For Dhorme, the eye has a unique position in the catalogue of organs because it is both the subject and the object of vision.[39] As the seeing subject, "l'œil est le principal instrument de connaissance" ("the eye is the principal instrument of knowledge").[40] In this capacity, it plays a key role in the discernment of good and evil.[41] The eye is the agent of judgment. For example, two of the refrains in the book of Judges concern the eyes and judgment: "The Israelites did evil in the eyes of (*bĕʿênê*) of the Lord . . ." (e.g. Judg 3:7, 12; 4:1), and its counterpart, "all the people did what was right in their own eyes (*bĕʿênāyw*)" (Judg 21:25). Knowledge is not limited to intellectual knowledge or moral knowledge for the Hebrew writers. The eye is also involved in emotional knowledge, for certain phrases carry with them the connotation of love or desire.[42]

In its relationship to the heart, the eye has a contradictory position. On the one hand, the eye and the heart can be opposed. "L'œil, comme la face, n'est pas seulement le subject, mais aussi l'object de la vision. Il s'opposera également au cœur, comme la chose visible à la chose invisible" ("The eye, like the face, is not only the subject, but also the object of vision. It is opposed equally to the heart, as the thing visible to the thing invisible").[43] The opposition is illustrated most strikingly in 1 Sam 16:7: "humans see the eyes, but the Lord sees the heart." On the other hand, the eye is the conduit between the internal and the external, and as such expresses the sentiments of the heart: "Les sentiments du cœur transpireront dans les yeux aussi bien que dans le visage . . ." ("The sentiments of the heart come out in the eyes as well as in the face . . .").[44] I will return to the relationship between the heart and the eye below.

Rivka Ulmer also notes that, in the Hebrew Bible, the eye is involved in a variety of contexts.[45] In addition to the uses noted above by Dhorme, Ulner adds that the eye is an essential and irreplaceable organ of the human body. The *lex talionis* is expressed first concerning the eye: "eye for eye (*ʿayin taḥat ʿayin*) tooth for tooth . . ." (Exod 21:24; cf. Deut 19:21).[46] Eyes express emotions, intentions, and desires. In Proverbs, one can have a "good eye" and engage in charitable actions: "One who has a good eye (*ṭôb-ʿayin*) shall be blessed, for he

Linda D. Maloney; Collegeville, Minn.: The Liturgical Press, 2001), 15 and 112. However, the privileging of hearing over seeing is present in the Hebrew Bible itself and not necessarily imposed by the biases of interpreters.

38. Edouard Dhorme, *L'emploi métaphorique des noms de parties du corps en Hébreu et en Akkadien* (Paris: Librairie Orientaliste Paul Geuthnes, 1963), 75–80.

39. Ibid., 76.

40. Ibid., 77. All translations from the French are my own.

41. Ibid., 78.

42. Ibid., 77. Dhorme notes that this nuance is central in Akkadian metaphorical use of the eye.

43. Ibid., 78.

44. Ibid., 76.

45. The following two paragraphs are dependent upon a brief survey of "eye" in the Hebrew Bible found in Rivka Ulmer, *The Evil Eye in the Bible and in Rabbinic Literature* (Hoboken, N.J.: Ktav, 1994), 1–4.

46. Even though the *lex talionis* begins in both instances a verse earlier with "life for life" the second term in the list (eye) is commonly used as a shorthand for the entire law.

gives of his bread to the poor" (Prov 22:9). Or, one can have an "evil eye" and do what is contrary to the good life: "He that hastens to be rich has an evil eye (*ra*ᶜ*-*ᶜ*ayin*) and considers not that poverty shall come upon him" (23:6).

God's eye signals God's intimacy, or omnipotence and watchfulness. For example, though the NRSV translates the following verse using "face to face," the Hebrew expresses the immediacy between the Israelites and God as "eye to eye": "They have heard that you, O Lord, are in the midst of this people; for you, O Lord, are seen eye to eye (ᶜ*ayin bĕ*ᶜ*ayin*) . . ." (Num 14:14).[47] Zechariah speaks of "the eyes of (ᶜ*ênê*) the Lord, which run to and fro through the whole world" (Zech 4:10) when referring to God's watchful omnipotence.

Dhorme and Ulmer both note that the eye is associated with both knowledge and desire. Power is also a part of this aspect of the eye. In Gen 3, the serpent explains to the first woman that the real reason God has forbidden the human creatures to eat the fruit in the middle of the garden is because "'God knows that when you eat of it your eyes will be opened, and you will be like God knowing good and evil'" (Gen 3:5). The opening of the eyes expresses the acquisition of knowledge (cf. Num 24:4; Isa 35:5). The story continues: "So when the woman saw that the tree was good for food, and that it was a delight to the eyes, and that the tree was to be desired to make one wise . . ." (Gen 3:6a). The woman directs her gaze toward the fruit as an expression of inquiry that transforms itself into desire which then manifests itself in an act of acquisition or power: ". . . she took of its fruit and ate" (Gen 3:6b).

Feminist interpreters have often noted that the eye in the Hebrew Bible is connected to issues of power and desire between men and women, and they have termed such a conjunction "the gaze." Men are the ones who look, whereas women are looked at, and this expresses the social hierarchy between them.[48] An example of "the gaze" is found in 2 Sam 11 when David sees Bathsheba and then summons her so that he can have intercourse with (rape?) her. According to one definition,

> The concept of the gaze describes a form of power associated with the eye and the sense of sight. Certain bodies can wield power over other bodies by looking at them in certain ways. When we gaze at somebody or something, we are not simply "looking." The gaze probes and masters. It penetrates the body and bounds it as a passive object.[49]

In sum, the look of the eye "can be understood as an act of engagement preceding interaction on other levels"[50]—interactions of judgment, power, desire, and knowledge.

---

47. Dhorme, *L'emploi métaphorique*, 77.

48. For example, J. Cheryl Exum grounds her work *Plotted, Shot, and Painted: Cultural Representations of Biblical Women* (JSOTSup 215; Sheffield: Sheffield Academic Press, 1996), upon this principle. "The gaze" received its theoretical conceptualization by psychoanalysts such as Lacan and its feminist critique by Laura Mulvey, "Visual Pleasure and Narrative Cinema," *Screen* 16, no. 3 (1975): 6–18. See also E. Ann Kaplan, "Is the Gaze Male?," in *Powers of Desire: The Politics of Sexuality* (ed. Ann Snitow, Christine Stansell, and Sharon Thompson; New York: Monthly Review Press, 1983), 309–27.

49. Dani Cavallaro, *The Body for Beginners* (New York: Writers & Readers, 1998), 115.

50. Ulmer, *The Evil Eye*, vii.

Qohelet's eye is an instrument of engagement in the realms of judgment, knowledge, power, and desire. At the conjunction between power and desire, Qohelet has three statements associating the eyes with the acquisition of pleasure: "whatever my eyes desired I did not keep from them" (Qoh 2:10a); "Light is sweet and it is pleasant for the eyes to see the sun" (11:7); and "Rejoice, young man, while you are young, and let your heart cheer you in the days of your youth. Follow the inclination of your heart and the desire of your eyes . . ." (11:9). Qohelet also makes three statements expressing the inability to be satisfied through the desire of the eyes: "their eyes are never satisfied with riches" (4:8); "When goods increase, those who eat them increase; and what gain has their owner but to see them with his eyes?" (5:10 [Eng 11]); "When I applied my heart to know wisdom, and to see the business that is done on earth, how one's eyes see sleep neither day nor night, then I saw all the work of God, that no one can find out what is happening under the sun . . ." (8:16–17). In all of these verses, Qohelet is associating pleasure (or the lack thereof) with the look of the eye, with the gaze, even if this is the only benefit of the object such as in 5:10 (Eng 11).

Looking at and desiring an object, or finding pleasure through the gaze, is not just about power and acquisition. Elaine Scarry points out that the total skin surface of an adult is about 3000 square inches. By comparison, the surface of the retina against which light is projected and transformed into electric impulses is minuscule:

> Yet, physiologically, 38% of all sensory experience takes place against that tiny surface. Eyes are, according to neurobiologists, the direct outcropping of the brain: not content to receive messages by mediation, the brain has moved out to the surface of the skull in order to rub up against the world directly (no wonder it is overwhelming to look into another person's eyes; one beholds directly the moist tissue of the person's brain).[51]

The eye is a sensuous organ.

Qohelet figures the ability to be wise—to be knowledgeable—in terms of the eyes, as well: "The wise have eyes in their head, but fools walk in darkness" (Qoh 2:14a). However, in typical Qohelet fashion, this wisdom does not get you anywhere in the end: "Yet I saw that the same fate befalls all of them" (2:14b). The wise can see, but it does not prevent them from experiencing death. In one instance, the eye is associated with knowledge and contrasted to desire: "Better is the sight of the eyes than the wandering of desire; this also is *hebel* and a chasing after wind" (6:9). Again, it is all ultimately worth nothing.

Some theorists on the body trace the ascendancy of the experience of seeing to the Renaissance ideal of perspectivalism.[52] It has been proposed that perspective was discovered by Renaissance artists as a way of representing the world more realistically through the application of mathematical rules. This connection between seeing and the scientific had implications that went beyond

---

51. Scarry, *Dreaming By the Book*, 68.
52. See, e.g., Cavallaro, *The Body for Beginners*, 105.

the artistic realm. "Perspectivalism says that the human eye can dominate the world and that its gaze can be structured scientifically."[53] The body was stripped down to just the eye, and the eye alone became the instrument of inquiry and objectivity.

Because of its associations with certain Western notions of objectivity and power, some feminists have decried the eye.[54] Recounting this vilification, Donna Haraway summarizes:

> The eyes have been used to signify a perverse capacity—honed to perfection in the history of science tied to militarism, capitalism, colonialism, and male supremacy—to distance the knowing subject from everybody and everything in the interests of unfettered power. The instruments of visualization in multinationalist, postmodernist culture have compounded these meanings of disembodiment.[55]

But the eye is embodied, situated, fallible. Emphasizing these aspects of the eye undermines the Western ideology of the eye: "objectivity turns out to be about particular and specific embodiment and definitely not about the false vision promising transcendence of all limits and responsibility."[56] The eye is not an organ of objective epistemology; rather, for Haraway, it is the site of situated knowledge.

Throughout history, the cultural configuration of the eye has shifted and changed. As we read Qohelet's eyes, these meanings accompany us, for they shape our understandings. The reader is always already entangled in an inter-textual web of meanings and associations for "eyes" and "seeing." It is difficult, and maybe even undesirable, to dis-entangle the reader from the text and avoid anachronism altogether. How much of our conceptualization of Qohelet's epistemology relies on our own ideology of the eye? Western culture has been governed by three main principles concerning sight:

> One: It has prioritized sight as the most reliable of the senses. Sight does not require physical proximity in the way the other senses especially touch and smell do. For this reason, it has been associated with the rational mind rather than the animal body. Two: It has endeavoured to standardize sight by codifying scientifically correct ways of seeing (e.g. through perspective). Three: It has used the sense of sight and the idea of regulated vision to fix the body.[57]

Qohelet references and then undermines each of these principles.

Michael Fox has written extensively about Qohelet's epistemology. For him, epistemology is the central question in the text.[58] And even though Qohelet's

---

53.   Ibid.

54.   For example, Exum's *Plotted, Shot, and Painted* references the visual in its title, and uses the rubric of "the gaze" to center its feminist critique.

55.   Donna Haraway, "The Persistence of Vision," in *Writing on the Body: Female Embodiment and Feminist Theory* (ed. Katie Conboy, Nadia Medina, and Sarah Stanbury; New York: Columbia University Press, 1997), 283–95 (284).

56.   Ibid., 285.

57.   Cavallaro, *The Body for Beginners*, 111.

58.   Fox, *A Time to Tear Down*, 71. See also Fox, "The Inner Structure of Qohelet's Thought," in Schoors, ed., *Qohelet in the Context of Wisdom*, 225–38.

method of knowing is "inchoate and unsystematic," it is not "chaotic." For Fox, what makes Qohelet's epistemology unique is the emphasis on seeing and experiencing the world: "Qohelet's investigation is based, in principle, on experience. He seeks experience, observes it, judges it, then reports his perceptions and reactions."[59] After a survey of the epistemologies of other Wisdom texts in the Bible, he concludes: "In brief, if one could ask a more conventional sage, 'How do you know this?' I believe he would answer: 'Because I learned it.' To this question Qohelet would reply: 'Because I saw it.' The shift is profound."[60]

But can the eye really guarantee knowledge? Qohelet sometimes thinks that it can but then always throws the value of that knowledge into doubt: the wise may have eyes in their heads, but they still suffer the same fate as the fool (2:14). Can even the reader's eye guarantee knowledge and the benefits that should then accrue? No, for there is a profound failure here too which happens well before death. The human eye only has 25 gradations for light (in other words, the pupil can only adjust 25 times in response to light), whereas there are over 10 thousand different light intensities.[61] We have an exceedingly limited ability to adjust to all of the different shades and degrees of illumination. Our view of the world lacks nuance. This alone should warn us against the privileging of sight in our own epistemologies.

Nor can the eye "fix" the body in Qohelet. First, the body is inscribed in pieces—an eye here, a hand there. It is fragmented and scattered across and through the text, and the reader's eye cannot pull it all together to stabilize it. The second reason for the lack of fixity of the body in the book is the ubiquitous decaying of the body toward death in the book of Qohelet. I will return to this later point in Chapter 6.

Billions of visual impulses enter our eyes at every instance of their opening, and these billions of impulses must be processed and interpreted. The interpretive frames are conditioned by our cultural moment. The technical and biological process of seeing is conventionally turned into a worldview: "light means enlightenment, truth, rationality, everything to do with the mind, whereas darkness means the unknown, basic instincts, the body."[62] Despite the abstractions of Qohelet's commentators, the eye in its epistemological capacity remains a part of the body, and thus it breaks down the dualism of mind/body. There is no seeing/knowing outside of the experience of the body. Qohelet's epistemological orientation is situated. The language of body and the language of mind are blended in Qohelet in a way that undermines their opposition, yet does not just simply collapse the two. The eye winks at us.

---

59. Fox, *A Time to Tear Down*, 77.
60. Ibid., 85.
61. Cavallaro, *The Body for Beginners*, 109
62. Ibid., 112.

The Language of the Heart

The word "heart" (*leb* or *lēbāb*) appears in the Hebrew Bible 858 times.[63] In the book of Qohelet, "heart" occurs 42 times,[64] a frequency greater than other characteristic words such as *hebel* and *ʿamal* ("toil"). Yet, rather than being at the top of any list enumerating Qohelet's distinctive vocabulary words and therefore his key concepts, it is largely absent from such word studies. The following will correct that oversight by examining the heart in Qohelet against the backdrop of the heart's uses in other biblical texts.

Human and animal bodies have one heart, but Qohelet's body has 42. What meanings are inscribed and what effects are produced by the redundancy of the heart in the body of the book? According to Gliserman, redundancy is the encoding of certain information in a variety of ways.[65] In a living body, redundancy begins at the level of the DNA and the RNA: "Why encode genetic information in DNA, when by representing it directly in proteins, you could eliminate not just one, but two levels of interpretation? The answer is: it turns out that it is extremely useful to have the same information in several different forms."[66] We have two eyes to take in light from two slightly different perspectives. We have two kidneys, two ears, two arms, two hemispheres of the brain. Qohelet has 42 hearts, each encoding in their rhythms various meanings, inviting multiple interpretations of the same word.

In none of the three major recent monographs on the language of Qohelet does an analysis of "heart" appear. As Daniel C. Fredericks notes, the language studies of Qohelet have been made with two interests in mind: determining the date and determining the influences.[67] He himself has only this dual project in mind.[68] Bo Isaksson's work concentrates on the verbal system, though it also examines the use of *ʾănî* in Qohelet (as discussed in Chapter 2).[69] He too is interested in dating Qohelet and charting its influences. Antoon Schoors has only published his study on the grammar of Qohelet, and he promises a forthcoming

---

63.   The count varies. Wolff (*Anthropology of the Old Testament*) tallies 858 times (p. 40); Francis I. Andersen and A. Dean Forbes (*The Vocabulary of the Old Testament* [Rome: Editrice Pontificio Istituto Biblico, 1989]) count 860 (p. 134); Marjorie O'Rourke Boyle ("The Law of the Heart: The Death of a Fool [I Samuel 25]," *JBL* 120 [2001]: 401–27) is satisfied with simply stating that "heart" occurs "more than eight hundred times" (p. 401) in the Hebrew Bible.

64.   Qoh 1:13, 16 (twice), 17; 2:1, 3 (twice), 10 (twice), 15 (twice), 20, 22, 23; 3:11, 17, 18; 5:1, 19; 7:2, 3, 4 (twice), 7, 21, 22, 25, 26; 8:5, 9, 11, 16; 9:1, 3 (twice), 7; 10:2 (twice), 3; 11:9 (twice), 10.

65.   Gliserman, *Psychoanalysis*, 15–16.

66.   Douglas Hofstadter, *Godel, Escher, Bach: An Eternal Golden Braid* (New York: Norton, 1979), 616–17, as quoted in Gliserman, *Psychoanalysis*, 15.

67.   Daniel C. Fredericks, *Qoheleth's Language: Re-evaluating its Nature and its Date* (Lewiston, N.Y.: Edwin Mellen, 1988), 1.

68.   Fredericks chronicles the language studies of the late nineteenth and twentieth centuries, from Delitzsch (*Commentary on Song of Songs and Ecclesiastes*) to Charles F. Whitley (*Koheleth: His Language and Thought* [New York: de Gruyter, 1979]). See Fredericks, *Qoheleth's Language*, 1–26.

69.   Isaksson, *Studies in the Language of Qoheleth*.

work on nouns.[70] Toward that later project, an article has been written, though if this recent article is a foretaste of this awaited volume, there will still be no examination of this frequently used word. He includes "heart" in a list of repeated words for further study, but does not indicate that he intends to accomplish this study himself.[71]

This omission is even stranger considering two things: (1) Qohelet has such a distinctive vocabulary that it has inspired countless studies on it; and (2) the human character of this book is often noted and emphasized over a more "divine" or "holy" orientation. Concerning the second point, how could one label Qohelet a "theological anthropology"[72] without a recognition and analysis of the bodily parts that comprise that anthropology? Hans Walter Wolff begins his major *Anthropology of the Old Testament* with precisely such a study, though he simply mentions Qohelet's 42 hearts without further examination.[73] Despite the fleshy language of the text, the flesh is abstracted and subsumed into discussions of observation and epistemology.

It is possible that commentators assume they know what Qohelet means when the word "heart" is employed. It does appear some 800 more times in the Bible and has been subjected to studies in these other contexts. As I will demonstrate, Qohelet not only has a distinctive vocabulary, but also tends to use common vocabulary in distinctive ways. "Heart" is one of these instances.

I begin at the beginning, with Brown, Driver, and Briggs's lexicon. BDB begins with a general definition of *lēb*: "inner man, mind, will, heart, seldom of things, usually of men." The work then elaborates upon this basic definition through an enumerated list. Definitions include "comprehending mind, affections and will," "knowledge, mind or wisdom, thinking reflection, memory," "inclinations, resolutions," "conscience" or "moral character," "the seat of the appetites . . . the emotions and passions . . . courage."[74] Other biblical dictionaries commonly slip into anachronism with definitions that presuppose modern medical knowledge.[75] For example, some biblical definitions begin with "the quivering, pumping organ, the heart"[76] thereby assuming Williams Harvey's 1628 discovery of the circulation of the blood through the pumping action of this "quivering" body part.

70. Schoors, *The Preacher Sought to Find Pleasing Words*.

71. Schoors, "Words Typical of Qohelet," 39.

72. Seow, *Ecclesiastes*, 54–60. Seow observes the reticence of commentators to speak of Qohelet's theology, substituting the word "philosophy" instead. Seow, while acknowledging that this reticence is understandable, and that Qohelet speaks more of humanity (*ʾādām*, 48 times) than of God (*ʾĕlōhîm*, 40 times), proposes a compromise between the two by arguing that Qohelet is a "theological anthropology."

73. Wolff, *Anthropology of the Old Testament*, 47.

74. BDB, 523.

75. See O'Rourke Boyle, "The Law of the Heart," for a survey and critique of this phenomenon. Dhorme disagrees with Boyle's contention that ancient peoples did not regard the heart as essential to the circulation of the blood; see Dhorme, *L'emploi métaphorique*, 113.

76. Ludwig Koehler and Walter Baumgartner, *The Hebrew and Aramaic Lexicon of the Old Testament*, Vol. 2 (Leiden: Brill, 1995), 514.

The widely used *HarperCollins Bible Dictionary* asserts that heart is "the most important anthropological word in the Hebrew scriptures"[77] and reckons its use at 814 times. As way of comparison, the next most widely used word of internal organs is "kidney" used 31 times, only 13 of which refer to human kidneys.[78] In biblical texts, unlike the body, hearts far outnumber kidneys. Physically, the heart is related to the movement of the limbs (see 1 Sam 25:37), and in 2 Sam 18:14 the stopped heart induces paralysis but not death. But the physical meanings account for only a fraction of the uses of *lēb*. Most are related to the heart as center of emotions and passions, thought and reflection. However, Edwards does not cite Qohelet in his discussion of the many meanings of the word "heart." Qohelet's usage may very well be connected to the other meanings and uses in the Bible, but there are distinctions that should warrant mention.

Perhaps Qohelet's heart is largely ignored because of its absence from English translations of the work.[79] The NRSV generally translates "heart" as either "mind" (e.g. 1:17) or "myself" (e.g. 1:13). Other popular translations such as the RSV and the JPS made translation decisions identical to that of the NRSV. Only the NIV will occasionally translate *lēb* literally (e.g. in 1:17, but not 1:13). The one study of bodily metaphors in Hebrew literature that does listen to Qohelet's heart is the French scholar Dhorme's comprehensive work noted above for its examination of the eye.

Qohelet's heart begins to beat in 1:13, a verse that introduces Qohelet's search for knowledge and wisdom—a prominent motif throughout the book: "And I gave my heart to seek and to search out wisdom . . ."—and again in 1:17, "I spoke to my heart saying, behold I will increase and add wisdom more than all who were before me in Jerusalem, and my heart saw the great wisdom and knowledge." Qohelet speaks of and to his own heart 18 times throughout the course of the text, the majority of these (12) clustering in the discourse on his investigations (1:13–2:26). Michael Fox believes that Qohelet "speaks of it [his heart] so frequently in 1:12–2:26 because he is reflecting on the process of perception and discovery and the heart has a central role in this process. Qohelet is not only exploring but also observing himself explore. He is his own field of investigation."[80] Qohelet turns in and out.

---

77.   Douglas R. Edwards, "Heart," in *HarperCollins Bible Dictionary* (San Francisco: HarperCollins, 1996), 407–8 (407); cf. Wolff, *Anthropology of the Old Testament*, 40.

78.   Wolff, *Anthropology of the Old Testament*, 65.

79.   A brief sampling of French and German translations of Qohelet yielded the following results. Luther translates *lēb* as "Herz" every time save one. In 9:7, *lēb* is translated as "Mut," a word that means "heart" in the sense of "courage" or "pluck." Another popular German translation (Elberfelder or ELB) uses "Herz" all the way through the book, including in 9:7. In French, the classic translation by Louis Segond (LSG) translates *lēb* as "cœur" ("heart"). Exceptions to the literal translation of *lēb* are the versions produced by the International Bible Society. In both French and German, *lēb* has various translations that correspond to the ways in which *lēb* is translated in English. For example, 1:16 reads "Ich . . . sagte mir" ("I . . . said to myself"). Since the IBS is an American-based organization (founded in 1809 in New York City), it is possible that its translations are influenced by English conventions.

80.   Fox, *A Time to Tear Down*, 78.

Not only does this passage introduce Qohelet's quest, but it also focuses on the most sensual part of the quest. The speaker conducts a series of experiments: he builds homes, gardens, parks, and buys slaves and animal herds; he gathers silver and gold, singers, and concubines. In short, he surrounds himself with sensual pleasures—he pursues a hedonistic lifestyle in the name of the pursuit of wisdom. Qohelet 1:12–2:26 will be discussed further in Chapter 4, but suffice it to say here that the body is central in and to the search for wisdom, and this is emphasized by figuring the search as a conversation between Qohelet and his heart.

The heart is the center of the junction of intellect and emotion, reason and passion. Dhorme sums up his study by concluding that "Toute la psychologie des Hébreux et des Akkadiens tourne donc autour du cœur" ("All of the psychology of the Hebrews and the Akkadians turns therefore around the heart").[81] As such, it demonstrates that what our culture tends to configure as binary oppositions are not oppositions at all.[82] The translation of "heart" as "mind" suppresses its emotional side. In English, we bifurcate the heart and the brain, the emotions and the intellect. Because of this exclusive association of the heart with the passions, translating heart as mind guards against the importation of English connotations and emphasizes the way in which the Hebrew heart is more akin to the English brain. However, the Hebrew heart is not the exclusive organ of the intellect, but rather it combines the thinking person and the feeling person. By translating *lēb* as "mind" in order to guard against the English connotations, this juncture is suppressed.

It is this very confluence that enables Qohelet to observe, to bring the observation into himself and consider it, and finally to learn from it. Taking one of the "heart" passages, we can chart the movement of the heart through the process of observation and knowledge: "I turned my heart to know and to search out and to seek wisdom and the sum, and to know that wickedness is folly and that foolishness is madness" (Qoh 7:25). In Hebrew, the first three words focus the reader on the speaker's own self. The "I" as carried on the suffix *yôd* is embedded in these first three words (*sabbôtî ʾănî wĕlibbî*), repeated one after the other, redundant for the surface meaning but essential for the deeper structuring of the body in the book. The three verbs (in infinitive form: *lādaʿat wĕlātûr ûbaqqēš*) that follow are the verbs of inquiry and motion, which the heart circles three times in the rhythm of the sentence. The heart is in motion though it never completes its quest, never comes to a final resting place.

What Qohelet finds in this passage is another heart: the woman's "heart is snares and nets, her hands are fetters" (7:26). As the woman embraces the

---

81. Dhorme, *L'emploi métaphorique*, 128.

82. Historical studies on the ancient Israelite idea of the body indicate that the body was seen as an integrated whole, unlike the Greeks, for example, who conceptualized the body as a body–soul dichotomy or body–soul–spirit trichotomy. See Douglas A. Knight, "The Ethics of Human Life in the Hebrew Bible," in *Justice and the Holy: Essays in Honor of Walter Harrelson* (ed. Douglas A. Knight and Peter J. Paris; Atlanta: Scholars Press, 1989), 65–88 (68–69). Knight also notes that the heart encompasses "reason, will, desires, and feelings" in the Hebrew Bible (p. 69).

unwary man and takes him to her bosom, it opens up to reveal an instrument of capture, and the enfolding arms are instruments of bondage. But does Qohelet's heart get caught during his investigations? Qohelet emerges on the other side of the woman to make a pronouncement: "See, this is what I found, says Qohelet, adding one to one to find the sum, which my soul (*nepeš*) constantly sought and I did not find: one man in a thousand I found, but a woman in all of these I did not find" (7:17–18). The Hebrew word *nepeš* is translated as "mind" in the NRSV, just like *lēb*. There is an identification between the *lēb* that begins the search and the *nepeš* that draws the conclusion.[83] But the words are not identical and it leaves me wondering if Qohelet is being dishonest with his readers. On the surface, he despises this woman. Yet, his heart is caught within her embrace. He leaves it behind, and his investigations conclude within this slippage. I will return to this passage in Chapter 5.

Qohelet's heart is sometimes separate from Qohelet's speaking self. The heart is spoken to, and then pursues part of the investigation on the heart's own—in other words, the heart is sometimes the subject of the verb. When Qohelet speaks of his heart, he is speaking to a semi-autonomous part of himself.[84]

Even though the heart functions semi-independently of its bearer, it is not uncommon to find definitions of the heart that emphasize the heart as the whole person. In the only book-length investigation of the heart in the Hebrew Bible, von Meyenfeldt concludes that "LEB (LEBAB) represents the *whole* person. In the deepest sense it marks this characteristic: the genuine, the authentic, the essential."[85] But even within this definition, there is a contradiction. How can the heart represent both the whole person and the most essential aspect of that person? Can a whole person be reduced to his or her essence? Or is the essence the only authentic part of the whole person?

There is another problem with thinking of the heart as the essence of the person. There are 814 instances of heart referring to the human. The remaining

---

83.   Fox (*A Time to Tear Down*, 78) cites these verses as an example of the heart's experience "enabling the person to attain knowledge."

84.   Speaking of and to one's heart in Qohelet is similar to Egyptian uses of "heart" in its wisdom corpus. Shannon Burkes discusses the importance of the heart as the source for both the emotions and the intellect in Egyptian wisdom texts (*Death in Qohelet*, 144). Fox also notes the Egyptian connection: "A similar conception of the heart's function is expounded in the Egyptian 'Memphite Theology': 'Sight, hearing, breathing—they report to the heart, and it makes every understanding come forth. As to the tongue, it repeats what the heart has devised' (AEL 1.54). In other words, the senses (Qohelet, less specifically says 'I') transmit sensations to the heart, which organizes them into knowledge. The heart then passes this knowledge to the tongue (again, Qohelet says 'I'), which speaks what it is told. Since Qohelet is more concerned with understanding, whose agent is the heart, than with the sense and speech, he subsumes the eyes, ears, and tongue to the 'I,' while frequently distinguishing the heart from the person" (*A Time to Tear Down*, 78 n. 9). Dhorme notes the similarities between Qohelet's speaking to his heart and Akkadian texts that use the same turn of phrase to express the process of thinking (*L'emploi métaphorique*, 125).

85.   F. H. von Meyenfeldt, *Het Hart (LEB, LEBAB) in Het Oude Testament* (Leiden: Brill, 1950), 218 (italics in the original). See also p. 221 where von Meyenfeldt reiterates this definition. I am quoting from von Meyenfeldt's English summary.

uses of heart include "the heart of the sea,"[86] "the heart of heaven,"[87] the heart of animals,[88] "the heart of the oak,"[89] "the heart of God."[90] According to Wolff, looking primarily at the Hebrew Bible's inanimate applications of heart, the "heart is always recognized as being an inaccessible, hidden organ inside the body."[91] Therefore, "the heart of the sea" refers to the sea's concealed, mysterious depths; "the heart of the oak" to the innermost, dark tangle of branches.[92] In the human, the heart always refers to the inner-person, but it is rare that the hiddenness, even mysteriousness of this inner-self is mentioned in definitions. Dhorme alone notes that the heart is the "organe central et mystérieux de la vie . . ." ("central and mysterious organ of life").[93] This hiddenness is present in the uses of heart in Qohelet, even if it is not the primary meaning of the word. Words cannot definitively mark themselves off—in this instance mean one thing, in this instance another. Rather, beneath the surface of the most obvious meaning in a particular context is the clamor of alternative meanings, clinging to the word from other usages in other (con)texts. In fact, different readers make different decisions about what is "the most obvious meaning." In the heart of Qohelet, along with the emphasis on reason, and will, and desire, is a core of mystery. Qohelet searches for wisdom with his heart, but this search can never be fulfilled or fulfilling, for the very organ with which he searches can also never be entirely known. If the heart is the essence, this essence is hidden and inaccessible.

Qohelet's text is full of heart—the heart that feels, listens, searches, desires. The heart is Qohelet's partner in his quest(ion)ing of life, not completely separate from the ʾănî but certainly distinct. There is a split at the root of Qohelet's identity between his I and his heart. He is (at least) two. And the relationship between the heart and the eye is complex and contradictory. As noted above, the eye sometimes represents the external as opposed to the internal, which is represented by the heart. But the eye also sometimes is the conduit between the internal and the external. Qohelet relies on the communication between his heart and his eye in order to gain knowledge and wisdom, but the contradictory position of the eye suggests that it cannot be relied upon. Knowledge is not unmediated, wisdom eludes.

It is unfortunate that modern translators obscure the language of the heart in Qohelet. The heart is an evocative concept in the Hebrew Bible, and it continues to function evocatively in our English language today. Qohelet's anthropology

---

86.   E.g. Prov 23:34; 30:18–19; Jonah 2:3.

87.   Deut 4:11.

88.   Five times: 2 Sam 17:10; Hos 7:11; Dan 4:13; 5:21; Job 41:24.

89.   Where Absalom's hair tangles and is caught, 2 Sam 18:14.

90.   Only in Job 10:13 is God's hidden heart explicitly named. Other instances such as 1 Sam 2:35 and 2 Kgs 10:30 emphasize God's will. See Wolff, *Anthropology of the Old Testament*, 55–58.

91.   Ibid., 42–43.

92.   Ibid., 43.

93.   Dhorme, *L'emploi métaphorique*, 113. For Dhorme, the heart does not represent the whole person, but only the interior person. It is only when *lēb* is paired with *bāśār* that the whole person is indicated (e.g. in Ps 84:3).

begins with the assertion of the self—the I. It is then fleshed out by repeated use of the word *ʾādām* (humanity, from the earth), and a *lēb* that searches the world, sensing, reasoning, communicating with the self who encompasses it but never completely controls it.

Qohelet is an *ʾādām* with 42 beating hearts, nine very active eyes, two ears, five mouths, one foot, and eleven waving hands. Bodies are always already fragmented by society and culture, which highlight certain body parts at the expense of others. For example, the gendered body is categorized by stressing certain body parts (primarily, reproductive organs) and not others. The racial body is constructed through emphasizing certain body parts (primarily skin) over others. The textual body is also necessarily fragmented. Certain body parts are emphasized, inscribed over and over again in the text, leaving others absent from the page. But there is something in this fragmentation, almost fetishization, which compels desire. And that leads us to the next chapter.

Chapter 4

QOHELET IN PLEASURE AND PAIN*

I am interested in language because it wounds or seduces me.

—*Roland Barthes*[1]

The speaker extols the virtues of wine, wanders through gardens resplendent with fruit-trees and cool pools of water, is surrounded by female singers, yet remains unfulfilled, searching for the elusive one that is desired above all. The body behind the voice experiences the sweetest pleasures and the bitterest pains. Where are we and into what book have we entered?

I am writing, I am reading, I am being read. And through your reading, you are touching me. Can you find me wrapped around the letters? Can you feel me as you hold these papers in your hand? Is it my body you are cradling and turning? Can you sense my desire between the words, embedded in a semi-colon, curved around this very question mark? You are reading me; who are you reading?

When I think of desire in biblical text, the first book that comes to mind is the Song of Songs. With its lyrical poems to love and the body, and with its tension between the lovers as they play their erotic game of hide-and-seek, the Song of Songs is the quintessential text of desire. As Fiona Black has demonstrated, the desire between the lovers in the text arouses desire between the reader and the text. She writes, "One could say that the Song engages its readers *as a lover*, that the reading relationship is amatory, even erotic."[2] But the body as a site of both pleasure and pain, and the desire that results from the vacillation between the two, is not just found in the Song of Songs. The picture in the first paragraph above describes the book of Qohelet. The words of Qohelet are a site of desire as well.

I saw the sign when I was eighteen. Made by a skillful hand, it stood out on the wall among the other signs. I noted the number. I considered. I came to college to shock myself out of shame. I called.

---

* I am indebted to Robert Paul Seesengood for seeing something in this chapter that I had not yet seen.

1. Roland Barthes, *The Pleasure of the Text* (trans. Richard Miller; New York: Hill & Wang, 1975), 38.

2. Black, "What is My Beloved?," 35.

He picked me up at my dorm—an older white man, hair just starting to thin, beard closely trimmed, body still slim and hard—in a pick-up truck. He was smoking. I breathed deeply the sharp cold air, held it in my lungs close and tight, exhaled. He leaned over and unlocked the door. I climbed in.

When we arrived at his house, the others were already there, pads of paper, pencils, pens, charcoal. He showed me to the bathroom—small, dark, lit by candles. Slowly, deliberately, I removed my shirt, pants, socks . . . I wrapped myself in my turquoise and silver robe, scalloped edges, sheer. I stepped out, around the corner, into the living room.

He had set up a raised platform, covered with pillows and blankets. On strong light illuminated the scene; a space heater glowed hot. He told me what to do. I dropped my robe and we began.

As a prelude to the contours of the desiring body in Qohelet, we should first understand desire itself, particularly desire as an effect of reading. But defining desire is precisely the problem—if desire could be defined, would it be desire anymore? Who knows the interpretation of this *dābār* ("word," Qoh 8:1)?

> I mean the word that teases, that allures, the word that entices exploration—intimate discovery of its curves and hollows, its warm, forbidden places; the word that must be covered up—for modesty's sake, or is it for fear of vulnerability?; the word that is made bare again, for explorers are ever curious, attracted, urgent. Lover-like, this word beckons, it seduces, it possesses, is possessed, then is cast away, only to be sought again, forever.[3]

Judith Butler writes, "The expectation that we might trust language to make something clear about desire presupposes that language itself has no vested interests in desire."[4] But language is invested and implicated in desire and, as such, is "bound to flounder on the question of desire."[5]

Language is implicated in desire because it is simultaneously the vehicle for the production of desire, and the vehicle for the displacement of desire. Caught in this tension, this back and forth rhythm, it can neither describe nor define desire. If we completely had what we wanted we would not need to speak of it. Desire is in the gap, and language is used to bridge the gap, but also, paradoxically, demonstrates and reifies the gap. Language divides us from that which we seek to obtain, even while we use it in the search. It is this "seeking" which signals desire, which *is* desire. In fact, for Butler, "Desire will be that which guarantees a certain opacity in language, an opacity that language can enact and display, but without which it cannot operate."[6] The book is a body. The eye gets caught up in the curves and hollows of the words, seduced by its warm and hidden places. The book is an opaque body and reading a drama of desire.

Roland Barthes has responded to this opacity in language, this dilemma of desire, not by trying to define the discourse of desire, but, in the words of Butler,

3. Ibid.
4. Judith Butler, "Desire," in *Critical Terms for Literary Study* (ed. Frank Lentricchia and Thomas McLaughlin; Chicago: University of Chicago Press, 1995), 369–86 (369).
5. Ibid., 370.
6. Ibid., 369.

by seeking "to reclaim pleasure as the production and proliferation of a polyse-mous textuality."[7] Barthes enacts pleasure in language in the process of both reading and writing. He even disingenuously denounces desire in favor of plea-sure; yet, pleasure is the fulfillment of desire and thus cannot operate in complete contradistinction from desire. Moreover, pleasure may be found within desire itself—pleasure may be experienced not just in the release of tension, but also in the tension, in the lack, even in the pain of desire. Commentators like Butler pull Barthes into their discussions on desire and thus acknowledge the desire present even in, even because of, his protestations.[8]

"Pleasure" (*jouissance*) and "bliss" (*jouir*) are words central to Barthes's writings, but he has difficulty defining them with precision.[9] He cannot keep all of the interrelated meanings away from the terms as he wants to employ them. Other meanings interpenetrate, leaving "pleasure" and "bliss" ambiguous and uncontrolled. In the end, he "must allow the utterance of [his] text to proceed in contradiction."[10] As Barthes himself is troubled by definitions, I find it difficult to define his theory and method. Taking a cue from Fiona Black,[11] I will enact his flirtatiousness by using his aphorisms to suggest readings of Qohelet.

I am full of secrets held in tight. I can feel them consuming me from the inside out, a slow burn. Later the burning will accelerate, so that even as I become naked under your gaze, I am vanishing, my ulcer forming the center of the implo-sion. I have closed my eyes. But you, here, right now, look at me. Through your eyes, I am new born. And I reconstruct my body through your gaze; I recon-figure the meaning of hands, breasts, belly, thigh. Look at me. Read me now.

I am an object; I am their object. I am signified; I am sign. Unmoving, I barely breathe, I barely blink, I hold my body taut and open to their eyes, how-ever they want me, however long they want me. I am good. They ask for me again and again.

Barthes's writings provide a lens through which to examine pleasure and pain, body and autobiography in Qohelet. In fact, Barthes notes that his auto-biography is primarily about the body, his body, a body that writes in pleasure and pain: "So you will find here, mingled with the 'family romance,' only the figurations of the body's prehistory—of that body making its way toward the labor and the pleasure of writing."[12] Qohelet too writes about the body as it

---

7. Ibid., 384.

8. See Karmen MacKendrick, *Counterpleasures* (Albany: State University of New York Press, 1999), 5–6, for another reading associating Barthes' pleasure with desire.

9. Barthes, *The Pleasure of the Text*, 19.

10. Ibid., 20.

11. And I wonder if she labored with her writing as I did, trying to make Barthes comply with a straightforward format: summary of theory, application of method. But Barthes refused me, ran around the room as I gave chase, confused my language the more I tried to force clarity. Black writes that she was never tempted: "Influenced by the whimsical and musing spirit that characterizes these works [*Pleasure of the Text, Roland Barthes on Roland Barthes*, and *A Lover's Discourse*], I am not tempted to 'apply' Barthesian 'theory' or 'method' to the Song [of Songs]" (Black, "What is My Beloved?" 36). I admit, I was tempted by mastery and I attempted control.

12. Barthes, *Roland Barthes*, 3.

experiments with the world of sensation, as it moves toward the point where it
will begin to write of these experiments in toil and in joy. And yet, neither text
reflects a reified, stable, coherent self. Both texts are written in fragments, and
both texts begin with a statement that undermines the very foundations of autobiography as a genre: the assumed coherence between the "I" on the page and
the "I" of the writer. Barthes opens his autobiography by writing, "It must all be
considered as if spoken by a character in a novel."[13] Qohelet's superscription—
the proclamation that he is a son of David, king in Jerusalem—cannot possibly
be true. When I write "I," to whom am I referring? Qohelet and Barthes's writings resist systemization, contain ambiguous key words and concepts, embody
longing, and thus cannot resist desire.

Although the body and desire is most obvious in the Song of Songs, Barthes
reminds us that "The text of pleasure is not necessarily the text that recounts
pleasures; the text of bliss is never the text that recounts the kind of bliss
afforded literally by an ejaculation."[14] If you believe that intellectual activity
(the search for wisdom in Qohelet) is not as sexy as, well, sex; if you see the
application of these categories to the Song of Songs but not Qohelet, I ask you
then to open yourself up to being seduced and wounded by Qohelet's words.

Artful Ambiguity

The meaning(s) of Qohelet are not self-evident, either in the grand sense or in
the smaller sense—meanings of phrases, sentences, and even individual words
are sites of debate:

> *Text* means *Tissue*; but whereas hitherto we have always taken this tissue as a product,
> a ready-made veil, behind which lies, more or less hidden, meaning (truth), we are now
> emphasizing, in the tissue, the generative idea that the text is made, is worked out in a
> perpetual interweaving; lost in this tissue—this texture—the subject unmakes himself,
> like a spider dissolving in the constructive secretions of its web.[15]

The very name (or title?) "Qohelet" is untranslatable; "heart" and "eye" carry
within them multiple meanings, both literal and metaphorical. Ambiguity is a
feature throughout the text of Qohelet, and it is this that layers the text, turning it
into a tissue, a skin stretched out and rolled up—not a tissue as a veil, hiding
meaning; but a tissue as a skin, producing meaning (and pleasure) through the
touch of the reader. The reader enters into and is enfolded.

*What does it feel like to become a piece of art? My skin has been painted,
black stripes on white. My hands have been drawn, charcoal on paper. My body
has been photographed, digital to be manipulated and conventional to be later
drawn out in darkness. I listen to conversations long and low about how best to
render my left breast—you see, how it is flat here but then here round and full,
see how the shadows fall here and here, the pencil tracing my shape nearly
touching, nearly touching my skin. Look at the way the hip curves when she*

13. Ibid., 1.
14. Barthes, *The Pleasure of the Text*, 55.
15. Ibid., 64.

stands like that, weight shifted to one side. Look at her chin. Everyone come over here, from this side, look at those angles: cheek, chin, light, dark.
I am good. I am alive while motionless, dynamic under the surface of my perfectly still skin. And I can remain still, sit still, stand still, lay still for hours. I turn into myself; my nose itches; my hand falls asleep; I become faint. And yet, I do not move. I am in control. Control. Focus, concentrate, meditate. Control.

Many scholars have noticed the literary device of ambiguity in Qohelet.[16] Two papers presented at a recent (1997) session of the *Colloquium Biblicum Lovaniense* devoted to Qohelet and published in the volume *Qohelet in the Context of Wisdom* address ambiguity directly.[17] With reference to Qoh 1:1–11, Lindsay Wilson notes, "this passage is full of words and expression with a broad semantic range, which makes it an ideal seedbed for ambiguity."[18] In an article on 2:24–26, Byargeon defines ambiguity as the aspect of the text describing "different options regarding the meaning of a word or phrase."[19] In other words, ambiguity is "multiple meanings."[20] Ambiguity makes the meaning of the word or phrase uncertain, doubtful, and ultimately inexplicable.

Wilson reads the first poem in Qohelet, word-by-word, line-by-line, stopping to spin out the various meanings each phrase could have. These include a few of Qohelet's standbys: *taḥat haššāmeš* ("under the sun"—the words alone are not ambiguous but together in a phrase they are enigmatic), and *hebel*; and also other words and phrases like *kol-haddĕbārîm* ("all words" or "all things"[21]) and *yĕgeʿîm* ("wearisome," "labor," "property," or "wealth"[22]). Wilson's reading of

16.   Ambiguity is also related to irony, which has been a fruitful interpretive framework for Qohelet study. The first to write about Qohelet in terms of irony was Edwin M. Good, *Irony in the Old Testament* (Bible and Literature Series 3; Sheffield: Almond Press, 1981 [first published 1965]). See also Izak J. J. Spangenberg, "Irony in the Book of Qohelet," *JSOT* 72 (1996): 57–69.

17.   Lindsay Wilson, "Artful Ambiguity in Ecclesiastes 1,1–11," in Schoors, ed., *Qohelet in the Context of Wisdom*, 357–65, and Rick W. Byargeon, "The Significance of Ambiguity in Ecclesiastes 2,24–26," in Schoors, ed., *Qohelet in the Context of Wisdom*, 367–72.

18.   Wilson, "Artful Ambiguity," 358.

19.   Byargeon, "The Significance of Ambiguity," 368.

20.   There has been some concern in studies of ambiguity in the biblical text about readers importing ambiguity when none exists in the text itself. Byargeon wishes to guard against this and cites P. R. Raabe's criteria for doing so: (1) do not base ambiguity on evidence from cognate languages alone; (2) make sure the ambiguity fits the context; and (3) the ambiguity should always have theological significance. See P. R. Raabe, "Deliberate Ambiguity in the Psalter," *JBL* 110 (1991): 213–27 (213–14), as cited in Byargeon, "The Significance of Ambiguity," 368 n. 7. For Byargeon, using these criteria enable the interpreter to produce a controlled ambiguity grounded in historical-critical study. I disagree with Byargeon on this point. Not only does it prove impossible to assert with certainty which ambiguities were intended by the author and which are imported by the reader, but also the inability to control exact meaning is precisely the point of ambiguity, which renders the phrase "controlled ambiguity" an oxymoron.

21.   The NRSV notes the ambiguity in v. 8 by translating *hadĕbārîm* as "things" but providing a footnote that indicates the alternative translation of "words." In v. 10, the NRSV simply translates *dābār* as "thing" without further comment.

22.   Whybray, for example, suggests translating Qoh 1:8a as "all things are constantly in activity," which sounds less pessimistic and defeatist than "all words are wearisome." For Whybray, Qohelet is essentially optimistic. See Whybray, "Qoheleth as a Theologian," in Schoors, ed., *Qohelet*

this passage demonstrates that many of the problems with translating and inter-preting Qohelet revolve around the question of contradictions and whether Qohelet is essentially an optimistic text or a pessimistic text, an opposition I will return to below. Wilson notes that commentators invariably choose one reading over the other and thus foreclose on any ambiguity in the passage.

Deliberate ambiguity is demonstrable throughout the passage. In the end 1:1–11 seems to introduce the theme of ambiguity by the concentration of many ambiguous words, phrases, and ideas. This is literary artistry at its best. It is not that a positive or negative reading alone is intended, but that the reader needs to see both the regularity and seemingly pointless repetition are true to life.[23]

As both comfort through the regular movement of the seasons and despair through endless and pointless repetition are possible in this passage and in life, the book of Qohelet enacts the "complex, ambiguous, enigmatic"[24] quality of living by being a complex, ambiguous, and enigmatic text.

The ambiguity is an invitation to the reader to step into the text, hold each word in his or her hand turning it over and over again. Meaning cannot be simply read and each word opens up new significations. "Is not the most erotic portion of a body *where the garment gapes?*,"[25] asks Roland Barthes. The garment gapes and hints at what is hidden underneath. Between the contradictions are the gaps where the language gapes, reappearing and disappearing meanings, creat-ing a texture of meanings, a tissue of sensation. This tissue is the location of both pleasure and pain through the excess of meaning. Readers are bound to read and read again, searching for meaning as Qohelet searches for wisdom—a search fraught with longing, sometimes satisfying, sometimes frustrating, always compelling.

Garden of Delights

After establishing an "autobiography" through repeated use of the word *ʾănî* and then establishing a physical presence through repetition of the words "heart" and "eye," Qohelet intensifies the focus on the body through the discourse on pleasure in 2:1–11. This passage is usually not called a discourse on pleasure. It falls under titles such as "Accomplishments of the Wise King,"[26] "The Futility

---

in the Context of Wisdom, 239–65 (249), and idem, "Ecclesiastes 1:5–7 and the Wonders of Nature," *JSOT* 41 (1988): 108–10 as cited in Wilson, "Artful Ambiguity," 360.

23. Wilson, "Artful Ambiguity," 363.

24. Ibid., 362. Wilson suggests that *hebel* should be translated with the phrase "complex, ambiguous, enigmatic." I have deliberately refrained from jumping into the *hebel* debate. As Wilson indicates, it is an ambiguous and enigmatic word, and as such enacts the ambiguous and enigmatic nature of both text and life. The word *hebel* means everything it has ever been proposed to mean and more. It is emblematic of the empty signifier. For a comprehensive survey of the previous attempts to define *hebel*, see Douglas B. Miller, *Symbol and Rhetoric in Ecclesiastes: The Place of Hebel in Qohelet's Work* (Atlanta: Society of Biblical Literature, 2002). Miller also argues that the word is multivalent—its meaning cannot be captured by a single English word.

25. Barthes, *The Pleasure of the Text*, 9.

26. Seow, *Ecclesiastes*, 150.

of Success,"[27] and "The Royal Experiment."[28] I want to shift the focus from accomplishment, success, and experiment to amusement, delight, and enjoyment. After all, the wise king is not commissioning projects for the greater good of his subjects; he is not building public parks; he is not participating in the expansion or protection of his borders. The tasks he pursues are not part of royal duty or achievement. Rather, he takes the wealth and power he already has and uses them for pleasuring himself.[29]

This passage of delights opens thus: "I said in my heart, let us make a test in pleasure and see what is good, and behold also this was *hebel*" (2:1). In this one sentence, there are all the marks of selfhood discussed in previous chapters. First, Qohelet emphasizes "I" through the use of *ʾănî* after the verb. Second, the heart is personified as a partner in the endeavor. Choon-Leong Seow notes that here, as elsewhere, Qohelet uses the heart as a conversation partner "to explore contradictory positions."[30] When observing the contradictions in the world, Qohelet underlines the contradictions in his own self through the split in his subjectivity. Third, Qohelet sets out to "see" the good. The verb *rʾh* is usually translated "experience" or "enjoy" in this context. While not incorrect,[31] this translation makes the body indistinct in the passage for English speakers. In the Hebrew, the role of the body in the pursuit of wisdom is highlighted here, thereby foreshadowing the role of the body in the passage that follows.

We begin with a series of quick poses to quicken the eye and limber the hand. I explore the limits of my endurance, tracing out the strength and flexibility of my muscles. I feel the inner thigh begin to shake; my left arm above my head weakens. I explore the limits of my endurance, tracing out the contours of my shame. I do not own a bathing suit; I have not worn shorts in years; my shirts are baggy. And yet, here I am naked before you, your eyes studying hands, breasts, belly, thigh. I feel the warmth of the space heater and smell the faint but sharp scent of my own perspiration.

Qohelet and his heart entice the flesh with wine as their first step in the exploration of wisdom and folly. The first phrase in 2:3 presents some difficulties in translation, as if the wine were already slurring speech. It begins, "I explored in my heart, inducing my flesh with wine and leading my heart in wisdom and grasping in folly. . . ." The opening verb *tûr* is translated in other places in the book as "explore" (1:13; 7:25), but it can also mean "to go about," "to turn," "to flow," "run."[32] It connotes a constant motion—Qohelet is staggering around/with/

---

27. NRSV.

28. Crenshaw, *Ecclesiastes*, 68.

29. As Seow points out in his article "Qohelet's Autobiography," this passage resembles Akkadian and West Semitic royal inscriptions in form and content. It was typical to enumerate building, planting, and irrigation projects. For Seow, the irony in Qohelet is heightened through the imitation of these inscriptions, for his accomplishments are not lasting monuments but *hebel*.

30. Seow, *Ecclesiastes*, 149.

31. See Pss 27:13; 128:5; Num 11:15; and Hab 1:13 for other examples of *rʾh* meaning "to experience."

32. Seow, *Ecclesiastes*, 126–27; see also BDB, 1064.

in (*bêt-*) his heart. The next word *limšôk* is even more difficult.[33] The root of the word *mšk* means "to lead along, carry along, take away, pull, draw, drag."[34] Hence, Qohelet induces, draws, leads along his body (*bāśār*) with wine. The pursuit of wisdom will begin quite literally in the flesh, through the open mouth.

Wine is an intoxicating drink of ambivalent virtue in the Hebrew Bible. It is introduced to humankind after the flood, cultivated first by Noah (Gen 9:20; see also Ps 104:15 where it is highly praised). Noah, however, excessively imbibed which resulted in his shameful exposure to his sons. Yet, isn't this precisely what Qohelet is pursuing? Truth, naked and exposed to all eyes? Wine also figures prominently in the Song of Songs, where the kisses of the beloved are better (*ţôb*) than the sweet, heady drink (Song 1:2). Qohelet is tipsy with all of these meanings of wine at the outset of his pursuit—gift, curse, unveiling, shame, pleasure, love. Qohelet is pursuing truth, naked and exposed.

The ambiguity of wine and drunkenness is reflected in the ambiguity of the verse as a whole. The verbs are unclear, as is the precise meaning of what Qohelet is about to do. The verb *tûr* may mean "to explore" or "to search," as it does in 1:13 and 7:25. Or it may not. The ancient versions are troubled by the verb, and translate it figuratively. The LXX reads *kateskpsamēn* ("I examined") and the Vulgate has *cogitavi* ("I thought"). Others also regard the passage that follows as a "thought experiment"[35]—Qohelet did not really pursue wisdom by literally drinking wine, then planting gardens, building pools, and accumulating wealth. But *tûr* is a verb of journeying, of physically moving about to look for something lost. As far as the text is concerned, the activities about to be described were physically experienced. To call them a thought experiment is another way to intellectualize the sensuality of the book.

Next begins the litany of accomplishments: "I built for myself houses, and I planted for myself vineyards. I made for myself gardens and orchards and I planted in them all fruit trees. I made for myself pools of water to irrigate forests bursting with trees" (2:4b–6). The word that I have translated "for myself" is the Hebrew *lî*. It is a common word meaning reflexively "to/for myself." But in the book of Qohelet, it is used in this passage alone, nine times in six verses. By the repetition of this word, Qohelet repeatedly draws the reader's attention back to himself. The focus is not on what Qohelet has built and planted, but on Qohelet himself, and on his own physical enjoyment of what he is creating.

According to Martin Gliserman, the second level of the encoding of the body in the book is symbolic representation of the body through description of spaces.[36] In 2:1–11, the body is reflected in the landscape that the body creates,

---

33. This is another place where the Song of Songs is glimpsed lurking in the margins of the text. The *BHS* suggests emending it assuming that the drunken Qohelet had a slip of the tongue and meant *lišmôk* ("to support"). The notes then direct the reader to Song 2:5 to confirm the decision. Other suggested emendations include *lśmḥ* ("to rejoice"). See Seow, *Ecclesiastes*, 127, though Seow ultimately rejects emendation because no textual witness supports any emendation.

34. BDB, 604.

35. Seow, *Ecclesiastes*, 127; Fox, *A Time to Tear Down*, 177.

36. Gliserman, *Psychoanalysis*, 30, 44–47.

and the landscape becomes another surface of the body. Houses are protective extensions of the body. There may also be here an allusion to having sons (the word for *bēn* and to build *bnh* are similar), behind which is a reference to the way people "build families," i.e., through sexual intercourse. Vineyards are for the production of wine, already mentioned at the beginning of this passage. Gardens in the Bible are places of peace, comfort, and delight. The first humans are placed in a garden that provides for all of their physical needs. When they are expelled, they enter the world of hardship and toil. Thus, gardens in the Hebrew Bible become places that hearken back to that original time of paradise.[37] Specific mention of all the different fruit trees also puts the reader in mind of the Garden of Eden.

This building of paradise, a place free from want and toil, continues in the planting of orchards. These gardens and orchards provide complete physical sustenance and sensual harmony. The pools of water invoke images of coolness, and sounds of bubbling and rushing. The forests "sprouting" or "bursting" with trees invokes images of lush abundance. The root *ṣmḥ* not only refers to the hyper-fertility of the earth as plants burst forth, but also to human fertility as children burst forth out of their parents.[38] Qohelet has created a place that pleases all of the senses—seeing, feeling, hearing, tasting, scent—with an underlying sexuality throughout it all.

Qohelet then goes on to recount how he filled the paradise he had created:

> I acquired male servants and maidservants, and sons of the house for myself; also cattle both oxen and sheep, they were numerous to me, more than all who were before me in Jerusalem. I also gathered to myself silver and gold, and the possessions of kings and provinces; I made for myself male and female singers, and delights of the sons of humanity, many concubines. (2:7–8)

A life of wealth, leisure, and sexual pleasure is portrayed here.[39] The last phrase (*šiddâ wĕšiddôt*) has a contested translation since both the syntax and the diction are unusual. The meanings range from male and female cupbearers; cups and pots; princes and princesses; female concubines; treasures in chests. Embedded in the consonantal roots are allusions to plunder and breasts.[40] Perhaps, again,

---

37. This is particularly true for the gardens in the Song of Songs. Although the relationship between the lovers is not as egalitarian or blissful as Phyllis Trible suggests, her argument of literary relationship between the Garden of Eden and the garden of the Song is convincing. See Phyllis Trible, *God and the Rhetoric of Sexuality*, 144–65.

38. See, for example, Ps 132:17 where God promises that "I will cause a horn to burst out (*ʾaṣmîaḥ*) of David."

39. The phrase "sons of the house" is disputed, but may refer to children produced by the slaves, perhaps even between the female slaves and the master (see Seow, *Ecclesiastes*, 129). The cattle are also become numerous through sex and reproduction. Both the people and the animals are enjoying themselves in this household. The penultimate phrase *wĕtaʿănûgōt bĕnê hāʾādām* also has an erotic connotation because of its association with a similar phrase in Song 7:7 (*battaʿănûgîm*, "daughter of delights"). Fox notes that this phrase "seems to allude to women" (Fox, *A Time to Tear Down*, 180).

40. Following Gordis and Whitley, Fox believes that Qohelet has acquired concubines: *šiddâ wĕšiddôt* is parallel to *taʿănûgōt bĕnê hāʾādām*, which Fox understands to mean "the pleasures of

we see "artful ambiguity" at work in the passage. All of the possible meanings indicate not only wealth and leisure, but also abundant sexual pleasure and gratification. The words and phrases all are open to erotic connotations, indicated not only by the ambiguous vocabulary, but also by the convoluted syntax. Like wine, the heat of passion can garble language.

In *The Body in Pain*, Elaine Scarry argues that material objects are extensions of the body, that they are even the "making sentient of the external world."[41] She begins with the quite obvious connection between a woven bandage over a wound as a "mime and substitute" for the missing skin. In the same vein, all clothing "will continue to duplicate and magnify the protective work of the skin, extending even its secondary and tertiary attributes."[42] The house as well becomes another protective layer, extending the skin outward. Not only are the body's limbs and organs replicated and projected outwards into the inanimate world,[43] but also less tangible bodily characteristics are as well. Writing, and all of its subsequent and supporting technological innovations (from the printing press to the Xerox machine) is an extension of the complex and elusive attribute of memory.

Qohelet builds houses and other spaces extending outward from his body to replicate and project it into the inanimate world. Qohelet also accumulates possessions—human slaves that quite literally multiply his own body's capabilities. Combining Freud and Marx, Scarry notes that all bodily projections "can be summarized in terms of the projection of sentient *desire* . . . [and] described in terms of the bodily capacity for *labor*."[44] The owning and controlling of male and female slaves for the purposes of labor, reproduction, and sexual pleasure reflect this. The speaker also builds and plants and begets as a way to guarantee his body's survival after death, for houses and orchards outlive those who built them, witnessing their life, testifying to their memory. Wealthy people build things to be remembered, and then they write inscriptions pointing to the buildings to aid memory further. The genre that Qohelet imitates here (Akkadian and West Semitic royal inscription) is precisely this type of bodily extension and memory continuation after death. Memory and writing, and the ways they deteriorate like the body, obsess Qohelet. Despite our best efforts, nothing is permanent, nothing can guarantee memory, all is *hebel*.[45]

men." Thus, both phrases are taken to refer to sexually available women. Traditional Jewish interpreters have also emphasized the connection between these phrases and women—ibn Ezra understands the word in questions to be a form of *šdd*, which means "to plunder"; thus, the words refer to booty and hence includes women. Gordis notes the shared root between these words and *šad* ("breast"). See Seow, *Ecclesiastes*, 131, and Fox, *A Time to Tear Down*, 180.

41.   Scarry, *The Body in Pain*, 281.

42.   Ibid., 282.

43.   Other examples that Scarry gives that reflect our modern world are eyeglasses and microscopes for eyes, pump-driven irrigation systems for the heart, and the computer for the nervous system. See ibid.

44.   Ibid., 284. Scarry does not cite specific Freudian or Marxian texts, but is summarizing their writings as a whole.

45.   Death and memory will be addressed further in Chapter 6.

Qohelet ends his recounting of his experiment with sensuous pleasure with the pronouncement,

> And I increased and I caused to be added more than all who were before me in Jerusalem, and also my wisdom served me. And all that my eyes asked I did not withhold from them, I did not withhold my heart from all pleasure for my heart was happy in all my toil, and this was my portion in all my toil. (2:9–10)

As at the beginning, Qohelet speaks of his heart and his eyes. His eyes are the indicators of desire, and that which is used to obtain and possess the desired. His heart is full of these pleasures and happiness. What begins as an experiment of heart and eye, ends well for both. And yet, when the eye turns another way, taking the reader with it, situating its knowledge—"And I turned to look at all my deeds which my hands had done . . ."—then the conclusion reached at the beginning (2:1c) is reiterated at the end—". . . and in the toil which I toiled to do and behold all was *hebel* and chasing after wind and there was no profit under the sun" (2:11).

What effect does this conclusion have after the catalogue of hedonistic activity? Is Qohelet ultimately pessimistic, despairing of everything even in the midst of having everything? Or is Qohelet ultimately optimistic, advocating an enjoyment of life even in the face of meaninglessness? Or, will we be lead to Barthes again? "The pleasure of the text does not prefer one ideology to another. *However*: this impertinence does not proceed from liberalism but from perversion: the text, its reading, are split."[46]

Pleasure and Pain

R. N. Whybray raised not a few eyebrows when he declared against all objections that Qohelet was a "preacher of joy."[47] Although readers of the book have always noted the positive statements commending the enjoyment of life, these statements were most often constituted as a problem to be solved rather than an indication of Qohelet's zest for living. For these scholars, the pessimistic statements in Qohelet, as well as the general tenor of the book, overwhelm the seven passages commending pleasure and joy.[48] Therefore, the positive and the negative statements are harmonized in a way that subsumes the positive to the negative and thereby preserves pointlessness or vanity as Qohelet's primary message.

Whybray argues, on the other hand, that there is a "steadily increasing emphasis and solemnity"[49] in these passages (2:24a; 3:12, 22a; 5:17; 8:15a; 9:7a, 8, 9a;

---

46. Barthes, *The Pleasure of the Text*, 31 (italics in original).
47. R. N. Whybray, "Qoheleth, Preacher of Joy," *JSOT* 23 (1982): 87–98.
48. Whybray ("Qoheleth, Preacher of Joy") outlines the history of interpretation on this issue in his article. He notes that a few others have read the expression of joy as "the keynote of the book" (p. 94). See also Gordis, *Koheleth*; M. A. Klopfenstein, "Die Skepsis von Qoheleth," *Theologische Zeitschrift* 28 (1972): 97–109; and R. K. Johnston, " 'Confessions of a Workaholic': A Reappraisal of Qoheleth," *CBQ* 38 (1976): 14–28, 94.
49. Whybray, "Qoheleth, Preacher of Joy," 87.

11:9, 10a; 12:1a), which indicates that they are more than just "marginal comments or asides."[50] Instead, they form a *leitmotif* in Qohelet. Viewed from this perspective, the negative comments become subservient to a general tenor of joy. In fact, contends Whybray, many of the verses understood to be depressed and depressing, are not really so at all.[51]

In addition to these verses brought forth by Whybray, the book of Qohelet is peppered (sweetened?) with words for joy and happiness. The words *śimḥâ* and *śāmaḥ*, *ṭôb*, *śĕḥôq*, and *śābāᶜ* are all used by Qohelet to indicate these positive emotions and experiences. Commentators have struggled to define these words precisely, and Fox in particular devotes a chapter to the uncovering of their meanings.

For example, the word *ṭôb* is the positive word used most frequently in Qohelet (59 times).[52] It means, according to Fox, beneficial, efficacious, virtuous, good fortune.[53] In the Hebrew Bible, *ṭôb* often has theological and ontological implications, as in the creation story in Gen 1 where God pronounces all parts of creation *ṭôb*. Similarly in Qohelet, *ṭôb* can mean moral goodness as it does in 7:20 and 9:2. Although *ṭôb* does not primarily indicate sensuous pleasure, this meaning is not entirely absent. The consumption of food and the imbibing of wine is called *ṭôb* in 1 Sam 25:36, 2 Sam 13:28, Judg 16:25, and Esth 1:10 and 5:9. All of these instances also imply a bit of drunkenness, like the lover's kisses that are more *ṭôb* than wine in the Song of Songs. Likewise in Qohelet, *ṭôb* can indicate personal enjoyment and can be applied to such activities as eating and drinking.

The quest to define these words of positive feeling, experience, and evaluation does help the reader understand, but not by pinning down meaning. Rather, such word studies proliferate definitions. These words, like many others in Qohelet, defy precise definition. But then again, the human emotions of pleasure, joy, happiness, satisfaction, amusement, bliss, and contentment are also multivalent, encompassing a complex range of associations and emotions, never able to be sorted out into individual packets of analysis. Roland Barthes expresses frustration at being unable to restrict the meanings of his words for pleasure and bliss (*jouissance* and *jouir*).[54] The same can be said for Qohelet's words of *śimḥâ*, *ṭôb*, *śĕḥôq*, and *śābāᶜ*. They create a web of meanings, touching not only each other and other biblical texts, but also spinning out into the world of the reader, evoking the sensations and associations of what is good in the world, and pulling these associations into the meaning of the text.

---

50. Ibid., 88.

51. The passages that Whybray argues are not so pessimistic after all include 2:17 ("so I hated life") and 6:3–5 (". . . a stillborn child is better off than he"). He believes that when read in their full context, they clearly are not statements reflecting Qohelet's general worldview. See ibid., 92–94.

52. Qoh 2:1, 3, 24 (twice), 26 (twice); 3:12 (twice), 13, 22; 4:3, 6, 8, 9 (twice), 13; 5:4, 10, 17 (twice); 6:3 (twice), 6, 9, 12; 7:1 (twice), 2, 3, 5, 8 (twice), 10, 11, 14 (twice), 18, 20, 26; 8:12, 13, 15; 9:2 (twice), 4, 7, 16, 18 (twice); 11:6, 7; 12:14.

53. Fox, *A Time to Tear Down*, 116–17. Also see Schoors, "Words Typical of Qohelet," 33–39.

54. See also Richard Howard's explanatory note on the translator's (Richard Miller) dilemma in Barthes, *The Pleasure of the Text*, v–vi.

Models always undress and dress in private, hidden from the gaze of their artists. Standing naked in front of strangers is not the intimate act; rather, the veiling, unveiling, re-veiling of the body are the moments saved for lovers. Here I am naked before you, and yet you are not my lover. My body is the raw materials of your labor; you will create with me, you will create me, over and over again.

I am an object, figured, configured, reconfigured. My body has come under multiple gazes, drawn at different angles, by different abilities. I fragment: a leg, my torso, a hand, my side. Never the same, I multiply on canvas, paper, film. And once drawn, I am gone. I fragment, I have multiplied, I am multiple, destroyed and remade, dissolved and fixed.

We settle into a longer pose. When first I recline upon the pillows and blankets they have arranged for me I feel warm, comfortable, soft. They tell each other stories as they draw and paint. Time passes and I feel the tension in my muscles as I hold my body in place. My lower left leg tingles and then goes numb. There are aches that are sharp and then fade; an itch that torments and then dissolves; ennui threatens and then releases. I am becoming by holding: still.

Whybray's analysis of the seven passages of pleasure neither dissolves the contradiction nor proposes a way of bringing the optimistic together with the pessimistic while retaining the tension between the two. He simply flips the hierarchy, maintaining the binary opposition. Usually commentators highlight the pessimistic tenor of the book and downplay or disregard the more optimistic strain. For example, W. H. U. Anderson labels the passages of enjoyment as "wishful thinking" that provided "psychological relief."[55] But it is in the tension between statements such as the seven above and "so I hated life" (2:17), and "What gain have the workers from their toil?" (3:9) that the body (and desire) emerges:

> The body of the text "speaks" about its primitive tensions as they occur within or at the surface of the body. . . . The body speaks of its needs, desires, fears, and anxieties as they have been generated within or manipulated by relations with others. Thus we find tensions in such polarities as pleasure and pain, anxiety and relief, release, symbiosis and separation, good and bad insides, creation and destruction, secure and anxious, passive and active.[56]

Another aspect of desire is the primary vacillation between pleasure and pain, joy and despair, that structures the book of Qohelet. "The pleasure of the text does not prefer one ideology to another."[57] As William Brown puts it, "Arguing over whether Ecclesiastes is either optimistic or pessimistic is sort of like trying to determine whether Stravinksy's *The Rite of Spring* is happy or sad. Such profound works cannot be shackled to simple categories."[58]

---

55. W. H. U. Anderson, *Qoheleth and its Pessimistic Theology: Hermeneutical Struggles in Wisdom Literature* (Mellen Biblical Press Series; Lewiston, N.Y.: Mellen Biblical Press, 1997), 73, as quoted in Seow, "Theology when Everything is Out of Control," *Interpretation* 55, no. 3 (2001): 237–49 (238).

56. Gliserman, *Psychoanalysis*, 31.

57. Barthes, *The Pleasure of the Text*, 31.

58. Brown, *Ecclesiastes*, 10.

The book is a catalog of this pain, both as observed and as experienced by Qohelet. After the passage of delights that opens ch. 2, Qohelet continues:

> And I hated all of my toil in which I had toiled under the sun: because I must leave it to the person who shall come after me. And who knows whether he will be a wise man or a fool? And he will rule over all my toil in which I have toiled, and in which I have been wise under the sun. This also is *hebel.* Therefore I went around to cause my heart to despair about all the toil, which I toiled under the sun. For there is a person whose toil is with wisdom, and with knowledge, and with skill. And to a person who has not toiled for it, he must give it for his portion. This also is *hebel* and a great evil. For what has a man of all his toil and of the striving of his heart, in which he toils under the sun? For all his days are pains, and his work is a vexation, even in the night his heart takes no rest. Also this is *hebel.* (2:18–23)

In this passage alone, ʿāmāl is used eight times,[59] interwoven with such negative evaluations as *hebel*, evil, despair, pain, vexation.[60]

Qohelet 2:18–24 immediately follows the experiment of pleasure (2:1–11). Both passages entail physical labor. The first passage begins by emphasizing the positive results of labor, but this second passage follows by declaring the agony of work. Qohelet 2:1–11 is fraught with fecundity, but this passage implies the failure of fecundity. Children are not the exact reproductions of their parents. Once the child leaves the womb, it is an independent being and it grows into greater independence and difference. Even in the womb, it takes over the body, feeding off of it, potentially even killing it in its own need. Qohelet acknowledges that one has only limited control over the wisdom or foolishness of one's own offspring. The book is full of the labor of the body to transform the world, and this labor is painful, disappointing, and inadequate.[61]

Commentators have struggled with how to resolve the "contradiction" between these passages of work and pain with the passages of enjoyment and pleasure, as if it is only in Qohelet's world (2:24; 3:22; 5:17) where the two exist simultaneously. But Scarry's study on the body notes that these associations are true in all of Western civilization:

> That pain and the imagination are each other's missing intentional counterpart, and that they together provide a framing identity of man-as-creator within which all other intimate perceptual, psychological, emotional, and somatic events occur, is perhaps most succinctly suggested by the fact that there is one piece of language used—in many different languages—at once as a near synonym for pain, and as a near synonym for created object; and that word is "work." The deep ambivalence of the meaning of

<hr>

59. The book of Qohelet contains 70 per cent of all of the biblical occurrences of ʿāmāl.
60. Such associations emphasize the "gloomy connotations" of the word, which match the meaning and connotation of the word in the rest of the Hebrew Bible, as well as the cognate languages (Fox, *A Time to Tear Down*, 97). For a complete study of the range of the meanings of ʿāmāl, see ibid., 97–102, and 121–31. While most exegetes agree that ʿāmāl has negative connotations, a few dissent; e.g. William Brown, "'Whatever Your Hand Finds to Do': Qoheleth's Work Ethic," *Interpretation* 55, no. 3 (2001): 271–84 (276).
61. Qohelet uses other words too to speak of his work: ʿāśâ ("do," "make," "earn"); maʿăśeh ("deed," "property," "event"); ʿānâ ("busy," "business," "task"). The word ʿānâ also means "affliction" and "poverty."

"work" in western civilization has often been commented upon, for it has tended to be perceived at once as pain's twin and as its opposite: in its Hebrew and Greek etymological origins, in our spoken myths and unspoken intuitions, and in our tradition of religious and philosophic analysis, it has been repeatedly placed by the side of physical suffering yet has, at the same time and almost as often, been placed in the company of pleasure, art imagination, civilization—phenomena that in varying degrees express man's expansive possibility, the movement out into the world that is the opposite of pain's contractive potential.[62]

For Scarry, the connection between pain and the imagination in work is a product of work being "an extremely embodied physical act,"[63] through which one produces something that had not existed in the world before. Qohelet works to create a paradise for himself, an ordered world that had not previously been in the world. He experiences both pleasure and pain through being a worker, a toiler, a creator.

For Scarry, pleasure and pain are inextricably bound in the creative process. However, she stops short of saying that pleasure can be found in the pain. Karmen MacKendrick, on the other hand, highlights precisely this relationship between pleasure and pain. In her book *Counterpleasures*, she addresses the writings of Sade and Masoch, sadism, masochism, and asceticism. For MacKendrick, all of these practices (inside and outside of texts) are complexly related, all "share a love of boundary-play,"[64] and all are a "new strategizing of pleasure, a new disruption in the relations of power."[65] Further:

> The pleasures collected here are pleasures that queer our notion of pleasure, consisting in or coming through pain, frustration, refusal. They are pleasures of exceptional intensity, refusing to make *sense* while still demanding a philosophical unfolding. This unfolding takes odd forms; that of an infinite self-reflexion or a rupture of language in the very act of description.[66]

The body in Qohelet vacillates between pleasure and pain. Moreover, the body in Qohelet finds pleasure in pain—pleasure in work, pain in creation. There is an excessive self-reflection not only at the level of content, but even in the very syntax and diction of the text itself. Qohelet seeks meaning, wisdom, knowledge, and is constantly frustrated in this search. The seeking is then mirrored in the reading experience. The text pleasures the reader through the frustration of meaning, in the refusal of clear signification. We are compelled to read and read again, to write about our readings, to write and write again. As such, Qohelet is a counterpleasure, as defined by MacKendrick. Qohelet is a book that, in general, disrupts the biblical canon and traditional theologies. Qohelet's discourse on the body becomes, then, another site of subversion in this already subversive book.

62. Scarry, *The Body in Pain*, 169.
63. Ibid., 170. Here she notes that even non-physical labor engages the whole mind and is thus an embodied act as well.
64. MacKendrick, *Counterpleasures*, 17.
65. Ibid., 18.
66. Ibid., 18–19.

Turn, Turn, Turn

Qohelet 3:1–8 may be the most widely known biblical passage in the English-speaking world. One reason for its popularity in such diverse contexts is the underlying eroticism in the passage, as well as the way it compels desire. It does, in fact, begin with a word of desire: "For every time there is a season, for every desire (*ḥepeṣ*) under heaven" (3:1).

It continues:

> A time to give birth,[67] and a time to die;
>> A time to plant, and a time to pluck up the planting.
> A time to kill, and a time to heal;
>> A time to break down, and a time to build.
> A time to weep, and a time to laugh;
>> A time to mourn, and a time to dance.
> A time to cast stones, and a time to gather stones;
>> A time to embrace, and a time to repel embracing.
> A time to search, and a time to forsake;
>> A time to keep, and a time to cast away.
> A time to tear, and a time to sew together;
>> A time to be silent, and a time to speak.
> A time to love, and a time to hate;
>> A time for war, and a time for peace (3:2–8).

This passage exemplifies the movement back and forth between contrasting poles that takes place throughout Qohelet. As Georges Bataille notes, love is the longing of two discontinuous beings to become one and desire is produced by the fact that this merging can never be accomplished.[68] There is pleasure in this desire. As Derrida notes, "Pleasure can accumulate, intensify through a certain experience of pain, ascesis, difficulty, an experience of the impasse or of impossibility."[69] Qohelet 3:1–8 is a catalog of oppositions that co-exist, interconnected and interdependent, but never merge into one. It is also a compelling passage because it mimics the two most steady and essential rhythms of our body: the beating of the heart, and the interrelated cadence of breathing;[70] on these

67.   The word *lāledet* means literally (with the more common female subject) "to give birth" or (with male subject) "to beget." The word cannot mean "to be born" for it would have to be the *nipᶜal* construction to have the intransitive meaning (see Qoh 7:1; Gen 4:18; Deut 23:9 for examples of the verb in the *nipᶜal* construction with the meaning "to be born"). The vast majority of translators and commentators mis-translate this word so that it is in a "proper" parallel relationship to *lāmût*, which does mean "to die." Few even bother to disclose that they are disregarding the literal meaning of the word. I will return to this phrase in Chapter 6.

68.   Georges Bataille, *Eroticism: Death and Sensuality* (San Francisco: City Lights Books, 1986), 20.

69.   Jacques Derrida, " 'There is No One Narcissism' (Autobiographies)," in *Points . . . Interviews, 1974–1994* (ed. Elisabeth Weber; trans. Peggy Kamuf et al.; Stanford, Calif.: Stanford University Press, 1995), 196–215 (198).

70.   The connection between Qoh 3:1–8 and breathing comes from Daniel C. Fredericks, *Coping with Transience: Ecclesiastes on Brevity in Life* (The Biblical Seminar 18; Sheffield: Sheffield Academic Press, 1993), 27–28.

interpenetrating rhythms our life hangs. The life of the book of Qohelet hangs on 3:1–8; it is its center (heart) and its life-rhythm.[71]

Athalya Brenner has noticed the erotic undercurrent in this passage. In her study of male and female voices in the Hebrew Bible, she proposes that 3:1–8 should be understood as a "male poem of desire."[72] First, Brenner explains what she means by reading this text as the product of a male voice. The identification is not necessarily a statement about the author or editor or compiler; rather, the "point to be discussed is the gender *positions* inherent in a text."[73] Second, Brenner reviews the history of interpretation of this passage and broadly categorizes it into two groups: a dominant pessimistic reading, and a less common optimistic reading. In either case, it is a meditation about time.

Brenner's alternative explanation begins by isolating the passage from the rest of the book.[74] She argues that, without its context, it becomes impossible to situate on either side of the optimistic–pessimistic divide. The key to understanding the original meaning, then, is in the poem alone, and the key consists of the opening (3:2), central (3:5), and concluding pairs (3:8).[75] While I do not think that the passage needs to be separated from the rest of the text and given an earlier date (Brenner relies on the same historical-critical assumptions that this book challenges), I am interested in Brenner's noting of the erotic undercurrent.

The central pair is the key to her interpretation. The beginning of v. 5 reads there is "a time to cast away stones, and a time to gather stones together."[76] Rejecting the literal meaning, Brenner links the casting/gathering of stones to the last part of the verse, "a time to embrace, and a time to refrain from embracing."[77] Conjoined, the sexual connotations emerge.

---

71. Many commentators have noted the centrality of this passage to the book of Qohelet. For example, Crenshaw notes how the author returns to the themes introduced in this section repeatedly (3:17; 8:5–6, 9; 9:11–12), and he calls the relationship between this passage and the remainder of the book "intimate" and central; see James Crenshaw, "The Eternal Gospel (Ecclesiastes 3:11)," in *Urgent Advice and Probing Questions: Collected Writings on Old Testament Wisdom* (Macon, Ga.: Mercer University Press, 1995), 548–72 (549).

72. Athalya Brenner and Fokkelien van Dijk-Hemmes, *On Gendering Texts: Female and Male Voices in the Hebrew Bible* (Leiden: Brill, 1993), 133. Brenner alone wrote the chapter on Qohelet.

73. Ibid., 134.

74. Brenner does this through the dating of the poem's verbs. Twenty-one of its verbs are common in both Classical and Post-Exilic Hebrew. The remaining five verbs are difficult to date. They may be later, but the evidence is inconclusive. Therefore, Brenner concludes, the "language of the poem is different from that of the introduction and conclusion enclosing it. . . . The poem seems to be linguistically and stylistically earlier and more conventional in its linguistic usage . . . [thus] the poem is quoted out of another context" (ibid., 137).

75. Following Loader's proposal of a chiastic structure, Brenner argues that the attention is then drawn to the central stanza. For the final line, since it comes after 13 pairs, it "cannot but be highly suggestive" (ibid., 139). See J. A. Loader, "Qohelet 3:2–8—A 'Sonnet' in the Old Testament," *ZAW* 81 (1969): 240–42.

76. Brenner's translation.

77. Not every instance of the use of *ḥbq* implies a sexual embrace, though the majority do denote intimacy sexual and otherwise. See ibid., 142, for the inventory.

Brenner takes her cue from rabbinic sources that interpret the casting and gathering of stones as sexual play. *Qohelet Rabbah* and *Yalqut Shimeoni* read the casting of stones as a man having sexual intercourse with his wife, and "gathering" as to abstain from sex.[78] Robert Gordis follows the Jewish sources as well, and also references the links between "stones" and sexual and/or reproductive matter in other biblical passages.[79] For example, millstones and grinding are sometimes used as a metaphor for sexual intercourse: "If my heart has been tempted by a woman and I have waited at my brother's door, Let my wife grind for another and others will kneel over her" (Job 31:9–10). Brenner notes the connections between "stones" and women's reproductive activities, as well as the connections between "stones" and testicles: "When you assist the Hebrew women in giving birth, look at the two stones. If it is a son, kill him; if a daughter, let her live" (Exod 1:16).[80]

Brenner argues that the poem has "a unified structure" separate from the structure of the book as a whole. For her, a unified structure indicates "a unified message."[81] And the key to the meaning is the central verse in the chiasm, v. 5. Therefore, the entire passage is not about the human life cycle or time, as it is often read, but a riddle about sex and love from a male perspective:

> The poem emerges as a love poem whose theme is the fluidity of love and sexual desire. Like everything else in life, love and sex are not constant but dynamic, in the sense that at times they inevitably change and mutate into their opposites. Nevertheless, they are subject—again, like everything else within the human order—to a continuous point–counterpoint movement.[82]

There are a couple of problems with Brenner's argument that detract from the insight of this observation. First, Brenner attempts to read every verse as a sexual reference, but her readings are not convincing. For her, the obvious sexuality in v. 5 and the lack of obvious references to sex in the rest of the passage is only an "apparent lack of consistency" because the poem is a "riddle."[83] She struggles to bring the text into compliance with her theory. Yet, eroticism does not necessitate explicit references to sex. The desire is enacted by the rhythm of the passage, by the rocking motion of the oppositions; desire is caught in the opacity of meanings; desire is experienced in the reader's search for wisdom. This search is necessitated not by an "apparent lack" but by an actual lack of consistency.

Second, to call the perspective of this text "male" is too simplistic.[84] The text is not as univocal in its gender identification as Brenner argues. For example, in her key verse—"a time to cast away stones, and a time to gather stones together" —she puzzles over what it could mean to gather stones. Yet, the solution seems

---

78. See ibid., 141–42.
79. Gordis, *Koheleth*, 230; cf. Seow, *Ecclesiastes*, 161.
80. The verses both from Job and Exodus are Brenner's translations.
81. Brenner, *On Gendering Texts*, 146.
82. Ibid., 149.
83. Ibid., 148.
84. Chapter 5 will address the question of gender more completely.

simple to me. If casting stones refers to the sexual act as executed by male bodies, the opposing line refers to sexual acts as received by male bodies—"stones"
gathered up in the embrace of a lover. Brenner claims, "the ejaculatory and
thrusting nature connoted by key expressions is perceived as especially blatant
when heard or read by a woman. . . ."[85] Not only is the poem consistently male,
but also female readers are consistent in their interpretations. Yet, this female
reader disagrees. Gender, sexuality, and perspective never simply and straight-
forwardly cohere.

But I do agree that one of the themes of this poem is desire, the way desire
rocks back and forth in "a continuous point–counterpoint movement," its fluidity
and dynamism, the way that this desire infuses all aspects of life. Seow points
out that this passage is "tantalizingly rhythmic" and yet it "leads to the utterly
surprising conclusion that mortals are not able to grasp what God has done
'from beginning to end.'"[86] It is all as elusive as the breath we bring into and
send out of our body. It is as mysterious as how our own bodily rhythms work in
concert to create the song that is the human being. And it is as evocative as the
symphony of humans called culture and community.

Qohelet turns round and round, he searches, he experiments, he does not find:
"Then I saw all the work of God, that no one is able to find out the work which
is done under the sun. However much one may toil in seeking, one will not find
it; even though one who is wise claims to know, no one is able to find it" (8:17).
There are moments of discovery, but these shimmer and fade as the object of
pursuit recedes once more. Desire is produced in the gap between what one
wants and what one has. The play between seeking and (not) finding is produced
in the reader through the vacillation between the oppositions named in Qohelet:
life and death, wisdom and folly, pessimism and optimism, light and dark,
enjoyment and toil, pleasure and pain. The commentator is compelled to read
Qohelet over and over, searching for an interpretation, being thrown back and
forth by the text, as Qohelet is thrown back and forth in his search for wisdom.
This is textual foreplay, exploring, building tension, risking rejection as one
comes closer and closer to possession: "To get the very complicated pleasure . . .
I suppose one must, at a given moment, stand at the edge of catastrophe or of the
risk of loss."[87]

Brenner isolates Qoh 3:1–9, but many commentators delineate the passage
differently. Crenshaw, for example, argues, "both style and content suggest that
3:1–15 is a separate unit."[88] In terms of stylistic features, Crenshaw notes that
these verses include rhetorical questions[89] and broken sentences.[90] Although

85. Ibid., 151.
86. Seow, *Interpretation*, 243–44.
87. Derrida, "'There is No *One* Narcissism,'" 198.
88. Crenshaw, "The Eternal Gospel," 548.
89. R. Kroeber, *Der Prediger* (Berlin: Akademie, 1963), 37, enumerates 29 rhetorical questions
in the book as a whole, as referenced in ibid., 549.
90. K. Galling, "Stand und Aufgabe der Kohelet-Forschung," *TRu* 6 (1934): 355–73 (369),
counts eight broken sentences in Qohelet, as referenced in Crenshaw, "The Eternal Gospel," 549.
A broken sentence, as defined by Galling, is a sentence that begins with one of the following words:

these are features found throughout Qohelet, the way in which they contribute to the structure of these verses indicate that vv. 1–15 should be read together as a passage. While Crenshaw is concerned with precise passage boundaries in order to illuminate meaning, I am more concerned with the ways these stylistic features impact the rhythm of the reading. The rhythm of the reading then becomes another mode of interpretation, another vehicle for meaning in this already meaning-full passage.

Rhetorical questions are Qohelet's way of engaging the reader in his meditations; rhetorical questions hook readers by pulling them into the passage. There is a rhetorical question in 3:9: "What profit have the workers in that which they toil?" The steady rhythm of 3:1–8 is like the perpetual intake and outtake of breath or the beating of the heart or the movement of lovers—our most central life-rhythms. In v. 9, the rhetorical question causes the inflection to rise, only to fall again into v. 10. Qohelet 3:9 is not a break-stop but a rise and fall, as if the reader has taken a big breath in preparation for the next few verses.

Upon reaching 3:11 the reader is stopped short by fragmentary phrasing.[91] First we are arrested by its unusual syntax (the breathe catches, the heart skips a beat). The verse begins with the direct object indicator (*ʾet*) rather than the verb, which is the more common construction in biblical Hebrew: *ʾet-hakkol ʿāśâ yāpeh bĕʿittô* ("He [God] made everything beautiful in its time," 3:11a). By beginning the verse in this way, Qohelet also connects it to the poem above (3:1–8). The Poem of the Times begins each phrase with the word *ʿēt*—a homonym of *ʾet*. The next phrase in v. 11 begins with *gam* followed again by syntax that places the direct object before the verb (3:11b).

The second phrase of v. 11 has puzzled readers because of the difficulties in translating the central word, *hāʿōlām*. God has given something into humanity's heart, but what that something is ranges from "eternity" (*aiōn*, LXX) to "the eternal work" (Isaksson);[92] "the world" (*mundum*, Vulgate) to "toil" (Fox);[93] "a sense of past and future" (NRSV) to "the unknown" (Crenshaw).[94] These six translations do not exhaust the possibilities proposed by commentators.[95] God

wĕgam ("and also," 2:14; 3:13; 7:6), *gam zeh* ("also this," 2:24), *ûbkēn* ("and then," 8:10), *kî gam-yôdēaʿ* ("this also I know," 8:12), and *w-* ("and," 9:18).

91.   Crenshaw uses Galling's definition of a "broken sentence" to describe the fragmented style of v. 11. According to Crenshaw (ibid), there are possibly two broken sentences in 3:11, which are introduced by the words *gam* and *mibbĕlî*.

92.   Isaksson, *Studies in the Language*, 183. Isaksson means "eternal work" in the sense of "creation in its widest sense, in time and space, the created and ongoing history."

93.   Fox, *A Time to Tear Down*, 192. He further explains his translation decision in pp. 210–11. Fox emends the word *ʿōlām* to *ʿāmāl* based on a similar phrase in 8:17, and concludes that the MT preserves "a mistake" (p. 211).

94.   Crenshaw, *Ecclesiastes*, 91. He further explains his decision on p. 97. Crenshaw notes that the root *ʿlm* is a verb meaning "to hide." And this root does occur in Qoh 12:14 with this meaning. Therefore, he emends the pointing of the MT and translates the word in 3:11 as "the unknown." See also Crenshaw, "The Eternal Gospel," where he labels the pointing as it stands in the MT as a "corruption" (p. 563).

95.   The most popular translations are: (1) "eternity"; (2) "world"; (3) "toil" (with emendation); (4) "knowledge" (*hapax legomenon* related to the Arabic noun *ʿilm*); and (5) "ignorance" (assuming

has placed something so infinite or mysterious or troubling into finite flesh that no one can decide quite what it is, and every translation possibility leaves something lacking. Perhaps the indecidability is the point. Whatever the word means, its meaning is too great to be contained in the flesh. This gift into the heart both wounds as it breaks the heart open, and seduces as it creates the conditions for desire. It is the risk embedded in every experience. Humans are compelled to exceed themselves, to overcome their finite, frail, and mortal nature, to seek outside of themselves for something other. It is this simultaneous desire and pain that compels the search for wisdom in Qohelet.

Am I beautiful? Do I care? I am signified and significant. I am remade and remaking. My body has become an object, an image, a figure on canvas, film, and paper. There I am, there and there. I can circle the room and see familiar curves and shadows, angles and colors. I am existing without name, existing without number, no longer myself or for myself but as someone else's vision. I am good. I am beautiful. I am signified. I am my own, controlled even as I am exposed; deep and full even as I am reduced to two dimensions; fragmented even as I am fully finally seen.

a noun related to the verb *ʿlm*, "to hide"). See Seow, *Ecclesiastes*, 162–63, for a complete survey. Seow himself concludes there is no evidence for either a corrupted text, or for favoring an obscure meaning from a cognate language over the face value of the MT. Therefore, he translates *hāʿōlām* as "eternity."

Chapter 5

IN LOVE AND (GENDER) TROUBLE

Bisexuality: that is, each one's location in self (*répérage en soi*) of the presence—
variously manifest and insistent according to each person, male or female—of both
sexes, non-exclusion either of the difference or of one sex, and, from this "self-permis-
sion", multiplication of the effects of the inscription of desire, over all parts of my body
and the other body.

—*Hélène Cixous*[1]

Who is Qohelet?

Qohelet is a fictional autobiography, an elusive "I," a textual body with many
eyes and multiple hearts (or is it just one large pulsating one?). Qohelet has skin,
which stretches over the binding of the book, feeling the pleasure of touch.
Qohelet eats and drinks. Qohelet labors endlessly and relentlessly, the weariness
of the body enacted in the weariness of the words on the page, their sometimes
inability to make sense like a stumbling tongue worn out by the day's activities,
or drunk on wine.

Who is Qohelet? This is Qohelet. We pick up Qohelet's body every time we
pick up the text, we read the body, turn its pages, touch its body with our own.

But a pressing question has been assumed but not asked: Is Qohelet male or
female? The centrality of this question is made manifest every time a woman is
pregnant. The first question—Is it a boy or a girl?—rises to the lips of every
family member, friend, and acquaintance. The first or second pronouncement of
the delivering midwife or doctor is the sex of the child. So central is the sex of a
person that it is difficult, if not impossible, to imagine someone un-sexed. And
persons cannot be inscribed in texts without the mark of gender, particularly in
gendered languages such as Hebrew.[2] So what is it—boy or girl?

---

1. Hélène Cixous, "The Laugh of the Medusa," in *New French Feminisms: An Anthology* (ed.
Elaine Marks and Isabelle de Courtivron; trans. Keith Cohen and Paula Cohen; Brighton: Harvester,
1981), 245–64 (254).

2. Monique Wittig demonstrates this for the French language in "The Mark of Gender,"
Feminist Issues 5, no. 2 (1985): 63–73. I am not, however, making an argument about the thought
structures of the ancient Israelites, particularly since "feminine" and "masculine" language categories are terms imposed by grammarians and do not necessarily correspond with feminine and
masculine roles and stereotypes in the culture. James Barr's critique of theological and historical
arguments about the Hebrew mind based upon syntax, grammar, and vocabulary of the Hebrew
language is operative here. See James Barr, *The Semantics of Biblical Language* (London: SCM
Press, 1961).

Sexual History

The sexed body in Qohelet is wrapped up in the gendered body. There has been a tradition in feminist thought that makes a strong distinction between sex, defined by the body's reproductive organs, and gender, the cultural stereotypes and roles imposed on these sexed bodies. This is summed up in the astute observation of Simone de Beauvoir that "one is not born a woman, but rather becomes one."[3] But the boundary marks between sex and gender have begun to blur under the scrutiny of such theorists as Michel Foucault, Donn Welton, and Judith Butler.

Michel Foucault began the contemporary re-theorizing of the body with his seminal work *The History of Sexuality*.[4] In the dominant ideology, sex, sexuality, and gender work in a natural concert. If one has female genitalia, one acts in ways defined as feminine (gentle, centered in home and family life, emotional), and one is only attracted to men. If one has male genitalia, one acts in ways defined as masculine (aggressive, oriented toward the world outside of the home, unemotional), and one is only attracted to women. Foucault works to "unhinge" the triptych, focusing specifically on sexual desire.[5] He continues his project with the publication of the diary of a nineteenth-century French hermaphrodite by the name of Herculine Barbin.

Foucault writes the introduction to this confession, opening it with the query,

> Do we *truly* need a *true* sex? With a persistence that borders on stubbornness, modern Western societies have answered in the affirmative. They have obstinately brought into play this question of a "true sex" in an order of things where one might have imagined that all that counted was the reality of the body and the intensity of its pleasures.[6]

Foucault goes on to trace the Western obsession with sexual duality to the biological interpretation of sexuality, the science of medicine, the legal definition (and therefore creation) of the individual, and state administrative control. In ancient times through the Middle Ages, a third sexual category—the hermaphrodite existed. In France, during the period of the Middle Ages through the Renaissance, a hermaphrodite had to decide upon reaching adulthood whether to live and marry as a man or a woman.[7] Once that decision was made, the person could not change his or her mind, and then must marry the "opposite" sex.

---

3. Simone de Beauvoir, *The Second Sex* (New York: Vintage, 1973), 301.

4. Michel Foucault, *The History of Sexuality: An Introduction* (trans. Robert Hurley; New York: Vintage, 1990).

5. Arguably, this all began with Freud's theory of infantile sexuality which stated that humans are born bisexual and it is through their later development that they must choose the "proper" object of desire and become heterosexually oriented. But, even though heterosexuality was part of the developmental process, it was still the natural development for Freud. See Sigmund Freud, *Three Essays on the Theory of Sexuality* (San Francisco: HarperCollins, 1962).

6. Michel Foucault, ed., *Herculine Barbin: Being the Recently Discovered Memoirs of a Nineteenth-Century French Hermaphrodite* (trans. Richard McDougall; New York: Pantheon, 1980), vii.

7. Ibid., viii.

In the post-Enlightenment West, this category was eliminated medically, legally, and morally.[8] Sex-assignment became not a choice based upon personal feelings of identification and desire but something imposed by the medical and clerical community and vigorously enforced by the juridical community at the moment the hermaphroditic body was discovered.

In the case of Herculine Barbin, her "condition" was not discovered until after she had already spent a very happy childhood and adolescence as a girl. Herculine was caught in a love affair with another young woman, which subjected her to scandal and scrutiny. A physical examination by a doctor and a priest when she was in her early twenties resulted in her re-assignment as a man. In France, in the 1800s, when gender roles shaped every aspect of a person's life—from dress to education to occupation—a person raised as a girl in an all-women environment (convent) had not acquired any skills that would allow her to function in society as a man. Unable to find gainful employment or companionship as a man, feeling as if her identity had been ripped away from her, Herculine Barbin committed suicide at the age of 25. For Foucault, this individual tragedy underscores the fictional nature of the stable, binary oppositions of male and female sex. Once sex is destabilized, gender and sexuality, which supposedly inhere naturally to certain bodies, are destabilized as well.

Judith Butler further destabilizes the gender–sex connection. She notes that despite Foucault's radical reading of sexuality, he still subtly maintains that the body is before culture and hence reinscribes the nature/culture dichotomy he ostensibly wishes to deconstruct. In her ground-breaking book, *Gender Trouble*, Butler proposes that the idea of two, mutually exclusive genders functions at the service of heterosexual ideology, and creates two, mutually exclusive sexed bodies. In other words, we have two sexes *because* we have two genders, not vice versa:

> Gender ought not to be conceived merely as the cultural inscription of meaning on a pregiven sex (a juridical conception); gender must also designate the very apparatus of production whereby the sexes themselves are established. As a result, gender is not to culture as sex is to nature . . .[9]

And we have two genders in order to maintain the heterosexual matrix.[10]

Thomas Laqueur supports Foucault and Butler's theories through further historical investigation. He examines medical texts from antiquity through the modern period, thereby demonstrating that the very shape of the body has changed over the centuries. Rather than assuming two separated sexes, there was only one human body in Greek and Roman antiquity. This one sex was in a form that was weak and incomplete in women, and was strong and complete in men. The re-conceptualization of the human body, bifurcating the sexes, took place in

8.   Ibid.

9.   Judith Butler, *Gender Trouble: Feminism and the Subversion of Identity* (New York: Routledge, 1990), 7. Butler is also responding to the idea that gender is a cultural construct imposed upon biological bodies. See Michelle Zimbalist Rosaldo and Louise Lamphere, eds., *Woman, Culture, and Society* (Stanford: Stanford University Press, 1974).

10.   Butler, *Gender Trouble*, 17.

the eighteenth and nineteenth centuries, not as a result of advanced scientific research (which came later to support the new conceptualization), but because of the need for post- Enlightenment political justification for the inferiority of women.[11]

So what is it—boy or girl? In a post-Butler world, the answer is never self-evident. And no matter the answer, the coherence assumed between sex, gender, and sexuality dissolves into un-intelligibility.

Resisting Qohelet

I am a body marked by sexual difference and inculcated in a gender ideology that names me "woman." And I begin this analysis of gender/sex in Qohelet with a concern. I am troubled by the way that Qoh 7:26–29 portrays women and how this portrayal has been read throughout the modern history of interpretation. The passage reads:

> And I found more bitter than death the woman. She is a snare and her heart is nets, her hands are fetters. One who is good before God escapes from her, but the sinner is captured in her. See, this I found, said the Qohelet: add one to one to find the reckoning, which my soul still sought but I did not find. One man in one thousand I found, but a woman in all of these I did not find. See, this alone I found: God made humanity right, but they sought many contrivances.

This passage troubles me, and my first response is to resist. Consequently, I am drawn first to Judith Fetterly's theories on reader response criticism and the resisting reader. Fetterly argues that the books in the American canon are "relentlessly androcentric and misogynist, as is the educational establishment in which the canon is taught."[12] We are all taught to identify male. For women, this means internalizing and identifying with androcentrism and misogyny and thus reading against their interests. Fetterly urges people to become resisting readers: "the first act of the feminist critic must be to become a resisting rather than assenting reader and, by this refusal to assent, to begin the process of exorcising the male mind that has been implanted in us."[13]

Although Fetterly is discussing literature produced in the United States during the nineteenth and twentieth centuries, her general theory is applicable beyond her particular specialization. For Fetterly, the misogyny and andro-centrism are inside the text itself. We can enter into the world of the text and be inculcated in its ideology, or we can refuse. Qohelet 7:26–28 is a misogynist passage in the Hebrew Bible. There have been other negative portrayals of women in the Hebrew Bible, especially of women in the Wisdom traditions. However, this is the only statement that categorically condemns all women.

---

11. Thomas Laqueur, *Making Sex: Body and Gender from the Greeks to Freud* (Cambridge, Mass.: Harvard University Press, 1990).

12. The Bible and Culture Collective, *The Postmodern Bible* (New Haven: Yale University Press, 1995), 37.

13. Judith Fetterly, *The Resisting Reader: A Feminist Approach to American Fiction* (Bloomington: Indiana University Press, 1978), xxii.

Tikva Frymer-Kensky calls this "the first openly misogynistic statement in the Bible,"[14] and I would have to concur. These verses describe women in general; they do not limit the type of women who are called "more bitter than death." Arguments that this passage is not misogynist smack of apologetic. And, empowered by Fetterly to read against the grain, I resist this text.

Scholarly literature that explicitly identifies itself as feminist often notes the misogyny in the text, but rarely devotes much space to it. For example, in *A Feminist Companion to Wisdom Literature*, Qoh 7:26–29 is discussed briefly in a survey essay on the portrayal of women in Wisdom Literature,[15] but there is not one feminist interpretive essay on Qohelet alone. This verse seems to be ripe for interrogation from a feminist standpoint. Is it because it is too easy? In *The Woman's Bible Commentary*, the only major commentary that squarely faces the misogyny in the text without excuse or qualification, Carol Fontaine writes that "the misogyny expressed (7:26) is no surprise."[16] She does not elaborate further.

The rest of the commentaries fall into four main camps. The first group, represented here by Whybray, denies that there is misogyny in the text:

> It has also been alleged, on very flimsy evidence, that Qohelet was that very rare phe-
> nomenon among the Jews of the Old Testament period, a bachelor, and even a misogy-
> nist. This notion is based mainly on a single very obscure passage, 7.23–29, which is
> certainly capable of being interpreted as expressing contempt or hatred of women in
> general, but is also capable of other interpretations.[17]

This is the only place in his commentary where he speaks of this passage. He does not state why these verses are "obscure," nor does he offer any other inter-pretation.

N. Lohfink offers another version of this denial. He argues that Qohelet quotes a common proverb against women in order to argue against it.[18] But his argument rests on some questionable translations.[19]

---

14. Tikva Frymer-Kensky, *In the Wake of the Goddesses: Women, Culture and the Biblical Transformation of Pagan Myth* (New York: Ballantine, 1992), 205.

15. Athalya Brenner, "Some Observations on the Figurations of Woman in Wisdom Literature," in *A Feminist Companion to Wisdom Literature* (ed. Athalya Brenner; Feminist Companion to the Bible 9; Sheffield: Sheffield Academic Press, 1995), 59–61.

16. Carol R. Fontaine, "Ecclesiastes," in *The Women's Bible Commentary* (ed. Carol A. Newsom and Sharon H. Ringe; Louisville, Ky.: Westminster/John Knox, 1992), 153–55 (154). The comments on Qoh 7:26–29 in the forerunner of all feminist commentaries, Elizabeth Cady Stanton's *The Woman's Bible* (Seattle: Coalition Task Force on Women and Religion, 1990), is reminiscent of Zimmermann's analysis in the *Inner World of Qohelet*. Stanton states, "Solomon must have had a sad experience in his relations with women. Such an opinion is a grave reflection on his own mother, who was so devoted to his success in the world" (p. 99).

17. Whybray, *Ecclesiastes*, 22.

18. N. Lohfink, "War Kohelet ein Frauenfeind? Ein Versuch, die Logik und den Gegenstand von Koh. 7:23–8:1a herauszufinden," in *La Sagesse de l'Ancien Testament* (ed. M. Gilbert; Leuven: Leuven University Press, 1979), 259–87.

19. Lohfink argues that *mar* may mean "strong" rather than "bitter." This verse then becomes a positive assessment of women, parallel to the verse in the Song of Songs that states that "love is as strong ($^c azz\hat{a}$) as death" (Song 8:6).

The second interpretive strategy in the commentaries is to stress the relative pronoun *ʾăšer* ("who") in v. 26: "the woman, the one who is a snare." The entire passage is not a condemnation of all women, then, but only the condemnation of a particular type of woman. Roland Murphy represents this position: "The description fits a certain type of woman against whom the sages railed; it is not a description of the female sex *per se*."[20] He goes on to note that this "certain type of woman" is the adulterous woman. It is only adulterous women who are as bitter as death. To emphasize his point about the particular woman whom Qohelet hates, Murphy chooses to translate *ʾiššâ* as "harlot" in his analysis of ch. 7,[21] but he does retain the translation "woman" for his commentary.[22]

Choon-Leong Seow also pursues this line of argumentation but he believes that it is Woman Folly who is "more bitter than death."[23] As Woman Folly, this woman is a *femme fatale*. But, he points out, these words are not "just clichés about women."[24] Men can also represent "the deadly seductive power of evil."[25] Seow also argues that a later copyist inserted the following lines in v. 28 ("And a woman in all of these I did not find"), perhaps as "an ancient sexist joke."[26] These scholars protest too much.

The third interpretive strategy is one that does not necessarily deny that Qohelet's statement is misogynistic or at least androcentric, but it does place the discussion of this androcentrism within its own androcentric frame. James Crenshaw opens his contribution with the following statement: "This section discusses two profound mysteries: wisdom and woman."[27] Even though he does confront the contempt and hatred for women expressed in these verses, he has already excluded women from the conversation by foregrounding it in a statement on their mysterious nature. This is a biblical commentary's version of Freud's infamous statement, "What do women want?" Before he even addresses the misogyny of the text, Crenshaw makes a stereotypical statement about women himself. He places them all in a category outside of the knowable.

Dominic Rudman has recently proposed the final interpretive strategy. Through a complicated inversion, the woman in Qohelet becomes an agent of the divine will rather than a snare for careless men. Using what he calls a "contextual method" and presupposing a deterministic worldview in the text, Rudman argues that women are God's instruments of punishment. Sinful men are entrapped by women and thereby prevented from acquiring the wisdom to

20. Murphy, *Ecclesiastes*, 76.
21. Murphy, "A Form-Critical Consideration of Ecclesiastes VII," in *SBL Seminar Papers, 1974* (ed. George MacRae; 2 vols.; Cambridge, Mass.: Society of Biblical Literature, 1974), I:77–85 (82).
22. Murphy, *Ecclesiastes*, 74.
23. Choon-Leong Seow, "Dangerous Seductress or Elusive Lover? The Woman of Ecclesiastes 7," in *Women, Gender, and Christian Community* (ed. Jane Dempsey Douglass and James F. Kay; Louisville, Ky.: Westminster/John Knox, 1997), 23–33.
24. Seow, *Ecclesiastes*, 262.
25. Ibid., 263.
26. Seow, "Dangerous Seductress or Elusive Lover?," 28.
27. Crenshaw, *Ecclesiastes*, 144.

which they are not entitled (for Qohelet does assume that wisdom and sex are antithetical). It is not in following the woman that that man sins. Rather, she is his punishment for sins already committed:

> Qoheleth's view of Woman is at once restricting and liberating. Like Man, she is a being controlled by the deity. Yet she is also an extremely powerful semidivine figure. Her weapons are allocated to her by God, and Man has no defense in the face of them. God may pull the strings from heaven, but on earth it is Woman who is the master. In a sense, Qoheleth's worldview is one in which Eve has ganged up with God against Adam.[28]

She has committed no moral transgression herself in her act of sexually snaring a man; rather, this is her role mandated in creation and it is in no way indicative of an essential wickedness.[29]

Rudman contrasts the woman in Qoh 7:26 with the negative portrayals of women in the book of Proverbs: "The woman of Eccl 7:26 is more a huntress of the masses than a temptress of the individual. She is an every-woman figure who works for rather than against God in her enactment of judgment upon those who have sinned."[30] The only similarity between her portrait and that of the women in Proverbs is that both are discussed in the context of the search for wisdom.

Yet, when I look at comparable texts within the Wisdom tradition,[31] I reach a different conclusion that throws Rudman's thesis into question. Qohelet has intensified the condemnation of women presented in Proverbs by taking a criticism directed at the *'iššâ zārâ*—translated alternatively "strange woman," "harlot," "loose woman," and connected to the "foreign woman"—and making it a blanket statement about all women. The *'iššâ zārâ* is characterized as one who leads men astray away from wisdom (e.g. Prov 7), captures men (Prov 6:25; 22:14; 23:27), and whose bitterness leads to death (Prov 5:4–5). These are the same ways in which *hā'iššâ* is characterized in Qohelet. In Proverbs, the "strange woman" is negatively characterized due to her actions, and Woman Wisdom and the faithful wife oppose her. In contrast to this, the woman in Qohelet is not negatively characterized because of her actions. She is never said to do anything evil. Rather, her very person is already corrupt.

The personification of wisdom as a woman (*ḥokmâ*, or more commonly referred to as Sophia, from the LXX *sophia*) in Proverbs is avoided altogether in Qohelet. In fact, instead of wisdom being a woman, no wisdom whatsoever is found in any woman: "And a woman in all of these I did not find" (7:28c). The lack of a female personified wisdom is particularly evident in the Hebrew text. There are no neutral pronouns for inanimate objects in Hebrew; in other words, there is no Hebrew equivalent to the English word "it." Whenever the passage refers to wisdom, the feminine third person pronoun *hî'* is used (e.g. Qoh 7:23).

---

28. Dominic Rudman, "Woman as Divine Agent in Ecclesiastes," *JBL* 116, no. 3 (1997): 411–27 (418–21).

29. Ibid., 421.

30. Ibid., 419.

31. See Brenner, *Wisdom Literature*, 51–56, for a full description of female characters in Proverbs.

But unlike Proverbs (e.g. Prov 8), Qohelet never takes the next step of representing wisdom as a woman. Within the bounds of the statements against women in 7:26 and 7:28, the author is unable to equate wisdom with woman. It would transgress the boundaries of the ideology of the text.

Despite the fact that Proverbs characterized certain women as foolish and dangerous to men, there are many other women in the text who are good and helpful. There is the mother whose counsel the son is commended to listen and to obey (Prov 23:22; 31:1). There is the *ʾēšet-ḥayil* (alternatively translated "woman of valor," "virtuous woman," "capable wife") who is the woman who supports and aids her family (31:10–27). She is a blessing to all (31:28–31). While it is true that these roles are still within the parameters of an androcentric society, and that there is still an opposition between the good and the bad woman, the variety of images continually challenge each other and the positive portrayals offer alternatives for women that are absent in Qohelet.

The negative characterization of all women in Qoh 7:26–29 is not mitigated by the positive spin Qohelet places on the pleasures one can derive with (or from?) one's wife (9:9).[32] The woman is not valuable and worthy in and of herself; but she is valued only in relation to the pleasure she can give to her husband in this limited and harsh world. The full verse reads thus: "Enjoy [literally 'see'] life with the wife whom you love, all the days of your vain life that are given you under the sun, because that is your portion in life and in your toil at which you toil under the sun" (9:9). To read this verse as a direct contradiction of 7:26–29 is to make misogyny and love antithetical, a proposition refuted by any critical look at the history of the relationships between men and women. An androcentric and misogynist worldview simply does not make love of one's wife (or mother, sister, daughter) impossible. If this were true, either misogyny or marriage would have failed a long time ago.

Neither is Qoh 9:9 a ringing endorsement of womankind, or even a praise of the good wife. A second look at Prov 31 will confirm this. The wife in Prov 31 is good and praiseworthy because of her actions. This wife provides clothes and food; she takes care of the financial concerns of her family; she is charitable and compassionate to others in need; she is wise and kind and industrious. Contrast this endorsement in Proverbs—"many women have done excellently, but you surpass them all" (Prov 31:29)—to the end of the passage in Qohelet—"And a woman in all of these I did not find" (Qoh 7:28c).

Certainly, men do not fare much better in 7:28. Only one man in a thousand is wise, but at least there is this one man. Also, the voice of the text is male, the entire book assumes a male audience, and men are characterized in a variety of ways and in a variety of contexts. Therefore, the statement in v. 28 does not become a general condemnation of all men (or even 999 men). A feminist interpreter must conclude that this text is unredeemable.

---

32.   Qoh 9:9 and 7:26–29 are seen as contradictions by most commentators. Delitzsch, *Ecclesiastes*, 363–64, was the first to frame the problem of women in Qohelet as the problem of resolving the contradiction between the negative 7:26–29, and the positive 9:9.

Inverting Qohelet

Do I really mean that? The passage is not as simple and stable as I have portrayed it. The feminist reader that I have employed mirrors the one-dimensional
woman of the text. She suppresses other readings in order to argue her one point.
She also invests the text with an androcentric and misogynist core, and then
reads from there. Fetterly's interpretation of the canon of literature does the
same. As the *Postmodern Bible* states,

> To argue that the canon of American fiction is at its core androcentric and misogynist
> presumes there is a determinant core already there in these texts. To read against the
> grain of these texts is to operate on the assumption that there is a grain against which to
> read.[33]

The same can be said of the Bible and my reader response and feminist interpretation of Qohelet. But no text has a stable core of meaning. Qohelet may have
a basic misogynist ideology, but that ideology has fissures and cracks. The mask
that I have used to be a feminist critic begins to show fissures and cracks, as
does the text itself. It has begun to mutate.

The first step in any interpretation is to read the text in Hebrew, attend to the
marginal notes, and stabilize the text. In the margins are variations, problems,
inconsistencies. These marginal notes threaten to pull the text apart; they challenge its integrity, and the interpreter must tame them before he or she can go
any further. Before I had even begun this study, I was the text critic searching
for the original, striping off layers of scribal error, clarifications, and theological glosses. Specifically, text-critical analysis requires the emendation of Qoh
7:22–27 in order to preserve the coherent gender identity of the speaker. But
what I thought I had stabilized in the beginning now begins to shimmer and
shake, shift and change. The letters are moving again, back to how they appear
without emendation in the MT. The stability that I have been seeking is an
illusion. And reading the MT without text criticism, coherent gender identity is
absent.

Language is not an absolute system inextricably bound to an external reality.
Instead, language is a system of differences. It is only possible to know the
meaning of a word through other words. The connection between the signifier
(the word or sound) and the signified (the concept or object) is a matter of con-
vention, and this relationship is inherently unstable. The words themselves are
unstable—letters can break off, change to another, or come together. With each
mutation of a letter, meaning can change subtly or radically. Only the difference
of a letter (a sound) separates "tree," "thee," "the," "tee"; and each of these
words (sounds) are intelligible only because of what they are not.[34] Words also
change meaning depending upon their contexts; they change as they wander in
and out of texts.

---

33.   Castelli et al., *The Postmodern Bible*, 38.
34.   Ibid., 124.

The feminist analysis above relies on a misogyny found in the text itself, as well as a reading that resists that misogyny. However, the reading above suppresses the instability of the text, and the inherent undecidability of language. There are moments in the text where the feminine unexpectedly erupts, thus undermining the androcentric ideology.

If one regards the unemended MT, the gender of the one spoken and the gender of the one speaking wavers. The first case is in v. 22. It reads, with vowels: "For also your heart knows that many times you (*ʾattâ* [masculine, singular]) also cursed others." But, without pointing and without emendation, it reads: "For also your heart knows that many times you (*ʾt*) also cursed others." The masculine and feminine second person pronouns differ by only one consonant: *ʾatt* (feminine "you") and *ʾattâ* (masculine "you"). With words so similar, the letters are incapable of staying in their place.[35] The letter *hê* has disappeared in the MT, thus the gender of the person addressed in this verse is inverted. Through this pronoun dysphoria, the coherent male audience slips.

The second case is in v. 27. It reads, with emendation: "See, this I found, said (masculine, third person, singular) the Qohelet (*ʾāmar hāqōhelet*)." However, it appears in the MT thus: "See, this I found, said (feminine, third person, singular) Qohelet (*ʾāmrâ qōhelet*)." Again, it is the matter of a *hê*. Does the letter belong at the end of the verb, thus rendering it feminine; or does it belong at the beginning of the next word *qōhelet* which would maintain the masculine gender of Qohelet but turn the proper name into an object with a definite article? The gender of Qohelet slips.

There are two texts here—the one that appears in the MT and the one that is formed through the emendations of the text critic.[36] In a deconstructive reading, neither of these texts is privileged; rather, they are superimposed upon each other and remain undecidable. From one angle, there is a coherent male speaker and audience. But out of the corner of my eye, I see bursts of the feminine interrupt the text's smooth surface.

In addition to these small, although intriguing, textual instabilities (as discussed in Chapter 2) the very word Qohelet is a feminine form of the root *qhl*. Although all of the verbs, except for the case noted above, are masculine, the form of the name—which is untranslatable and unattested anywhere else—retains its feminine side. The more that Qohelet attempts to suppress these feminine facets of language and text, the more that feminine breaks out at other textual sites. Who is Qohelet and what is Qohelet trying to hide?

Qohelet is a figure with an untranslatable and femininely formed name, and there are places in the text where feminine forms unexpectedly emerge, like slips of the tongue. Qohelet is more invested and entangled in the feminine than

35. Qoh 7:22 is not the only place in the MT where *ʾt* is pointed as *ʾattâ* (or *ʾatā*) and is therefore taken as a masculine "you." This form also occurs in 1 Sam 24:18; Ps 6:4; Job 1:10; and Neh 9:6. In addition, there are occasions when the pointing is *ʾatt* but the "you" in understood to be masculine so the reader is asked to re-point (Num 11:15; Deut 5:24; Ezra 28:14).

36. The LXX reads *eipen o Ekklēsiastēs*. Greek does not distinguish between masculine and feminine third person singular verbs, but the LXX does include the definite article.

the condemnation of women in 7:26–29 first suggests. In the body, gender, sex, and sexuality do not work in a natural accord despite a culture's demand that they do so. In the book, gender, sex, and sexuality do not cohere. Language shifts and changes, revealing inconsistencies and instabilities, which reflect the instability of the body.

Marjorie Garber names this type of unstable, boundary-crossing, category-confusing figure "the transvestite." "The transvestite willfully creates a third space beyond the masculine/feminine dichotomy, the homo/hetero binary, the real/artificial antithesis . . ."[37] The transvestite is not always the obvious. Garber argues "for an *unconscious* of transvestitism, for transvestitism as a language that can be read, and double-read, like a dream, a fantasy or a slip of the tongue."[38] And this third category is what compels desire. Building on Lacan's dictum that "the object of desire remains potent only when veiled,"[39] a cross-dressing Qohelet covers and uncovers herself/himself, herself/himself. . . . A cross-dressing Qohelet creates the desire that compels the reader.

Lacan writes: "desire is neither the appetite for satisfaction, nor the demand for love, but the difference that results from the subtraction of the first from the second, the phenomenon of their splitting."[40] By definition, desire is that which cannot be satisfied. And desire leads us to the deeper level of the feminine, one that threatens to undermine the entire book. As a text about wisdom, the feminine is the very subject of the text, the feminine structures the text, and the feminine is what is desired above all else. Wisdom is a feminine noun and as such demands feminine pronouns and verbs. Although this is obscured in the English translation, in the Hebrew it is an unavoidable aspect of the text: "All of this I tested in wisdom; I said, 'I will be wise,' but *she* was far from me" (Qoh 7:23 [my italics]). Qohelet is searching for this elusive feminine word/concept. And the more he desires and pursues his desire for wisdom, the more he negates women.

Although Qohelet is searching for wisdom throughout the text, the search intensifies in Qoh 7. Throughout this chapter, the language of searching and (not) finding links the pursuit of wisdom with the woman condemned as more bitter than death. Words of searching are used eleven times in six verses: *bqš* ("to seek") in 7:25, 28, 29; *mṣᵓ* ("to find") in 7:24, 26, 27 (twice), 28 (three times), 29; *twr* ("to explore") in 7:24. The high concentration of such language implies franticness, as if the search has reached a fever pitch. Wisdom is personified in Proverbs as a woman, and this woman lurks around the edges of the Qohelet text. One cannot read the one without the other. Qohelet's silence on her presence is glaring. By refusing the personification, Qohelet is in effect

---

37. As summarized in H. Aram Veeser, ed., *Confessions of the Critic* (New York: Routledge, 1996), xxi. Marjorie Garber lays out her thesis in *Vested Interests: Cross-Dressing and Cultural Anxiety* (New York: Routledge, 1992), 9–13.

38. Garber, *Vested Interests*, 354.

39. Veeser, *Confessions*, xxi.

40. Jacques Lacan, "The Signification of the Phallus," in *Ecrits: A Selection* (trans. Alan Sheridan; New York: W. W. Norton; 1977), 281–91 (287), as quoted in Garber, *Vested Interests*, 75.

neutering Wisdom, veiling the feminine in such a way that even Wisdom becomes a third term, neither male nor female. Qohelet has substituted the woman for the . . . what? For the changeling, the change, the crossing, the *search* itself.[41] It too is the third term, thus making Wisdom a transvestite herself/itself.

And rather than hiding the feminine aspect of wisdom in this search, Qohelet's silence draws attention to her notable absence. The more he is silent, the more he suppresses, the more he tries to hide the feminine, the more he is betrayed by its insuppressible presence. Garber cautions us against simply collapsing the transvestite into either male or female categories, thereby looking *through* rather than looking *at* the third term.[42] In other words, Qohelet is not simply a matter of a male desire for and fear of the feminine. Rather, the feminine and the masculine cannot remain in their own mutually exclusive categories. Qohelet is full of anxiety, because the feminine is there, in the book and in the body, producing desire through the effect of the transvestite.

There is another intertext here: "Love is as strong as death" (Song 8:6). Is the proclamation that "woman is as bitter as death" a response to this climatic moment in the Song of Songs, a text where the narrative voice is female, and love and pleasure is lauded? Or vice versa? The texts echo each other, calling each other into question, destabilizing each in a dance between death, love, and women. Because of its character as a general maxim, these verses represent a little piece of wisdom embedded in the love lyrics of the Song.[43] It is wisdom countering wisdom.

Georges Bataille enters the dance with another maxim: "Eroticism . . . is assenting to life up to the point of death."[44] Sex, death, and life are intimately bound together because of humanity's ambivalent feelings about our own discontinuous being. It is this desire for and fear of discontinuity that compels our relationships with other bodies. Life begins with the continuity of our being with another body—the maternal body. Birth brings discontinuity and this discontinuity becomes more and more apparent as the child grows. This is not a negative state, for independence of being brings satisfaction, and our consciousness of our separate and unique selves is what makes us human. However, there is also profound loneliness at the heart of humanity, and this loneliness results in a nostalgia for the continuous life.

During sex both individuals "are simultaneously open to continuity. But nothing persists in their imperfect awareness. The crisis over, the discontinuity of

41. In folklore, the changeling is one child exchanged for another. Garber uses the term with a twist. Garber's use of the term "changeling" is influenced by Shakespeare's *A Midsummer Night's Dream*, where a changeling boy enters the plot as the locus of conflict and desire between Titania and Oberon. But even though there is a struggle for possession of the changeling, "The changeling himself is never present—or, at least, he never speaks. His absence, his elusiveness, is part of what makes him desirable." In the economy of the play, "the changeling boy is change itself," and this is understood by Garber as "the transvestite effect" (*Vested Interests*, p. 85).

42. Ibid., 9.

43. M. Sadgrove, "The Song as Wisdom Literature," *StudBib* 1 (1978): 245–48.

44. Bataille, *Eroticism*, 11.

each is intact."[45] But sex is more than the hearkening back to the continuity experienced before birth. It is also a drive toward the continuity of death. First of all, reproduction goes hand-in-hand with death. Life grows out of the decomposition and decay of the deceased. And even with human life, where parents survive the birth of their offspring, "the reprieve is only temporary."[46] Reproduction is super-abundance, excess, and the death of the parents must eventually follow from this excess. Bataille writes:

> One need look no further for the cause of the fear associated with sexual activity. Death is exceptional, an extreme case; each loss of normal energy is indeed only a little death [exhaustion following orgasm] . . . but whether obscurely or clearly this little death is what is feared. On the other hand it is also desired. . . . No one could deny that one essential element of excitement is the feeling of being swept off one's feet, of falling headlong. If love exists at all it is, like death, a swift movement of loss within us, quickly slipping into tragedy and stopping only with death. For the truth is that between death and the reeling, heady motion of the little death the distance is hardly noticeable.[47]

Qohelet desires and fears women, wisdom, even the feminine inside of Qohelet's own self. It is in the interplay of desire and fear in the book of Qohelet that the body of Qohelet contemplates death. Qohelet 7:26 is only one more instance of a discourse on death that runs from the first chapter to the last.

Qohelet knows that that which he desires most is feminine—women and wisdom contaminate each other and become inextricably bound. The text and its ideology cannot remain stable and contained. Instead, it quickly unravels as Qohelet frantically grabs at its loose ends.

True Confessions

This is a true story. Once upon a Monday night, I was reading Fernando Segovia's introduction to *Reading from this Place*, volume 2.[48] Curled up in bed, I finished the essay. I turned off the light, and began to drift thinking of Qohelet and my social location. I began to dream.

What is my social location? What are the components of my identity that read Qohelet and why my attraction to this text? I am an interpreter who bases my interpretation primarily on my own assumptions about identity. I look into the mirror and see inconsistency, incoherence, fragmentation. My own identity is as contradictory as this text; I am alienated from parts of my own self, and these parts shift and change under examination and over time. Neither my class position, nor my sexual orientation, nor my Jewish identity has remained unproblematic or stable. I have always been a woman, but my understanding of my sex and gender has changed. Who is reading when "I" look at Qohelet?

---

45. Ibid., 103.
46. Ibid., 100.
47. Ibid., 239.
48. Fernando F. Segovia, "Cultural Studies and Contemporary Biblical Criticism: Ideological Criticism as Mode of Discourse," in *Reading from this Place*. Vol. 2, *Social Location and Biblical Interpretation in Global Perspective* (ed. Fernando F. Segovia and Mary Ann Tolbert; Minneapolis: Fortress, 1995), 1–17.

Qohelet rises up before me. It is an architectural structure of words, a building unlike any building I have ever encountered. Its angles are unpredictable; there are places to enter in the most unlikely locations—neither doors nor windows but something else altogether. The spaces between the words are white and the black lines run in all directions without order. It stretches up vertically further than I can see. I fracture. Different aspects of my identity split off and become independently animated. Like pieces of a jigsaw puzzle they stand before Qohelet and start to fit themselves into its structure. They scatter up and around the edifice, some disappearing into its strange openings, some climb further up and on.

Each one is a persona, but not a false front that hides something more authentic or real. Each persona tells part of the story but at the same time obfuscates other identities. Pealing off one mask only reveals others in an endless chain of changelings, never getting closer to some essential core. This is my multifaceted and sometimes contradictory social location. Hélène Cixous writes: "the human subject is not singular, which is why one should never say 'who am I?' but 'who are I?'. . . We are all the ages we were and will be, all the characters we dream, all of our combinations with others, exchanges between languages and sexes, each one changing us with others."[49] And finally, we even have the "I who escapes me"[50]—like those figures in my dream that climb up and on, escaping my gaze to have their own encounters with the body of Qohelet.

49. Susan Sellers, ed., *The Hélène Cixous Reader* (New York: Routledge, 1996), xvii.
50. Ibid., xviii.

Chapter 6

DECOMPOSING QOHELET*

> However condensed or displaced, the body carries with it a tale it is dying to tell.
>
> —*Martin Gliserman*[1]

Death permeates the book of Qohelet to such an extent that H. Wheeler Robinson has voiced a visceral reaction: Qohelet has "the smell of the tomb about it."[2] As signaled by this almost physical recoil, death is encoded in the body of the book in a variety of overlapping ways. We have already seen death in the proper name in Chapter 2. "Qohelet" lives on after the death of its author and thus unbinds the name and the text from their origin. And in the previous chapter, Qohelet labels women more bitter than death and thus initiates a dance between death and desire. In this chapter, I look at death in Qohelet more explicitly.

The first part of this chapter briefly reviews the ways in which Qohelet speaks of death. The second part demonstrates how death is manifest not only in the content of the book but also in its very form. In other words, the structure of the book, often called a "riddle," is in a state of decay. But perhaps the most significant inscription of death, for it is the one that constitutes the very (im)possibility of the others, is God's gift of death. God "gives" (*nātan*) in Qohelet more than God is involved in any other activity. Employing Jacques Derrida's analysis of the gift, the third part of this chapter will illuminate God's giving in and giving to Qohelet.

Qohelet's Vigil

It is almost a truism that Qohelet is the most philosophical book of the biblical corpus. Despite the frequency of Qohelet's references to God (40 times), the philosophical as opposed to the theological dimensions of this book persist in the minds of readers. The mournful tolls of the death knell drown out any other

   * A version of this chapter appears in *Derrida's Bible: Reading a Page of Scripture with a Little Help from Derrida* (ed. Yvonne Sherwood; New York: Palgrave, 2004), 247–59. I would like to thank Joel Beaupré for his philosophical guidance and insightful editing of this chapter.
   1. Gliserman, *Psychoanalysis*, 29.
   2. H. Wheeler Robinson, *Inspiration and Revelation in the Old Testament* (Oxford: Clarendon, 1946), 258.

note sounded, and death is the intimate partner of philosophy. As Derrida writes, "Philosophy isn't something that comes to the soul by accident, for it is nothing other than this vigil over death that watches out for death and watches over death, as if over the very life of the soul."[3] In Qohelet's confrontation with death, we see him as a philosopher, a philosopher watching and waiting and writing.

In the opening poem, the cycle of birth and death is part of the workings of nature: "A generation goes, and a generation comes, but the earth remains forever" (1:4). Intertwined here with the concern about death is the concern about memory: "The people of long ago are not remembered, nor will there be any remembrance of people yet to come by those who come after them" (1:11). For Qohelet as for Derrida, the name may survive death, but once detached and remaindered—left on its own—the memories it evokes cannot be controlled or guaranteed. Reading Sarah Kofman after her death, Derrida writes: "But there is no longer any doubt: such testimonies survive us, incalculable in their number and meaning."[4] The name after death continues on, proliferating endlessly, mutating in each new context, multiplying meaning, "keeping the last word— and keeping silent."[5]

In Qoh 2, where Qohelet makes a test of pleasure, death is also in attendance: "I explored in my heart, inducing my flesh with wine and leading my heart in wisdom and grasping in folly, until I will see what is good for the children of humanity, what they will do under the sun for the number of the days of their life" (2:3). The concern with memory, and its connection to writing is present implicitly in this section. Qohelet is imitating royal inscriptions of the ancient Near East, particularly West Semitic and Akkadian. These texts were often written in stone and intended to preserve the memory of the king and of his deeds. The similarities include the lauding of the wisdom of the king, the boast of surpassing all predecessors, and a series of first person singular perfect verbs. There are also similarities in content. For example, the Assyrian rulers Sargon II and Sennacherib boast of great building projects, the creation of a garden, orchards, and irrigation canals.[6] Yet, as Qohelet points out, it is all *hebel* (vanity, nothing, ephemeral, absurd, vapor). There is no permanent monument in memory to one's name, not even those written in stone by conquering kings.

After this garden of delights, Qohelet has his first extended meditation on death:

> So I turned to see wisdom and madness and folly; for what can one do who comes after the king? Only what has already been done. Then I saw that there is more profit in wisdom than folly as there is more profit in light than darkness. The wise have eyes in their head, but fools walk in darkness. Yet I know also that one fate befalls all of them. Then I said in my heart, "What happens to the fool will happen to me also; why have I then been so very wise?" And I said in my heart that this also is *hābel*. For there is no eternal

---

3. Jacques Derrida, *The Gift of Death* (trans. David Wills; Chicago: University of Chicago Press, 1996), 15.

4. Derrida, *The Work of Mourning* (ed. Pascale-Anne Brault and Michael Naas; Chicago: University of Chicago Press, 2001), 170.

5. Ibid.

6. For a full comparison, see Seow, "Qohelet's Autobiography," 279–84.

remembrance of the wise or of the fool, all too soon in the days to come all will have been forgotten. How can the wise die just like the fool? So I hated life, because what is done under the sun was evil to me; for all is *hebel* and a chasing after wind. (2:12–17)

Besides the theme of memory, another important aspect of Qohelet's obsession with death is introduced here. Death is the great leveler. It comes for all, indiscriminately and without warning. And one has no control over who or what comes after one's death (cf. Qoh 6:12).

Death levels all of the deeds of the living, and this includes leveling human and animal:

For the fate of humans and the fate of animals is one fate; as one dies, so dies the other. They all have the same breath, and humans have no advantage over the animals; for all is *hābel*. All go to one place; all are from the dust and all return to dust. Who knows whether the breath of humans goes upward and the breath of animals goes downward to the earth? (3:19–21)

And despite the advice Qohelet gives about correct relationship with the divine (see especially 5:1–7), in the end there is no distinction:

Since the one fate comes to all, to the righteous and the wicked, and to the good and the evil, to the clean and the unclean, to those who sacrifice and those who do not sacrifice. As are the good, so are the sinners; those who swear are like those who shun an oath. This is an evil in all that happens under the sun, that there is one fate for all. (9:2–3a)

There is no living on (French: *sur-vivre*, "over-living"), either in the sense of survival, or resurrection. There is only, minimally, Sheol (9:10), a shadowy underworld or place of shades, where all go together.[7]

Death, then, for Qohelet, entails these two themes: (1) the extinguishing of memory and (2) the leveling of differences. Ostensibly, writing should preserve memory, should stabilize the sign. But the book is a body as well. "This book stands up to, and stands in for, the body: a *corpse* replaced by a corpus, a *corpse* yielding its place to the bookish thing. . . ."[8] Just as the body grows old and its memory becomes confused, the book is unstable—it enacts in syntax, diction, and structure Qohelet's concerns with the decaying body and its fading memory.

In order to signify, the sign must be repeatable and thus engaged in memory, yet it also must be distinguished from others, to stand out, to be significant. Without these two features, a sign is meaningless. As discussed in Chapter 2, Derrida refers to this phenomenon as "iterability." In order to be meaningful, the name or word must be as unique (singular) as the person who or object that bears it; and yet, in order to function, it must be repeatable (conform to a general law). It must be able to be used in a variety of contexts, repeated and understood, and function in the absence of its bearer.[9] As Qohelet meditates on the corrosive power of the death of the body to extinguish memory (v. 16a: "For there is no eternal remembrance of the wise or of the fool, all too soon in the days to come

---

7. In this manner, Qohelet is right in line with the predominant biblical viewpoint. See Antoon Schoors, "Koheleth: A Perspective of Life After Death?," *ETL* 61 (1985): 295–303.
8. Derrida, *The Work of Mourning*, 176.
9. Jacques Derrida, "Signature Event Context."

all will have been forgotten") and level differences (v. 16b: "How can the wise die just like fools?"), death renders signification impossible by erasing both repeatability and differentiation. Qohelet's book becomes a meditation on meaninglessness both at the level of the physical body and in the body of the book. We are all together caught in the natural processes of flesh. Qohelet's vigil is over death as the limit of signification, the open wound of meaninglessness. "No one has power over the wind to restrain the wind, or power over the day of death" (8:8a)—*hebel* blows all around.

"The Riddle of the Sphinx"

The search for the structure of this strange little book has dominated past scholarship. In his recent commentary, Choon-Leong Seow sums up the history of this study by noting that the "Scholarly opinion regarding the structure of the book falls between two poles. There are those who find no order whatsoever, and those who discern a carefully constructed structure."[10] As with almost every other aspect of the book of Qohelet, the debate is between mutually exclusive hypotheses.

One of the major proponents of a theory that discern an elaborate structure is Addison Wright. For Wright, until the structure of the book of Qohelet is discerned, the other "essential riddles" of message, genre, and unity cannot be solved.[11] Using a truncated version of New Criticism[12] in which he investigates such structural indicators as repetitions, inclusions, chiasm, symmetry, and refrains, Wright concludes that there are "three successive patterns of verbal repetition" in Qoh 1:12–11:16.[13] The title (1:1) and the introductory poem on toil (1:2–11) as well as the final poem on youth and old age (11:7–12:8) and the epilogue (12:9–14) are outside of this schema.

The outline of his structural proposal is as follows:[14]

> Title (1:1)
> Poem on Toil (1:2–11)
> I. Qohelet's Investigation of Life (1:12–6:9)
>> Double Introduction (1:12–15, 16–18)
>> Study of Pleasure-Seeking (2:1–11)
>> Study of the Fruits of Toil
>>> One has to leave them to another (2:18–26)
>>> One cannot hit on the right time to act (3:1–4:6)
>>> The problem of a "second one" (4:7–16)
>>> One can lose all that one accumulates (4:17–6:9)
> [Each of the above sections ends with *hebel* and "chasing after wind"]

10. Seow, *Ecclesiastes*, 43.
11. Addison G. Wright, "The Riddle of the Sphinx: The Structure of the Book of Qoheleth," *CBQ* 30, no. 3 (1968): 313–34 (313).
12. He employs a "careful verbal and structural analysis" but dispenses with the theory of the intentional fallacy. Though at the heart of New Criticism, Wright sees this dictum as a "weakness." See ibid., 317–19.
13. Ibid., 313.
14. Ibid., 325–26.

II. Qohelet's Conclusions (6:10–11:6)
    Introduction (6:10–12): humans do not know what God has done, for humans cannot
    find out what is good to do and they cannot find out what comes after.
    A. Humans cannot find out what is good for them to do
        Critique of traditional wisdom
            on the day of prosperity and adversity (7:1–14)
            on justice and wickedness (7:15–24)
            on women and folly (7:25–29)
            on the wise man and the king (8:1–17)
  [Each of the above sections ends with "not find out/who can find out"]
    B. Humans do not know what will come after them
            They know they will die; the dead know nothing (9:1–6)
            There is no knowledge in Sheol (9:7–10)
            They do not know their time (9:11–12)
            They do not know what will be (9:13–10:15)
            They do not know what evil will come (10:16–11:2)
            They do not know what good will come (11:3–6)
  [Each of the above sections ends with "do not know/no knowledge"]
  Poem on Youth and Old Age (11:7–12:8)
  Epilogue (12:9–14)

Wright later expands upon this initial proposal through a calculation of the numerical values, which, he claims, underlie the structure.[15] He begins with the observation that there are 222 verses in Qohelet, with the halfway point being at the break between 6:9 and 6:10. He argues that this number is not an arbitrary result of later versification but part of the deliberate intention of the author. The key to this proposal is 1:2. The recurrent phrase and theme *hăbēl hăbālîm hakol hābel* has the numerical value of 216 (using Hebrew numerology, or *gematria*). In addition, the numerical value of *hebel* is 37, and the term is used three times in this verse for the total value of 111. There are two groups of 111 verses (6:9 being the middle), disregarding the epilogue, which Wright assumes is added by an editor. In the first line, *dibrê* ("words of") has the value of 216. The first verse of the epilogue contains the word *wĕyōtēr* ("and more"), the *wāw* having the value of 6. The *wāw* signals to the reader that the author is adding six additional verses. The value of *dibrê* (216) plus the value of *wāw* (6) equals 222, the total number of verses in the book. Wright continues on in this manner, spinning a web of interrelated words and numbers throughout Qohelet. For Wright, these are not coincidences. Instead, the author Qohelet deliberately structured his book using this numerical plan.

    In the end, Wright must manipulate the data to fit the theory. For example, sometimes the refrain that Wright is using to mark the end of a section actually occurs in the middle of a unit (see Qoh 11:2). Sometimes Wright ignores one of the formulaic phrases because it does not appear where he needs it to appear (e.g. 4:4). And there are many repeated phrases that are integral parts of Qohelet's distinctive vocabulary that Wright overlooks altogether ("under the sun,"

"I turned to see").[16] Problems multiply in his numerical analysis. He even goes so far as to suggest that one of the verses containing the word *hebel* is a later addition (either 5:6 or 9:9) since its removal would decrease the total *hebel* count from 38 to 37, thereby making the number of times *hebel* appears in the book equal to the numerical value of the word. This is one of the moments in his argument where the numbers control the interpretation rather than vice versa; consequently, the reasoning becomes hopelessly circular.

After the "making many books" (Qoh 12:12) on the subject of Qohelet's structure, we are no closer to discerning it than we were before the modern era of scholarship. Rather than siding with one proposal or another, with one pole of the debate or the other, I believe that the contours of the question must be changed.

Michael Fox has moved in this direction. He wryly observes that proposals of structure rarely persuade anyone but their authors.[17] Instead of following the typical paradigm, Fox looks to Ludwig Wittgenstein's *Philosophical Investigations*. Excerpting here what Fox quotes in full, Wittgenstein describes his own book's structure:

> I have written down all these thoughts as *remarks*, short paragraphs, of which there is sometimes a fairly long chain about the same subject, while I sometimes make a sudden change, jumping from one topic to another. . . . After several unsuccessful attempts to weld my results together into such a whole, I realized that I should never succeed. The best that I could write would never be more than philosophical remarks; my thoughts were soon crippled if I tried to force them on in any single direction against their natural inclination. —And this was, of course, connected with the very nature of the investigation.[18]

Comparing his remarks to landscapes through which he has long journeyed, Wittgenstein warns readers that they will not find a structure more coherent than this. Readers too are about to enter sketches of scenery through which they will journey. Fox believes that Wittgenstein's description fits Qohelet's structure exactly. Thus, for Fox, while Qohelet offers no clear division of segments, or progression of content, there is a "conceptual organization . . . reinforced by uniformity in tone, ideas, and style"[19] and it is in this that the book coheres.

What Fox gives with one hand—a proposal that resists imposing a structure —he takes away with the other—his own proposal of coherency. I would rather "take hold of the one without letting go of the other" (7:18). While it is true that there is a certain uniformity of tone, this does not overshadow the incoherence of structure—both are present in Qohelet; they exist in an uneasy tension, and the book cannot be tamed by highlighting one over the other. As will be demonstrated through an investigation of Qoh 3:2–8 and 12:1–7, it is death that intervenes to subvert any coherence in the body and in the book alike. "[A]s a

---

16. Crenshaw outlines these problems in *Ecclesiastes*, 42.

17. Fox, *A Time to Tear Down*, 148.

18. Ludwig Wittgenstein, *Philosophical Investigations* (Oxford: ETG Anscombe, 1958), ix, as quoted in Fox, *A Time to Tear Down*, 149–50.

19. Ibid., 150.

book always comes to take the place of the body,"[20] corpse into corpus, the book of Qohelet reflects the death and decay of the body.

As discussed above, Martin Gliserman argues that the body is encoded in the book at three progressively deeper levels: content, symbol, and syntax. Between the levels,

> The drama of the body configured by language is often one of disintegration and reintegration in dynamic tension. It is a drama of fragmenting, severing, and loss, over against cohesion, union, and re-creation. The drama is one that Freud talked about as Thanatos and Eros. . . .[21]

We have seen how the tension between pleasure and pain structures the book in Chapter 4. In Chapter 5, this desire approaches death through the condemnation of women and the allusion to the Song of Songs. If the book of Qohelet is the body of Qohelet, what is the overall form or structure of this body? And how does it interrelate with the other levels of the body in the book?

Death is enacted in the overall structure of the book, a structure that decays and disintegrates like the dying body. Wright's inability to embalm Qohelet in his theory is emblematic. Verses encroach, while others are lacking where they are wanted. Wright ignores whole phrases and they clamor for attention, repeating themselves throughout the text. And finally, an extra *hebel* intrudes to fracture his numbers theory. It is telling that one of the words that Wright needs to delete in order to make his theory perfectly fit the text is *hebel*. This should be a warning to us. The word *hebel* means nothing; it is a word that signals absence and ephemerality like vapor, like death itself. It is the very principle by which all desire for stable meaning must unravel.

The text approaches coherency only to pull away again; the structural theory almost fits but in the end the text slips away in a dance between disintegration and integration. The body grows and lives, but from the moment we are born, we are growing toward nothing but death. The grave pulls us inexorably toward its dark embrace—it is our fundamental seducer. Living is a dance between integration and disintegration, because life is predicated on death, the most permanent and pervasive absence of them all. All proposals of structure are motivated by a search for meaning that Qohelet, in principle, can never satisfy. These analyses of structure necessarily fail because Qohelet is an attempt to speak to the absence at the heart of meaning. Body and text alike decompose.

The Conqueror Worm

Qohelet 3:2–8 is arguably the most rigidly structured passage in the entire book. It contains seven stanzas of seven pairs of binary oppositions. Seven is a perfect number in Hebrew numerology. The number is built into the very structures of the universe, for it took six days to create the world and one day to rest from that

---

20.   Derrida, *The Work of Mourning*, 169.
21.   Gliserman, *Psychoanalysis*, 56.

creation (Gen 1:1–2:4a).[22] This passage is rhythmic like the steady beat of the heart, or the inhale/exhale of breath through the nose, lips, mouth, chest rising and falling. As our heart and lungs form the core of our fleshy being, Qoh 3:2–8 is the core of the book's structure. But, upon closer examination, there are moments when the beat skips and the breathing falters.

The majority of the verses move at a fast clip, being composed of four words only for each couplet, in this pattern: *wĕ‘ēt l–‘ēt l–*. However, the *lāmed* (*l*) that introduces the infinitive is missing in two of the fourteen pairs: Qoh 3:4c–d, and 3:8c–d.[23] Moreover, the verses in 2d and 5a–b and 5d are longer than the other verses. Additional words added after the infinitive weigh down the sentence and slow down the reader. In the most rigidly constructed poem in the book, there are slippages in its strict style.

It is a common method to elaborate further on the structure of this passage by dividing the couplets into negative and positive poles. Commentators then look for some sort of pattern. For example, Loader discerns a chiastic pattern based upon his positive and negative division.[24] Wright also has a structural proposal that divides the couplets into two sections (3:2–4 and 3:5–7) each of which ends with a remark about mourning.[25] The obvious difficulty with such proposals is determining if a particular act or event is "positive" or "negative." While it may be clear that peace is better than war, 3:5a has been particularly vexing: Is it better to cast stones or to gather them up? In the end, these structural systems can only be maintained by assigning (somewhat arbitrarily) value and then suppressing textual elements that contradict.

But these are not the only disruption in the smooth surface of structure. The poem twists out of our control at the first verb: *lāledet*. As discussed in Chapter 4, a prominent interpretation of this poem as a whole is that the 28 acts or events enumerated in its verses instruct the reader in the importance of knowing the right way to act and the right time to do so. The first actions—"a time to be born, and a time to die" (as generally translated by, for example, the NRSV, NIV, JPS)—are not actions that one can choose to perform. The person is the passive

---

22. Gen 2:2 does, however, state that God finished (*klh*) the work of creation on the seventh day, implying that something was indeed created on this day. The LXX and the Syriac text record the verse differently—God finished on the sixth day in these versions, which accords with Exod 20:11 ("In six days the Lord made heaven and earth"). When confronted with Gen 2:2, the rabbis of *Genesis Rabbah* concluded that creation did take seven days rather than six, and that rest itself was created on the seventh day (*Gen. Rab.* 10:9).

23. R. N. Whybray, "'A Time to be Born and a Time to Die'? Some Observations of Ecclesiastes 3:2–8," in *Near Eastern Studies Dedicated to H.I.M. Prince Takahito Mikasa on the Occasion of his Seventy-Fifth Birthday* (ed. M. Mori; Wiesbaden: Harrassowitz 1991), 469–83. Whybray also argues that the order is inverted in v. 8c–d. He sees a positive action followed by a negative action throughout the passage except in this stiche where "war" precedes "peace." The conclusion that Whybray draws from these small anomalies is that Qoh 3:2–8 had a long history of composition. Each variation in the structure is the trace of a different hand.

24. Loader, "Qohelet 3:2–8," 241.

25. A. G. Wright, "For Everything there is a Season: The Structure and Meaning of the Fourteen Opposites (Ecclesiastes 3:2–8)," in *De la Torah au Messie: Mélanges Henri Cazelles* (ed. J. Doré, M. Carrez, and P. Grelot; Paris: Gabalda, 1981), 321–28.

recipient of the events in this verse only, but it makes sense that a pair that encompasses the outer limits of human experience and existence would intro-duce the poem.[26]

However, this is where the problems begin, for *lāledet* does not mean "to be born." It is not in a passive construction; rather it is an infinitive construct which should then translate as "to bear a child" or "to beget"[27] depending on the sex of the subject (which in Qohelet's case is undecidable).[28] Commentators and trans-lators twist the literal meaning of the word in order for it to be a perfect counter-part for *lāmût* ("to die"). Commentators desire this parallelism because if *lāledet* is translated accurately as "a time to bear" or "beget," then *lāmût* becomes the only event in the 28 that is outside of human control. Therefore, interpreters mistranslate *lāledet* in order to pull *lāmût* ("death") into the structural system. By making birth a complement to death, death is given a role and thus becomes a "manageable" alterity. But death cannot be tamed and managed. In the Hebrew *lāmût* stands alone in an alterity that interrupts life just as it disrupts stable and enduring meaning. Death cannot be contained by any system, for it is always in excess of our systems, or the lack at their heart. In Qoh 3:2–8, death quite liter-ally upsets the structure of the text and thereby disrupts meaning and interpreta-tion. The text decomposes.

Qohelet 12:1–8 is "one of the most exegetically challenging sections in Ecclesiastes" in the words of D. C. Fredericks.[29] This passage is difficult for several reasons. It contains many textual and grammatical problems, as well as words of uncertain meaning. Moreover, the referent(s) of the words on the page are indeterminate and no one knows what Qohelet means. Why are the heavenly luminaries darkening (12:2)? Who are the guards, the strong men, the women who grind (12:3)? What are the birds doing exactly, and why (12:4)? The dominant interpretation has been to read the passage as an allegory for the aging and dying body.[30] It is, in fact, the only passage in Qohelet that is consistently read in terms of the body, yet this body appears only symbolically, and its

---

26. Joseph Blenkinsopp, "Ecclesiastes 3:1–15: Another Interpretation," *JSOT* 66 (1995): 55–64 (56). After reviewing the history of translation, Blenkinsopp argues for translating *lāledet* literally, but he draws conclusions different from mine. He believes that the person who penned the bulk of the book did not author 3:2–8; instead it is a quotation. The poem originally did contain 28 acts sub-ject to human will—"a time to die" was originally "a time to take one's life." Obviously, this went against Qohelet's ideology (in sharp distinction from other similar ancient Near Eastern texts [e.g. the Egyptian "Dispute of a Man with his Ba"] Qohelet never contemplates suicide). Therefore, the author altered the second part of the couplet, leaving the first part as it was written.

27. Both the LXX and the Palestinian Targum understand the verb in this way. Seow argues that the verb is a gerund and should be translated "birthing." See Seow, *Ecclesiastes*, 160.

28. The first verb is the only one that requires a gender identification in order to translate pre-cisely. Since none is given here, *lāledet* becomes another site of gender undecidability in Qohelet.

29. D. C. Fredericks, "Life Storms and Structural Unity in Qoheleth 11:1–12:8," *JSOT* (1991): 95–114 (95). This is not an uncommon assessment. Fox calls Qoh 12:1–8 "the most difficult passage in a difficult book," in his "Aging and Death in Qohelet 12," *JSOT* 42 (1988): 55–77 (55).

30. This reading is at least as old as *Qoh. Rab.* 5:1–6:7 (650–900 C.E.). More recently, see Rachel Z. Dulim, "'How Sweet is the Light': Qoheleth's Age-Centered Teachings," *Interpretation* 55, no. 3 (2001): 260–70 (268–69).

presence in the passage is far from certain. The connections between the signifying words and the signified body are tenuous and rely on a reader's hard work. The body here persists in the commentaries, but, paradoxically, in the text it is a veiled body, obscure, elusive, slippery, perhaps not even there at all.

The list of geriatric maladies that are diagnosed from these textual symptoms are extensive: blindness, deafness, impotence, constipation, ischuria, acrophobia, agoraphobia, anorexia, white hair, osteoporosis, isolation, tooth decay and loss. . . .[31] But in order to sustain the allegory or extended metaphor, the interpreter must sweat and strain. How else can one explain the equation of the locust in 12:5 with an aging penis?[32] The failure to make the text fit this hermeneutical framework is usually blamed on the author, instead of seeing the failure as a problem with the interpretive device. George A. Barton, for example, blames Qohelet's "Oriental richness of imagination and carelessness in exact use of metaphor"[33] for the difficulties he has keeping his allegory up.

There have been a few alternatives proposed. Some reject the allegorical meaning and present some sort of literal reading instead. These include the actual experience of the old (M. Gilbert[34]), description of winter and the coming of spring (O. Loretz[35]), a gathering thunderstorm (Ginsburg[36] and Leahy[37]), a ruined house (Sawyer[38] and Witzenrath[39]), and a description of a community in mourning (C. Taylor[40]). As this short list demonstrates, "literal" has a very different meaning for each interpreter.[41] Apocalyptic readings have also been proposed. For example, Timothy K. Beal reads these last words of Qohelet as "envisioning cosmopolitical disjuncture and breakdown" as well as "a longing for and a beckoning of what is beyond it."[42] Similarly, Yvonne Sherwood writes that Qohelet is "hollowing out the genre of eschatology" by contracting it "to the

---

31. A. D. Power, *Ecclesiastes or The Preacher* (New York: Longmans, Green & Co., 1952), 123–26, has a full list of body parts and maladies that have been read from Qoh 12.

32. This is a common interpretation. See, for example, Gordis, *Koheleth*, 336–37; Seow, *Ecclesiastes*, 362–63

33. Barton, *A Critical and Exegetical Commentary*, 187.

34. M. Gilbert, "La description de la vieillesse en Qohelet XII 1–7 est-elle allégorique?," in *Congress Volume: Vienna, 1980* (ed. J. A. Emerton; VTSup 32; Leiden: Brill, 1981), 96–109.

35. Oswald Loretz, *Qohelet und der alte Orient: Untersuchungen zu Stil und theologischer* (Freiburg: Herder, 1964).

36. Christian David Ginsburg, *Coheleth* (London: Longman, 1861; repr., New York: Ktav, 1970).

37. Michael Leahy, "The Meaning of Ecclesiastes (12:2–5)," *ITQ* 19 (1952): 297–300.

38. J. F. A. Sawyer, "The Ruined House in Ecclesiastes 12: A Reconstruction of the Original Parable," *JBL* 94 (1975): 519–31.

39. Hagia H. Witzenrath, *Süss ist das Licht . . . Eine literaturwissenschaftliche Untersuchung zu Koh 11,7–12,7* (St. Ottilien: EOS, 1979).

40. C. Taylor, *The Dirge of Coheleth in Ecclesiastes XII* (London: Williams & Norgate, 1874).

41. For a more detailed analysis of each of these proposals, see Fox, "Aging and Death in Qohelet 12."

42. Timothy K. Beal, "C(ha)osmopolis: Qohelet's Last Words," in *God in the Fray: A Tribute to Walter Brueggemann* (ed. Tod Linafelt and Timothy K. Beal; Minneapolis: Fortress, 1998), 290–304 (292–93). Beal does not argue for a consistent and exclusive apocalyptic reading. Rather, he sees it as another layer of the text in addition to the symbolic level of an aging body.

end of the world that all of us know—the 'end of my world, creeping up on me.'"[43]

The difficulties in interpreting the poem as a whole are a reflection of the difficulties in interpreting each word and phrase. For example, the passage begins with the command to "Remember your creator (*bôrĕʾêkâ*) in the days of your youth. . . ." Qohelet uses an unusual word for the divine here, unique in the text and in the Bible as a whole.[44] The uniqueness of the word in conjunction with doubts about how well any reference to God fits the context of the passage, has caused many to propose dropping the clause altogether, or at least emending the word.[45] Dropping the *ʾālep* yields "your pit" which can also be a reference to "your grave." However, there is no textual witness to support such an alteration. And, although this designation for God is unusual, the idea of creation both human and divine is seen throughout the text. Qohelet is full of unusual constructions and unique words. Its phrases are plurivocal, equivocal, evocative, and unsubsumable—no overarching interpretation can suffice to bind all the diverse elements together. It could be that Qohelet uses this unusual word for God precisely because it also conjures up images of the grave. In this case, nothing stands between "your creator" and "your grave" but an *ʾālep*, and since the *ʾālep* is nothing more than a hard breath of air, nothing stands between "your creator" and "your grave, " birth and death, but a gasp.

Reading this line as a wordplay is not unprecedented. Rabbi Akabya ben Mahalalel says: "Consider three things and you will not come into the power of sin: Know whence you came; where you are going; and before whom you are destined to give an accounting."[46] This interpretation is based upon three different words alluded to by the one: *bĕʾērkā* ("your source"), *bôrkā* ("your pit"), and *bôrĕʾêkâ* ("your creator"). One can also hear the resonance of death in the similar English saying, "time to meet your Maker."[47]

One of the major themes of Qohelet is that of *ʿāmal*, human creation. Qohelet creates and builds and orders throughout his text but always despairs that such endeavors are *hebel* and chasing after wind. One cannot always enjoy the fruits of one's labors, or control who inherits them after one is gone, and they cannot guarantee the continuation of one's name. Humans create in imitation of the

43. Yvonne Sherwood, "'Not with a Bang but a Whimper': Shrunken Eschatologies of the Twentieth Century—and the Bible," in *Apocalyptic in History and Tradition* (ed. Christopher Rowland and John Barton; JSPSup 43; Sheffield: Sheffield Academic Press, 2002), 94–116 (113–14). Like Beal, Sherwood does not argue for an exclusive apocalyptic reading.

44. The word potentially has a grammatical problem, as well. The position of the letter *yôd* in the pronominal suffix generally indicates a plural noun ("your Creators"). Rather than seeing the form as a plural, Seow argues that the *yôd* is "the result of the frequent confusion in late Hebrew of III-ʾAlep and III-Weak roots . . ." (*Ecclesiastes*, 351).

45. An example of this position is Crenshaw, *Ecclesiastes*, 184–85. Crenshaw emends *bôrĕʾêkâ* to *bĕʾērkā* and understands "your well" to mean "your wife" (following the use of the word in Prov 5:15). See also Seow, *Ecclesiastes*, 351–53.

46. Rabbi Akabya ben Mahalalel was a first-century C.E. rabbi; this saying appears in *Abot* 3:1. As quoted in Seow, *Ecclesiastes*, 352.

47. Those who favor reading the MT as it stands include Gordis, *Koheleth*, 340; Fox, "Aging and Dying in Qohelet 12," 55; Seow, *Ecclesiastes*, 351–52; Beal, "C(ha)osmopolis," 294–95.

divine.[48] At the beginning of Qohelet, there is a sense that God's creation is the only thing that is permanent, enduring, solid: "Generations come and generations go, but the earth remains forever" (Qoh 1:4). By the time one reaches the end of Qohelet, the sun and the moon and the stars are blinking out (12:2). Could Qohelet, by calling God "creator" here, be subtly suggesting that God's work is *hebel* also; for all of God's creatures die and decay; even the earth and the heavens do not abide?

The poem continues with a list of actions that have been understood to refer to the loss of eyesight and teeth, weakness of limbs, deterioration of the digestive system, sleepless nights, deafness, stiff joints, white hair, the lack of sexual desire, and the inability of plants considered aphrodisiacs (caperberry) to do anything about it. There is also a dying down of all spheres of human life and activity as well as strange happenings in nature. The social world of the street stops; the commercial and/or family activity of grinding ceases; the natural world fades.

The final stanza is replete with imagery suggesting the cessation of human activity, the ways in which human objects remain after a general catastrophe, possible allegories for the human body, and eschatological imagery: "before the silver cord is snapped, and the golden bowl is crushed, and the jar by the spring is broken, and the wheel by the well is crushed" (Qoh 12:6). There is evidence to suggest that the breaking of pottery was a funerary practice, perhaps representing the breaking of the body in death.[49] The prophets describe God as a potter making humans out of clay (Isa 29:16; Jer 18:6). The allusion is to the second creation story, where God forms *hāʾdām* out of *hāʾădāmâ* (Gen 2:7). The connection between this passage and the creation story in Genesis is strengthened in the next verse where Qohelet specifically mentions the dust of the earth out of which human flesh was created. The final verse of this poem is "and the dust (*ʿāpār*) returns to the earth as it was, and the breath returns to God who gave it" (Qoh 12:7). In Genesis, when God creates the human being, the flesh comes from the dust (*ʿāpār*) of the earth, and the animating breathe[50] comes from God. In the "evil days," God's creatures disintegrate into their constituent elements. All is *hebel*, God's creation is undone.

In Qoh 12:1–8, the stars blink out (v. 1), the grinders disappear (v. 3), the body returns to the earth (v. 7). Creation is undone. Qohelet describes and enacts the uncreating of the world experienced at one level as decay in the body, at another level as the dissolution of the social world and the cosmos, at another level in the decomposing of the book. In the text there are gaps, fragments,

---

48. William Brown makes the connection between human work and divine creation in the book of Qohelet in his article, "'Whatever Your Hand Finds to Do.'" However, he draws the connection in order to redeem human work and put a positive spin on Qohelet's use of the word *ʿāmal*. I am using the connection to question God's work.

49. Seow, *Ecclesiastes*, 366. Seow cites several archaeological studies to support this contention. Broken pottery in Jewish tombs from the Persian period has been found at Jericho, Shechem, and other settlements in the Judean desert.

50. Qohelet uses a different term for God's breath. In Gen 2:7, God breathes *nišmat ḥayyîm* into the earth-creature; whereas in Qoh 12:7, the *rûaḥ* returns to God.

uncertain words, convoluted grammar, corrupted syntax. The pervasiveness of the allegorical interpretation (the poem as an allegory for the body) among commentators from pre-modern to post-modern times is ironic. The body is a superimposition upon the text to resolve the resistances in the text to interpretation. The text is resisting interpretation because meaning itself is subject to death.

As a result, the meanings imposed on the text by interpreters multiply as if the text in its own death throes spews forth an excess of signification. At one moment the text is perhaps speaking about the body, the next a storm, house, scene of mourning, then the universe, social world, cosmos. . . . The interpreter moves back and forth among allegory, symbol, literal meaning, metaphor, never able to secure the text to any one interpretation. Re-enacting in a radical manner the condition of all language and the fate of all bodies, Qohelet decomposes.

The Gift of Death

God is the subject of the verb *nātan* ("to give") more than God is the subject of any other verb in the book. God gives twelve times in the book of Qohelet. God gives that which makes up human life: eating, drinking, and enjoyment; wisdom and knowledge; gathering and heaping; wealth, possessions, and honor—all of the business with which we are busy. In sum, God gives life itself and, by implication, the death that makes life possible: "The affirmation of life is nothing other than a certain thought of death; it is neither opposition nor indifference to death—indeed one would almost say the opposite if this were not giving in to opposition."[51] They are the same giving, the same gift: "a gift of life, or, what amounts to the same thing, a gift of death."[52]

God's giving begins early in the book and continues through the final chapter:

There is nothing better for humans than to eat and drink, and find enjoyment in their toil. This also, I saw, is from the hand of God; for apart from him who can eat or who can have enjoyment? For to the one who pleases him God gives wisdom and knowledge and joy; but to the sinner he gives the work of gathering and heaping, only to give to one who pleases God. This also is *hebel* and chasing after wind. (2:24–26; cf. 6:2)

I have seen the business that God gives to humanity to be busy with; he has made everything beautiful in its time; moreover he gives eternity into their hearts. (3:10–11)

Also, it is God's gift that all humanity should eat and drink and take pleasure in all their toil. (3:13)

Behold, this is what I have seen to be good: it is beautiful to eat and drink and find enjoyment in all the toil with which one toils under the sun the few days of the life God gives us; for this is our portion. (5:17 [Eng 18]; cf. 8:15; 12:7)

Also all humanity to whom God gives wealth and possessions and whom he enables to enjoy them, and to accept their portion and find enjoyment in their toil—this is the gift of God. (5:18 [Eng 19])

51. Derrida, *The Work of Mourning*, 175.
52. Derrida, *The Gift of Death*, 97.

And the dust returns to the earth as it was, and the breath returns to the God who gave it. (12:7)

What is a gift? This question is not as simple as it may at first appear. A gift, according to Derrida,[53] must be freely given and freely received. It must not be a part of any system of return, barter, or debt. If it is, it ceases to be a gift and enters into an economy of exchange: "If the other *gives* me *back* or *owes* me or has to give me back what I give him or her, there will not have been a gift, whether this restitution is immediate or whether it is programmed by a complex calculation of a long-term deferral or *différance.*"[54]

So, in order for the gift to escape the economy of exchange, there must be a radical forgetting on the part of the giver as well as on the part of the one who receives: "If he recognizes it *as* gift, if the gift *appears to him as such*, if the present is present to him *as present*, this simple recognition suffices to annul the gift."[55] Giving involves a complete act of forgetting, both on the part of the giver and on the part of the receiver:

> For there to be gift, not only must the donor or donee not perceive or receive the gift as such, have no consciousness of it, no memory, no recognition; he or she must also forget it right away and moreover this forgetting must be so radical that it exceeds even the psychoanalytic categoriality of forgetting.[56]

But is this ever possible? Derrida points out that the conditions of the possibility of the gift are the conditions of its impossibility as well.

Because the gift is both possible and impossible, the gift is an aporia. It signals alterity because it must be outside of the economy of human purpose. It must not be known, it must not be acknowledged, and it must not be remembered. It exceeds any categorization or systematization. In Qohelet, death is the eraser of memory and the extinguisher of differences. It comes from outside of us without warning, without expectation. All categories—animal and human, pious and impious, rich and poor, wise and foolish—are overcome by death. "There is gift, if there is any, only in what interrupts the system as well as the symbol, in a partition without return and without division. . . ."[57] Perhaps the only gift possible is the gift of death.

The giving of death orients Qohelet's worldview—it (mis)shapes his theodicy, and his ethic. It is around "that" which the other systems in the book gather and constitute themselves, but cannot be included or contained in any system "itself." The question of theodicy arises in the first statement of God's giving (2:24–26). In this passage, God is responsible for both the pleasures and pains of living. What any one individual receives is dependent upon that person's ability to please the divine. Or so it seems at first. But the summary statement ("This

---

53. Derrida is building his own idea of the gift on the work of other theorists, especially Marcel Mauss's *Sociologie et Anthropologie* (Paris: Presses Universitaires de France, 1950).
54. Jacques Derrida, *Given Time: I. Counterfeit Money* (trans. Peggy Kamuf; Chicago: University of Chicago Press, 1992), 12.
55. Ibid., 13.
56. Ibid., 16.
57. Ibid., 13.

also is *hebel* and chasing after wind") introduces the undecidable—*hebel*—that undercuts Qohelet's traditional piety in a manner typical of the book as a whole. The word *hebel* is the undecidable because it is a word that means nothing, a word that is empty and thus always signals the absence of meaning. The book continues with a fundamental questioning of a just system of reward and punishment (or at least a just system that humans could know and predict). As Qohelet states, "All that I have seen in the days of my *hebel*, there are the righteous who perish in their righteousness, and there are the wicked who prolong their lives in their wickedness" (7:15; cf. 8:14).

For Qohelet, death levels differences and this leveling undermines any system of ultimate reward and punishment. How, then, should one act? Does death render ethical action meaningless as well? Not quite, for Qohelet holds *hebel* in tension with a poignant concern for the wellbeing of others: "Again I saw all the oppressions that are practiced under the sun. Look, the tears of the oppressed—with no one to comfort them! On the side of their oppressors there was power—with no one to comfort them" (Qoh 4:1). For Derrida, too, the gift of death does not annul ethical action but rather arouses an even more deeply felt impulse toward responsibility; it is in fact that which incites responsibility:

> The gift made to me by God as he holds me in his gaze and in this hand while remaining inaccessible to me, the terribly dissymmetrical gift of the *mysterium tremendum* only allows me to respond and only rouses me to the responsibility it gives me by making a gift of death, giving the secret of death, a new experience of death.[58]

The gift of death is made "to me." It cannot be taken (if someone sacrifices himself for another, his death only postpones the other's death, it does not in fact replace it), nor can it be given in the sense of murder (if someone kills another, that death is still irreducibly the other's own).[59] It is in this sense that the gift is dissymmetrical and absolutely singular. It is out of this space of dissymmetrical gift (the infinite given to the finite, see Qoh 3:11) and "irreplaceable singularity" that responsibility arises.

In Qohelet, death renders the desire for determinacy, memory, presence, and coherence—in short, the desire for meaning—*hebel*. The gift of death is an experience beyond our control, transgressing our boundaries, breaking our limits. Death literally breaks our bodies and Qohelet enacts this breaking in the fracturing of the book's structure, the intrusion of death that resists systematicity (3:1–8) and coherent interpretation (12:1–8). The breaking open of the body and the book thereby opens us up to responsibility. The open wound of meaninglessness in Qohelet opens us up to the *mysterium tremendum*, the wholly other, and to the responsibility that the face of the other demands.

---

58. Derrida, *The Gift of Death*, 33.
59. Ibid., 44.

Chapter 7

READING THE EPILOGUE THROUGH THIS BODY*

> Finally, is it necessary to posit an interpreter behind the interpretation? Even this is an invention, hypothesis.
>
> —*Martin Gliserman*[1]

Readers tend to look for closure at the end of texts. This has been particularly true in modern Western conceptions of literature, and these ideas have shaped how biblical commentators regard ancient literature as well.[2] At the end of a biblical story, readers look for meaning, closure, and a tidy wrap-up that "makes sense" and brings a certain satisfaction. In Qohelet, however, we have a text that resists meaning through its discourse on death. The structure of the book is in a state of decay, meaning is unstable through ambiguity at the level of individual words as well as whole passages, and the very conditions of signification are called into question through death's erasure of repeatability and differentiation. The end of Qohelet's life remains messy, as does the end of Qohelet's text.

Commenting on the state of scholarship on Qohelet in *Old Testament Interpretation*, Carol Newsom writes: "it is always interesting to see where the 'interpretative sweat' breaks out in dealing with such an iconoclastic book."[3] The epilogue of Qohelet (12:9–14) may be the sweatiest place in the text. It challenges any interpretation, and from the source critics of the late nineteenth century to the literary critics of the late twentieth century, no one can resist attributing these verses to another hand. It has routinely been dismissed as contradicting the primary message of the original author, and its words have been seen as those

---

* A version of this chapter was originally presented at the Mid-Atlantic Regional Meeting of the Society of Biblical Literature in New Brunswick, New Jersey, March 2001. Another version has been published in Ingrid Rosa Kitzberger, ed., *Autobiographical Biblical Criticism: Between Text and Self* (Leiden: Deo Publishing, 2002), 183–92. I would like to thank Robert Paul Seesengood and Ingrid Rosa Kitzberger for their comments and suggestions for this chapter.

1. Friedrich Nietzsche, *The Will to Power* (trans. Walter Kaufmann and R.J. Hollingdale; New York: Vintage, 1968), 267 para. 481.

2. See Robert Alter, *The Art of Biblical Narrative* (San Francisco: HarperCollins, 1981), for a full examination of the differences between Western conceptions of literature and biblical, and the ways in which modern ideas influence the interpretations of ancient texts. See especially his Conclusion (pp. 178–85) in which he summarizes the biblical narrative aesthetic.

3. Carol Newsom, "Job and Ecclesiastes," 191.

that made the text tame enough to be included in a religious corpus. But is this the only solution possible?

I begin my reading of the epilogue with the simple personal observation that I have never read these verses as being radically incongruous with the rest of the book, nor do I believe that an espousal of traditional piety necessarily contradicts the pessimistic questioning in the book. I come to my interpretation through a focus on the body—the text's, the speaker's, and my own. First, an examination of the language demonstrates that the features that are cited as distinguishing these verses are not absent from the rest of the book. Nor, on the other hand, is the epilogue a seamless pietistic coda. Second, keeping the commandments (12:13) is an injunction to right ritual—a function of the body—and not a demand for proper theological thinking. Finally, recognizing that the commentators' assumptions about coherent identities and unified texts shape their interpretations, reflections on my own assumptions about identity will be interwoven throughout this chapter.

The scholarship concerning the contradictions and consequently the authorship of Qohelet has been dependent upon a more general discourse on the relationship between integrity of identity and consistency of text. The single, unified, individual author guarantees the coherence of the narrative which he or she signs. The foundation of modern biblical criticism—source criticism—is based upon this presumed relationship. Any deviation in style or theme is understood as evidence of an intruder: a different source, the sentiments of a latter redactor, even the comments of a presumptuous scribe. The limitations of source criticism have been widely sounded, but its basic presuppositions continue to permeate readings of Qohelet. Postmodern theories radically undermine these presuppositions by promulgating ideas about identity that highlight its fragmented and contingent nature. Identity is disjointed, inconsistent, multivalent, lacking a stable center.[4] And the texts these identities produce can be the same without indicating one way or the other how many authors or sources contributed to the final form. Intentions, identities, texts are all complex phenomena with no simple formula for tracing out their interrelationships. The complexities of the relationships are compounded with biblical books because they have been transmitted to us with hidden authorial, temporal, and spatial origins.

As a result of these considerations, I am not making a contribution to the scholarship on Qohelet that argues for single authorship against the dominant opinion of at least two hands involved in the production of the final form. Rather, I am demonstrating that any theory of authorship is shaped primarily by the interpreter's assumptions about texts and identities, and only secondarily by the information in the text itself. In fact, there is no information that inheres independently within the text. All such information is always already in relationship with the reader. One project of postmodern biblical criticism is "to challenge

---

4.   For a synopsis of postmodern definitions of "identity" and their use in biblical interpretation, see Francisco Lozada, Jr., "Identity," in Adam, ed., *Handbook of Postmodern Biblical Interpretation*, 113–19.

modernism's long-reigning assumption that interpretation is [or should be] independent of one's identity."[5] Prominent scholars such as Gerhard von Rad have noted disparagingly that the study of Qohelet has always been wrapped up in the identity of its readers.[6] However, whereas von Rad laments that Qohelet is an exceedingly difficult book to study precisely because interpreters are always writing themselves into the text, I am going to revel in this very "problem." This chapter is an exploration of how, with different notions of identity and texts, a different picture of the epilogue of Qohelet emerges.

Autobiographical criticism rejects the fiction of scholarly objectivity. It is a form of interpretation that foregrounds the body, personality, and experience of the reader. In the words of Rachel Brownstein, it is a piece of critical writing "that reveals or pretends to reveal those attributes of the writing subject that are personlike, personal—the person, more usually than not, in the sense of the word that means the body."[7] In short, "Personal criticism is about the reader in the process of reading, the embodied critic."[8] I want to highlight a phrase Brownstein uses in this definition, a phrase she almost throws off like a parenthesis— "or pretends to reveal." The highlighting of the reader's self in interpretation does not reify modern theories of authors and identities. Autobiographical criticism acknowledges the contingent nature of identity and recognizes that any story about our selves is essentially just that—story. It necessarily leaves out information, constructs connections between events, and ascribes import. Autobiography is never a straightforward accounting of the facts of someone's life. The relationship between self and text defies the classifications of fiction and fact. And even the interpreter's self is not "capable of expressing itself without misrepresenting itself" when engaged in personal criticism.[9]

Continuing his critique of a Qohelet scholarship mired in the personal, von Rad's words sound like a prescient warning to projects such as mine: "It is clear, however, that in an approach which is burdened with such an obvious bias, inappropriate, ideological presuppositions can become entangled in the exposition and can lead to problematical assessments."[10] To that I affirm that what follows is burdened with bias, but I leave it to the reader of my reading to decide whether my assessments are inappropriate, ideological, and problematic—or, at least, any more so than those of any other interpreter.[11]

---

5.   Ibid., 113.

6.   Von Rad, *Wisdom*, 231–32.

7.   Rachel M. Brownstein, "Interrupted Reading: Personal Criticism in the Present Time," in Veeser, ed., *Confessions of the Critics*, 29–39 (31).

8.   Ibid., 32.

9.   Stephen D. Moore addresses this "pretending" or "performance" more thoroughly in "True Confessions and Weird Obsessions: Autobiographical Interventions in Literary and Biblical Studies," in Janice Capel Anderson and Jeffrey L. Staley, eds., *Taking it Personally* (Semeia 72; Atlanta: Scholars Press, 1995), 19–50.

10.   Von Rad, *Wisdom*, 32.

11.   The role of autobiography in literary criticism has been posed by such scholars as Nancy K. Miller (*Getting Personal: Feminist Occasions and Other Autobiographical Acts* [New York: Routledge, 1991]); Jane Tompkins (first in an [in]famous article entitled "Me and My Shadow," in

I have a mezuzah hanging on the doorframe of my apartment . . . "and write them on the doorposts of your house and on your gates" (Deut 6:9). I unlock my door, swing in and open, kiss fingertips, touch mezuzah, step over the threshold, I am home.

A History of Athletic Virtuosity

I have been reading people reading Qohelet. The rabbis of the Talmud conversed about this book from time to time. In fact, the first recorded conversation about Qohelet resolved rabbinic anxiety about its inconsistencies by noting the pious epilogue: "R. Judah b. Samuel b. Shilath said in Rav's name: The sages sought to withdraw the book of Qohelet because its words are mutually contradictory. Why then did they not withdraw it? Because it begins with words of Torah and it ends with words of Torah" (*b. Shab.* 30b).[12] What worried the rabbis has continued to worry modern scholars. According to Craig Bartholomew, so central are these final words that the way in which an interpreter deals with the epilogue provides the key to his or her hermeneutic.[13]

I have been reading people reading Qohelet. Sometimes I can feel the sweat dampening the pages of the commentary from the beginning. They flex their source-critical muscles by splintering the text into a thousand separate pieces. During the early, heady days of source criticism, up to nine separate authors for these twelve chapters were posited. In C. Siegfried's analysis, the original Qohelet had a radically pessimistic message that was toned down by a series of four glossators, two redactors, and two epilogists.[14] Positing different hands has continued to be a popular method of explaining (away) the inconsistencies in the text. The major early commentaries of A. H. McNeile (1904),[15] George A. Barton (1908),[16] and Emmanuel Podechard (1912)[17] followed this method as did the later commentaries of Friedrich Ellermeier (1967)[18] and Aarre Lauha (1978).[19]

The Intimate Critique: Autobiographical Literary Criticism [ed. Diane P. Freedman, Olivia Frey, and Frances Murphy Zauhar; Durham, N.C.: Duke University Press, 1993], 23–40; see also idem, *A Life in School: What the Teacher Learned* [Reading, Mass.: Perseus, 1996]); and Veeser (*Confessions of the Critics*). Biblical studies has followed suit in full-length works by Jeffrey L. Staley (*Reading with a Passion: Rhetoric, Autobiography, and the American West in the Gospel of John* [New York: Continuum, 1995]); Moore (*God's Gym*); and edited volumes by Janice Capel Anderson and Jeffrey L. Staley (*Taking it Personally* [Semeia 72; Atlanta: Scholars Press, 1995]), and Ingrid Rosa Kitzberger (*The Personal Voice in Biblical Interpretation* [New York: Routledge, 1999] and *Autobiographical Criticism*).

12. As quoted in Fox, *A Time to Tear Down*, 1.
13. Bartholomew, *Reading Ecclesiastes*, 69.
14. C. Siegfried, *Prediger und Hoheslied* (Göttingen: Vandenhoeck & Ruprecht, 1898).
15. A. H. McNeile, *An Introduction to Ecclesiastes with Notes and Appendices* (Cambridge: Cambridge University Press, 1904).
16. Barton, *A Critical and Exegetical Commentary*.
17. Emmanuel Podechard, *L'ecclésiaste* (Paris: Librairie Victor Lecoffre, 1912).
18. Friedrich Ellermeier, *Qoheleth* (Herzberg: Jungfer, 1967).
19. Aarre Lauha, *Kohelet* (Biblischer Kommentar Altes Testament; Neukirchen–Vluyn: Neukirchener Verlag, 1978).

More recently, scholars have streamlined their gymnastics routines, and as a consequence sweat less upon their pages. James L. Crenshaw (1981, 1987) understands there to be glosses on the original text (3:17; 7:18; 8:12–13; 11:9b) and at least two epilogues (12:9–12 and 12:13–14).[20] Although Roland E. Murphy (1992) employs a more literary-critical method to Qohelet, he too follows this standard explanation. For him, there are verses that simply cannot have been written by Qohelet, and some that may not have been written by him. So, even though he suggests that it is best to read the book as a whole, for Murphy the epilogue is certainly from a different hand and should be excluded from this unity.[21]

I have been reading people reading Qohelet. Michael Fox nearly makes it through the whole book without sweating about the epilogue. Almost. His 1999 reworking of his 1989 book begins with the primary thesis: "The contradictions in the book of Qohelet are real and intended. We must interpret them not eliminate them."[22] He then reviews the history of attempts to harmonize the discords, all of which he subjects to trenchant critique. Fox contends that the book was written by a single author who can be conflated with the frame-narrator—the person responsible for the epilogue. The frame-narrator then writes in the fictional persona of Qohelet, and this constitutes the body of the book.[23]

But in the end, even he panics. Fox separates out the final two verses of Qohelet: "The book of Qohelet contains two statements about wisdom that do not come from Qohelet. These belong to the epilogist (12:9–12) and the author of the postscript (vv. 13b–14), who are probably different persons."[24] The author of the postscript, Fox posits, was one of the first copyists of the book. This scribe could have eliminated the pessimistic refrain *hăbēl hăbālîm* (or "all is absurd" as Fox translates it) but did not do so. Instead, he added the postscript (vv. 13b–14) to delimit Qohelet's type of wisdom.

I have been reading people reading Qohelet. Although there has been a growing scholarly consensus that Qohelet should be read as a whole, the legacy of source criticism persists often in the interpretation of the epilogue (12:8–12) and always in the postscript (12:13–14).[25] This is based upon the understanding that

20. James Crenshaw, *Old Testament Wisdom: An Introduction* (Atlanta: John Knox, 1981), 146. In his subsequent commentary (*Ecclesiastes*, 48) the list of glosses is slightly altered, but the contention that there are two different epilogues remains.

21. Murphy, *Ecclesiastes*, xxxiv.

22. Fox, *A Time to Tear Down*, 3.

23. Fox first proposed this idea in his article "Frame Narrative and Composition in the Book of Qoheleth," *HUCA* 48 (1977): 83–106.

24. Fox, *A Time to Tear Down*, 95. This position is a change from the earlier essay, in which his thesis is "that all of 1:2–12:14 is by the same hand—not that the epilogue is by Qohelet, but that Qohelet is 'by' the epilogist" (Fox, "Frame Narrative," 91).

25. Bartholomew, *Reading Ecclesiastes*, 95. Also see Choon-Leong Seow, "'Beyond Them, My Son, Be Warned': The Epilogue of Qoheleth Revisited," in *Wisdom, You Are My Sister* (ed. Michael L. Barré, SS; Washington D.C.: The Catholic Biblical Association of America, 1997), 125–41 (125–27), for another succinct review of the history of separating the epilogue out from the body of the book.

the sentiments expressed in these passages are incongruous with the book as a whole and that a single person cannot express opposing views in the same text. Both of these are assumptions, cast back upon the book of Qohelet. Rather than regard the end of Qoh 12 as part of a later epilogue or postscript, added on as an attempt to domesticate the more radical message of the book's interior, I see this passage as an integral part of the text.

I heard a rabbi tell this story: He was teaching a young man how to wear tefillin . . . "bind them as a sign on your hand, fix them as an emblem on your forehead" (Deut 6:8). One day the young man come to the rabbi, worried. He says, Rabbi, I put on tefillin in the morning and I say the prayer and it feels right to do so. But Rabbi, I do not know if I believe in G-d. The rabbi responded: What does belief in G-d have to do with putting on tefillin?

Examining the Body of the Book

In the final verses of ch. 12 there is a change in the speaking voice and an espousal of traditional piety, which are seen by commentators to contradict the general tenor of the book. However, neither of these features is absent from the rest of the text. There are shifts in the speaking voice and general piety throughout the twelve chapters. If the end of ch. 12 is to be removed on these accounts, the entire book unravels.

I unlock my door, swing in and open, kiss fingertips, touch mezuzah, step over the threshold, I am home.

First, the speaking voice does not shift in v. 9 but in v. 8 of ch. 12: *hăbēl hăbālîm* says the Qohelet, all is *hăbel*. Some commentators do ascribe this verse to an editor. However, it expresses the major theme of the book as a whole, and it seems strange to sheer it off from Qohelet's authentic text. For example, Whybray, in an article exploring the theology of Qohelet, states that the refrain *hăbēl hăbālîm* in 1:2 and 12:8 is an "editorial interpretation of what was supposed to be the essence of Qoheleth's teaching." As such, he argues, "It should not be assumed that this is a correct interpretation of his thought."[26] In order to maintain consistently that any speech in the third person is an editorial intrusion, Whybray is forced to disavow this core theme of Qohelet.[27] Other moments in the text which speak of Qohelet in the third person are Qoh 1:1 (the superscription), 1:2 (parallel to 12:8), and 7:27.

Second, there is no change in the language of the text in 12:9–14. Even words and grammatical constructions that are unique to Qohelet continue through these verses without break or interruption. For example, the first word of 12:9, *yōtēr* ("more")—occurs six other times in this book (2:15; 6:8, 11; 7:11, 16; 12:12) and is related to the word *yitrôn* ("advantage"), which occurs only in Qohelet (e.g. 1:3). In 12:10, the use of the word *ḥepheṣ*, meaning literally "desire,"

26.   Whybray, "Qoheleth as a Theologian," 263.
27.   Whybray does caution against removing the final two verses from Qohelet, however ("Qoheleth as a Theologian," 260). I will address Whybray's interpretation of the epilogue further below.

shares the unique connotation of "enjoyment" or "pleasing," sometimes trans-lated "matter," with its use in the remainder of the text (3:1; 5:3 [Eng 4]; 8:6; 12:1).[28]

Even the particularly troublesome instruction to fear God (12:13) is not absent from the body of the book. This phrase also occurs in 3:14; 5:6 [Eng 7]; and 8:12–13. It is a typical maxim in Wisdom Literature. The beginning of the book of Proverbs declares the fear of the Lord to be the foundation of all wisdom (Prov 1:7). There is, however, a difference in language in the book of Qohelet in comparison to Proverbs and other Wisdom books. Qohelet instructs its readers to fear *hā'ĕlōhîm*, literally "the God," rather than the tetragrammaton ("the Lord") in all four verses (3:14; 5:6; 8:12–3; 12:13). There are two peculiar fea-tures of Qohelet present here: the tetragrammaton is absent, and God is almost always referred to with the definite article.[29]

Third, although commandments are not mentioned in the body of the text (except for 8:5, which refers to human commandments and not divine), some interpreters who maintain that Qoh 12:13–14 are from a later editor note that they do not really contradict what precedes them. Choon-Leong Seow concedes: "It must be said that the perspective in vv. 13b–14 is not contradictory to the rest of the book. Nowhere does Qohelet, or the writers of Proverbs for that matter, deny the importance of obedience to divine commandments. Nor is the possi-bility of an eschatological judgment explicitly rejected."[30] Fox reaches a similar conclusion through an analysis of the concept of justice in Qohelet:

> The book concludes with another resounding profession of divine judgment (Qoh 12:14): "For God will bring every deed into judgment, (even) every secret deed, whether good or evil." This tenet, whether written by an editor or by the author, is not without parallel in the body of the book (compare 3:17 and 11:9b), although it is more emphatic and dogmatic in tone than most of Qohelet's pronouncements on justice.[31]

In another article, Seow even discusses Fox's earlier position that these verses should not be separated out, and then notes that since this idea was first promul-gated in 1977 it has not been systematically refuted but it has been largely ignored.[32] Seow himself does not refute Fox's early argument, but still states that 12:13b–14 is written by a later editor.[33] If these verses do not express sentiments that clash absolutely with the remainder of the book, why insist upon their removal?

One can, and many do, argue that every time there is a change in the speaking voice in this book, there is a change in the author. One can, and some do, argue that the epilogist simply mimicked the language of the primary author. One can, and Seow and Fox do, argue that even though the pious sentiments expressed in vv. 13 and 14 do not contradict the body of the work, they are still the writings

28. Seow, *Ecclesiastes*, 385.
29. I will address these two peculiarities further below.
30. Ibid., 395.
31. Fox, *A Time to Tear Down*, 57.
32. Seow, "'Beyond Them, My Son, Be Warned,'" 127.
33. Ibid., 141.

of a different person. But, taking all of these points together, the argument for separating the epilogue (and/or the postscript) out from the body of the book rests on shifting sands.

I contend that it is impossible to demonstrate that these verses come from another hand based upon structural differences, semantic differences, or differences in meaning. Through these lenses, the epilogue coheres with the body of the book.

Do I believe in G-d? I stretch my arm out to touch the Torah with my prayer book as it is cradled, wrapped in its garments, in the arms of my rabbi, my heart beating, my eyes transfixed on the holy object, black fire written on white fire. My prayer book brushes it as it is walked by and I bring the book to my lips to kiss the place where it touched Torah . . . let me kiss you with the kisses of my mouth (Song 1:2). I feel the worn binding of the siddur against my wet lips.

A Second Opinion

The body of the book presents moments of piety throughout the text, not just in the final words. In the same vein, the epilogue is not the seamless pietistic coda presented in the commentaries. It is just as troubling as other more obviously troubling parts of the book. And it does undermine the rest of the book—though not in the way that commentators have commonly understood its subversion.

I unlock my door, swing in and open, kiss fingertips, touch mezuzah, step over the threshold, I am home.

The first thing that strikes me about this passage is that Qoh 12:11–12 does not fit comfortably with the book as a whole. In fact, it seems to undermine the very activity of study and book writing without which this book would have never come into existence. It begins: "The words (*dibrê*) of the wise are like goads, and like nails firmly fixed are the collected sayings that are given by a shepherd." On the surface, this sentence appears to be saying that the words of the wise should compel one ("goad one on") to act wisely—and this is the standard understanding. However, there are two problems with this interpretation. First of all, Qohelet is full of the elusive nature of wisdom. For example, 7:23–24 reads: "And this I tested with wisdom. I said, 'I will be wise.' But it was far from me. How far this is, and deep, very deep. Who will find it?" And 8:1 repeats: "Who is like the wise man? And who know the interpretation of a word (*dābār*)?" Is the speaker being ironic here? Wisdom certainly does not seem like "nails firmly fixed" in the rest of the book. Moreover, there is a menacing tone to v. 11. Wisdom does not give pleasure or ease.[34] Wisdom is painful, uncomfortable, even dangerous and torturous—it prods like nails threatening to puncture the skin. Perhaps it is a good thing that it is also elusive.

Continuing, v. 12 reads: "Of anything beyond these, my child, beware." Again, there is a threat contained in these words: "beware." For "of making many books

---

34.   Seow, *Ecclesiastes*, 393; and Fox, *A Time to Tear Down*, 354–55 also note this aspect of this passage.

there is no end, and much study is a weariness of the flesh." Is this a warning against other people's books? This has been a popular interpretation, and commentators have sensed a "canonical consciousness" in the line. Crenshaw believes that the epilogist is "warning against an open attitude toward the canon."[35]

Or is the warning really against all books, including this one? After all, a book that begins with the emptiness of life (*hăbēl hăbālîm*, "there is nothing new under the sun") could not believe its own self to be full of weighty meaning. Qohelet seems constantly to be engaged in self-critique. In the words of deconstruction, Qohelet writes under erasure.

Language is a system of differences. Texts, which are composed of language, are unstable and always already deconstructing themselves. Deconstructive criticism is equally subject to deconstruction since it too is a system that relies on language. Part of its awareness of its own instability is its introduction of the concept of writing under erasure. One writes, but recognizes the lack of stable meaning in the writing; one writes, but in a way that refuses writing as an act of domination. Qohelet writes, but this one verse is a giant gesture of erasure. I imagine the author here crossing out each and every one of the twelve chapters that precede this verse. Maybe, to paraphrase Hélène Cixous's statement about the relationship between God and writing, wisdom "is the phantom of writing; her pretext and her promise. [Wisdom] is the name of all that has yet to be said."[36] Perhaps this is Qohelet's only way of approaching wisdom, and through wisdom perhaps the divine—by unsaying what has just been said.

Do I believe in G-d? I excuse myself before the food comes and go into the bathroom. There, I run the water warm, and as it pours out over my hands I shape my mouth and tongue to the blessings.

The Ritual Body

In the final verses of Qohelet, the emphasis is on the keeping of the commandments: *ʾet-miṣôtāyw šĕmôr* (12:13b). In the Hebrew Bible, the *miṣôt* include commandments concerning belief, religious practices, and ethical action. All three types of *miṣôt* are interwoven together. The Decalogue (Exod 20:1–17 and Deut 5:6–21), for example, includes each of these three types of injunction. The Israelites are enjoined to believe in their God (Exod 20:2–3 and Deut 5:6–7), observe the Sabbath (Exod 20:8–11 and Deut 5:12–15), and refrain from murder, adultery, and theft (Exod 20:13–15 and Deut 5:17–19). Even though there is a command to believe in God, the precise perimeters of such belief are never drawn. Qohelet does believe in God, but within his belief he is open to question and comment about the nature of the divine. Such questioning does not constitute the breaking of a commandment, and Qohelet's recommending the commandments does not contradict the sentiments expressed in the remainder of

35. Crenshaw, *Ecclesiastes*, 191.

36. Hélène Cixous, "Writing Blind: Conversation with the Donkey" (trans. Eric Prenowitz) *TriQuarterly* 97 (1996): 7–20; repr. in idem, *Stigmata: Escaping Texts* (New York: Routledge, 1998), 139–52.

the book. The final verses are an espousal of basic belief, proper ritual, and ethical action rather than an advocacy of a particular type of theology judged "proper" by later readers.[37]

I cover my closed eyes with my right hand and in the darkness that I have created I sing—mouth open with the sweet minor vibrations of my throat, tongue shaping the waves into the sounds of the Sh'ma, I hear the words breathing out of the open mouths and the closed eyes that I know and feel around me—shma yisrael adonai elohenu adonai ehad (Deut 6:4).

According to Catherine Bell, the "study of ritual has always assumed the close association of rite with belief."[38] When Qohelet instructs the reader to keep the commandments, commentators assume a contradiction between this injunction and the questioning of the knowability of the divine expressed in the rest of the book. Therefore, an editor who desired to tone down Qohelet's radicalism must have written the instruction. Bell's study of ritual suggests something different: "These studies give evidence for the ambiguity and instability of beliefs and symbols as well as the inability of ritual to control by virtue of any consensus based on shared beliefs. They also suggest that ritualized activities specifically do not promote belief or conviction."[39] Bell argues that there is no clear connection between certain beliefs and their ritual actions. The ways in which individual persons negotiate belief systems through their bodies are complex, and sometimes contradictory. The point is not a mind/body dualism. Rather, it is an acknowledgment of the multiplicity of selves within one body, the various meanings that a single action can have, and the impossibility of drawing conclusions about what any individual person believes based upon ritual participation.

The epilogue of Qohelet reminds me of Elie Wiesel's work, specifically the novel *The Gates of the Forest*,[40] and the essay "The Death of My Father."[41] In both of these writings traditional faith and theology are thrown into question by the events of the Holocaust. Yet, at the end of each of these works, the protagonist participates in ritual, while still quarreling with the world and with God.

The Gates of the Forest is clearly a work of fiction; the genre of "The Death of My Father" is not clear. The classificatory note on the back of the book that contains the essay signals the bifurcation: "Literature/Judaica." Wiesel himself destabilizes the genre classification of this book in the introduction. He tells a story (fact? fiction?) of meeting a Rebbe in Tel Aviv, a Rebbe of whom Wiesel's grandfather was a disciple. The Rebbe asks what Dodye Feig's grandson was doing with his life. When Wiesel answers that he is writing stories the Rebbe responds with disbelieving reproach. The questioning continues:

---

37.   See Catherine Bell, *Ritual: Perspectives and Dimensions* (New York: Oxford University Press, 1997), 191–97, on the differences between orthopraxy and orthodoxy with special attention to the ways in which Judaism and Christianity manifest them, respectively.

38.   Catherine Bell, *Ritual Theory, Ritual Practice* (New York: Oxford University Press, 1992), 182.

39.   Ibid., 186.

40.   Elie Wiesel, *The Gates of the Forest* (New York: Schocken, 1966).

41.   Elie Wiesel, *Legends of Our Time* (New York: Schocken, 1968), 1–7.

"What are you writing?" the Rebbe asked. "Stories," I said. He wanted to know what kind of stories: true stories. "About people you knew?" Yes, about people I might have known. "About things that happened?" Yes, about things that happened or could have happened. "But they did not?" No, not all of them did. In fact, some were invented from almost the beginning to almost the end. The Rebbe leaned forward as if to measure me up and said with more sorrow than anger: "That means you are writing lies!" I did not answer immediately. The scolded child within me had nothing to say in his defense. Yet, I had to justify myself: "Things are not that simple, Rebbe. Some events do take place but are not true; others are—although they never occurred."[42]

"The Death of My Father" interplays with the book of Qohelet on several levels. Like Qohelet, it is written in the first person and the reader has a strong sense of the author behind the text. Like Qohelet, although true, fiction and fact are interlaced and therefore indistinguishable. Both are, in this sense, fictional autobiographies.

In his essay, Wiesel reflects upon a way in which to commemorate the anniversary of his father's death. He begins with the *Shulchan Aruch* by Rabbi Joseph Karo.[43] Perhaps, Wiesel thinks, I should "Obey tradition. Follow in the footsteps . . . go to the synagogue three times, officiate at the service, study a chapter of Mishna, say the orphan's Kaddish and, in the presence of the living community of Israel, proclaim the holiness of God as well as his greatness."[44] But the problem with following this traditional program is that Wiesel's father did not die in a traditional way. The Nazis at Buchenwald murdered him. His death was not his own. Should he go to synagogue then, "to praise the God of dead children?"[45]

Wiesel continues by describing his father in words that make his father seem much like how I would imagine the sage Qohelet. He "observed tradition" but "preached an open spirit toward the world. . . . He refused to sacrifice the present to an unforeseeable future, whatever it might be. He enjoyed simple everyday pleasures and did not consider his body an enemy. . . . [He] refused to cloister his mind . . . within any given system."[46] I hear echoes of Qohelet's injunctions to enjoy life, to pursue knowledge and wisdom, to test the world, to eat and drink.

After this general description, Wiesel speaks of what his father did. He quotes two sayings from his father—two proverbs: "Your duty is to fight solitude, not to cultivate or glorify it," and "God, perhaps, has need of saints; as for men, they can do without them."[47] Then he describes the good deeds of his father—always in government offices, involved in rectifying every misfortune that befell the community; he aided the sick and impoverished, those in prison, refugees looking for sanctuary.

When his father died, Wiesel was robbed of any knowledge about the meaning of his death. He did not know what his father felt or believed in those final

42. Ibid., viii.
43. A halakhic guide written in the sixteenth century.
44. Ibid., 1–2.
45. Ibid., 2.
46. Ibid., 3.
47. Ibid.

moments. He speculates upon some possibilities, but the one with which he concludes strikes the knell of meaninglessness: "In dying, my father looked at me, and in his eyes where night was gathering, there was nothing but animal terror, the demented terror of one who, because he wished to understand too much, no longer understands anything."[48] This is the death that permeates Qohelet and always threatens to undermine any meaning he manages to wrestle out of the experiences of life.

Again, Wiesel returns to ritual. After all, this was how his father commemorated his own father's death. But doubt creeps in once more: "The holocaust defies reference, analogy. Between the death of my father and that of his, no comparison is possible. It would be inadequate, indeed unjust, to imitate my father. I should have to invent other prayers, other acts."[49]

There is no resolving the theological problem of death, especially the deaths of the Holocaust. There is no justifying God. And this may mean one has to give up ritual, or at least create new ones. But in the end, Wiesel comes to rest (not a final resting place, but a temporary one nevertheless) on the tradition. He concludes his essay thus: "All things considered, I think that tomorrow I shall go to the synagogue after all. I will light the candles, I will say Kaddish, and it will be for me a further proof of my impotence."[50]

Wiesel is the frame narrator, telling the story of his father. But Wiesel is also Qohelet. In the face of the unpredictability of life, in the face of radical human evil, in the face of theological despair, Wiesel goes to synagogue, he lights the candles, and he says the Kaddish. Nevertheless, his actions do not in any way blunt the pain of his experience, nor do they domesticate the radical questioning of his faith in human and divine. To argue that this gesture of traditional ritual piety does these things is an affront to Elie Wiesel's experiences, his thoughts, his writings. Qohelet's epilogue is the same.

Do I believe in G-d? My body is weak from absence of food; my mouth is dry, my lips beginning to crack, and my head throbs without its daily dose of caffeine. I feel the sins of the world in my flesh; I feel my absolute dependence on a few simple things—a drop of water, a bit of bread. My knees are weak as I stand in synagogue, hand beats chest, stand, sit, stand, sit, waiting for the final sound of release, the sound of the shofar as the sun descends and I leave, unlock my door, swing in and open, kiss fingertips, touch mezuzah, step over the threshold, I am home. I run the water warm and as it pours out over my hands, I shape my mouth and tongue to the blessings. I hold the bread in my hands, break it, and touch it to my tongue.

48.   Ibid., 5.
49.   Ibid., 7.
50.   Ibid. Wiesel is not alone here. All post-Holocaust theologians re-examine traditional belief systems and the rituals that correspond. The most radical example is Richard Rubenstein (*After Auschwitz: Radical Theology and Contemporary Judaism* [Indianapolis: Bobbs-Merrill, 1966]) who claims that after the Holocaust "we live in the time of the death of God." However, the death of God does not negate religious community or ritual. Instead, it makes them even more imperative. For Rubenstein, all 613 commandments are still valid for the Jewish people. In both his unorthodox theology and his traditional ritual approach, Rubenstein exceeds the book of Qohelet.

Qohelet's Theology

Readers of Qohelet have taken two routes in analyzing Qohelet's theology. Either the theology is radical and unorthodox, and all passages that affirm a more orthodox theology are later accretions added to tone down this radical questioner, or the verses that espouse traditional theological understandings are the interpretive key to the entire book and therefore Qohelet's pessimistic questioning is undermined. For either reading, at least one aspect of the text must become subservient to the other. I resist both options.

As the sun descends on Friday I light my candles, circle the flame three times with my hands, feeling the heat, and then raise my hands to my closed eyes, breathe in the smell of burnt match, burning candle, and shape my mouth and tongue to the blessings.

In order to judge if Qohelet's belief system is orthodox or heterodox, one must have a standard against which to judge. Because there is no conclusive theory about where and when this book was written, it becomes difficult to determine what was orthodox in Qohelet's milieu. We have very few sources about either official or popular religiosity during the Persian or Hellenistic eras. We have almost no information about what was considered traditional belief and practice during the possible times of Qohelet's writing, and therefore no way of ascertaining with certainty if Qohelet was conventional or breaking with convention.

The argument that Qohelet is unorthodox rests on a presumed idea about of what orthodox thinking is comprised. Often, the definition of "orthodox" is based upon a general notion of biblical theology—Qohelet is unorthodox because the book expresses ideas that are in tension with the remainder of the Bible. However, the very category of "biblical theology" is problematic.[51] The history of biblical-theological study has been characterized by a tendency to "find" the theme that unifies the Hebrew Bible.[52] In recent years, such a project has been discredited. Jon Levinson, for example, writes, "this notion that all the literature of the Hebrew Bible . . . has one message presents grave historical problems."[53] The Hebrew Bible is a various, complex, and contradictory set of texts.

51. Its critics have called nearly every aspect of "biblical theology" into question. See James Barr, *The Concept of Biblical Theology* (Minneapolis: Fortress, 1999), 1–17, for a concise appraisal of the term's problems.

52. The first major biblical theological work was Walther Eichrodt's *Theology of the Old Testament* (trans. John A. Baker; 2 vols.; Philadelphia: Westminster, 1961 [3 vol. German original published 1933–39]). He proposed that "covenant" was the central principle in the Bible. Next, Theodorus C. Vriezen offered "communion" as his center in *An Outline of Old Testament Theology* (trans. S. Neuijen; Oxford: Blackwell, 1970 [German original published 1949]). Gerhard von Rad used the saving acts of God in history to organize his theology of the Bible in his *Old Testament Theology* (trans. D. M. G. Stalker; 2 vols.; San Francisco: HarperCollins, 1962 [German original published 1959]).

53. Jon Levinson, *The Hebrew Bible, The Old Testament, and Historical Criticism* (Louisville, Ky.: Westminster/John Knox, 1993), 55. Jon Levinson discusses the problem of biblical theology in terms of the differences between Christianity and Judaism. However, there have been Christian scholars who remark on the same difficulties in the discipline. See, in particular, Rolf Rendtorff,

As such it lacks a coherent theological center. Since the Bible presents a wide variety of theological beliefs, it is impossible to argue that one is more orthodox than another, and therefore arguments about the ways in which Qohelet does or does not conform to biblical theology are untenable.

James Crenshaw represents the first path commentators take in their analy sis of Qohelet's theology—he believes that it is radical and that any comment that is in contradistinction from this radicality is the work of a later editor.[54] Crenshaw opens his commentary on Qohelet by stating,

> Life is profitless; totally absurd. This oppressive message lies at the heart of the Bible's strangest book. Enjoy life if you can, advises the author, for old age will soon overtake you. And even as you enjoy, know that the world is meaningless. Virtue does not bring reward. The deity stands distant, abandoning humanity to chance and death.[55]

In his book on Wisdom, Crenshaw argues that God only acts at the personal level in Qohelet when God acts with malice (3:18 and in 3:1–11).[56] By present ing such an anti-religious picture of the deity, and by claiming that God's order of the world is ultimately unknowable, Qohelet undermines the entire wisdom tradition. Why then was this book accepted into the canon? Because the second epilogue (12:13b–14) "removed the sting from Qohelet's skepticism and advo cated traditional views concerning observance of Torah."[57]

Whereas I agree with Crenshaw's general picture of a distant deity and the effect of death on the meaning of life, I disagree with the distinction between un-traditional and traditional as applied to the body of the book and the epi logue, respectively. In an article entitled "Popular Questioning of the Justice of God in Ancient Israel," Crenshaw does endeavor to investigate "the actual relig ion of the 'man in the streets' in ancient Israel."[58] Toward this goal, Crenshaw uses prophetic quotations in order to gain access to the thinking of the general populace. What these prophetic quotations reveal is that the questioning of God's justice was an integral part of popular religiosity. In light of this, Crenshaw concludes that Qohelet's message is in kinship with popular religion though opposed to official Yahwism.[59] Crenshaw may be read as maintaining that the bulk of Qohelet coheres with popular conceptions of God's justice (or lack thereof), whereas the epilogue is the official religion's attempt to curtail the radicalism of the theological perceptions of the "man on the street."[60]

Canon and Theology: Overtures to an Old Testament Theology (trans. Margaret Kohl; Minneapo lis: Fortress, 1993), and Rolf P. Knierim, *The Task of Old Testament Theology* (Grand Rapids: Eerdmans, 1995).

54. Also see J. A. Loader, *Ecclesiastes: A Practical Commentary* (Grand Rapids: Eerdmans, 1986), 14–15.

55. Crenshaw, *Ecclesiastes*, 23.

56. Crenshaw, *Old Testament Wisdom*, 137.

57. Crenshaw, *Ecclesiastes*, 52.

58. Crenshaw, "Popular Questioning of the Justice of God in Ancient Israel," in his *Urgent Advice*, 175–90 (186).

59. Ibid., 188.

60. To my knowledge, Crenshaw does not state this explicitly, but it can be inferred from his other statements about the relationship of the epilogue to Qohelet as a whole.

There are several problems with Crenshaw's proposal. First, there is no way of knowing with certainty if the quotations in the prophetic books do represent the views of the people the prophets are addressing (or even if they are quotations). Even if the supposition about prophetic quotations is granted, a second problem emerges. The material Crenshaw uses ranges in date from the eighth to the sixth centuries B.C.E.[61] Since the earliest possible date of Qohelet would be the Persian period (based upon the Persian loan words and Aramaisms in the text), prophetic quotations are not accurate evidence of popular religion during Qohelet's time. In fact, the very categories of "popular religion" and "official religion" are problematic. For this, I turn to Rainer Albertz's comprehensive work on the religion of ancient Israel.

Rainer Albertz finds a similar split between popular and official religion in the time of the late monarchy and in the Persian period due to similar economic conditions.[62] For Albertz, not only is there a division between the upper classes and the general populace, but there is also a split within the upper classes. The upper classes were divided between those who sympathized with the plight of the lower class and those who did not. The complex stratification of the fifth century resulted in a social and economic crisis. This crisis then was the setting for a theological dispute played out in post-exilic literature between the "righteous" who were ethically committed to alleviating the suffering of the poor, and the "wicked" who exploited the poor.[63] Albertz arrives at his portrait of a stratified society based upon the contradictions within the biblical text itself. The diversity within the Bible reflects the diversity in society. The picture of society based on the contradictions in the biblical text is then used to interpret the biblical text. Since there is no evidence outside the textual evidence of the Bible itself, the argument about "official" and "popular" religion becomes circular.[64]

Although Albertz then assesses Proverbs and Job against this backdrop, he ignores Qohelet. In fact, the book of Qohelet is completely absent from his two-volume study, so how Qohelet would fit into his schema can only be surmised. With Albertz we have a picture of "the theological legitimization of riches and property . . . raised at the level of official Yahweh religion"[65]—so post-exilic, official religion was not a monolithic entity, but deeply conflicted and engaged in debate. Since the categories are not mutually exclusive, Qohelet could be both part of the religious establishment and question the religious establishment. The epilogue cannot be neatly separated out from the bulk of the book.

61. Dating biblical material is a perilous enterprise. The dates I use above represent the narrative situation of the prophets—the ends of the Northern Kingdom and Southern Kingdom. The prophetic books may have reached their final forms at a later time.

62. Rainer Albertz, *A History of Israelite Religion in the Old Testament Period* (trans. John Bowden; OTL; Louisville, Ky.: Westminster/John Knox, 1994), 497–503. These similar economic conditions include increased taxation and the "harsh laws of credit," which enabled creditors to seize the property of debtors.

63. Ibid., 499–500.

64. I am not necessarily objecting to the idea that society was stratified, that different groups held different opinions, and that these groups then debated their differences. Rather, I am calling into question our ability to know based on the biblical material alone.

65. Ibid., 507.

Whybray represents the opposing view to the dominant assessment of Qohelet's theology. He has taken the second path of analysis affirming that Qohelet is an advocate of traditional belief and that any verse to the contrary is to be re-interpreted or even re-translated. Whybray's ideas do differ from Crenshaw's, but they are equally bound to his assumptions about tradition. Whybray argues that Qohelet is a "religious and theological work concerned to defend rather than attack the Jewish faith."[66] He grounds his argument in who he believes Qohelet is—a conflation of the flesh-and-blood author and the speaker in the text—based upon the "strongly personal tone" of the book.[67] He constructs a picture of a teacher in Jerusalem under Hellenistic rule, instructing young men about how to maintain the orthodox faith under very trying circumstances. Jerusalem, he believes, was a place with great reverence for the wisdom tradition and a place where the clever and ambitious could succeed.[68] As such, Qohelet is conservative in affirming such doctrines as belief in a monotheistic, transcendent, creator God. On the other hand, because he must make orthodox belief relevant to the young men of his day who are beset with Hellenistic cultural imperialism, he has some interpretations of this orthodox belief which are radical.[69]

Whybray acknowledges that the view that Qohelet is a radical thinker overstates the gap between this book and the rest of Hebrew Bible theology.[70] There is no single consistent theological position in the Bible, and much of Qohelet's teaching has precedents elsewhere in the scriptures:

> It is true that Qoheleth makes no direct reference to divine action in history, the so-called *Heilsgeschichte*, but this is also true of the earlier wisdom books of Proverbs and Job. The sense of human desolation—that God hides himself from human distress—is also a frequent theme in the psalms of lamentation, and also in such popular sayings as that cited by the woman of Tekoa, "We are like water spilled on the ground, that cannot be gathered up" (2 Sam 14,14). That men and women are left by God in a state of helplessness and frustration because God has his own hidden plans for them is clearly stated in the book of Proverbs in contradiction to that book's otherwise "optimistic" tone. . . .[71]

But this statement appears more as a caveat not taken than grounding for his subsequent article.

In fact, Whybray's thesis rests upon an argument dependent upon removing many of Qohelet's more pessimistic statements. According to Whybray, much of the pessimism ascribed to Qohelet is based upon mistranslations and misinterpretations of the text. For example, 1:3–11 has commonly been understood to teach the futility of human life. Whybray denies this by arguing that *dôr* (v. 4) and *yĕgiᶜîm* (v. 8) are mistranslated. The former is not "human generations" but

---

66. Whybray, "Qoheleth as a Theologian," 245.

67. Ibid., 239.

68. Ibid., 256.

69. Ibid., 246.

70. In other contexts, Whybray has been very critical of the project of biblical theology. See R. N. Whybray, "Old Testament Theology—A Non-Existent Beast?" in *Scripture: Meaning and Method* (ed. Barry P. Thompson; Hull: Hull University Press, 1987), 168–80.

71. Whybray, "Qoheleth as a Theologian," 247.

rather "time past and present." The latter is not "weary" but "constant activity." Whybray retranslates other troubling passages that indicate an impersonal fate and lack of human free will (such as 2:14; 3:19; and 9:2–3) and the line in 7:16 ("do not be too righteous") to make them more palpable to what he believes is a more traditional theology. Whereas Whybray is right about noting the plurality of theologies in the Hebrew Bible, he still differentiates between "traditional" and "radical" and then tames some of Qohelet's most shocking statements through his own idiosyncratic translations. And though he acknowledges our lack of knowledge of what he calls "the 'unofficial' religion of the ordinary Israelites,"[72] the lack does not prevent him from arguing his thesis that Qohelet is "a religious and theological work concerned to defend rather than attack the Jewish faith"[73]—an argument dependent upon some kind of idea about what that faith must look like.

So how can Qohelet's theology be categorized? Is it radical, anti-religious, and heterodox? Or is it conventional, deeply religious, and orthodox? These categories are based more on the interpreter's assumptions than on textual or historical evidence. On the one hand, I believe that Qohelet is promulgating ideas of the divine that are not typical of biblical literature. They are not, however, without precedent and differ more in quantity than in kind. On the other hand, we have to be cautious in making any historical argument about the unorthodox or traditional quality of Qohelet's work. With these points in mind, I would like to discuss a couple of unique features in Qohelet's God-talk, and to draw some conclusions from them.

The book of Qohelet, which is more often called a philosophy than a theology, speaks of God more often than the former designation would indicate. The word *hāʾĕlōhîm* ("the God") appears in Qohelet 40 times. Qohelet acknowledges God. The commentators never question this belief though sometimes it is looked at with a disbelief of their own. How can the radical questioning of this book support theism? Crenshaw notes how modern "thinkers find Qoheleth's theism somewhat puzzling, for it would seem more natural to abandon belief in God altogether."[74] The standard explanation is that atheism was quite simply out of the purview of this sage. It was not an option.

There are three unique aspects of Qohelet's God-talk. First, Qohelet uses the definite article in front of *ʾĕlōhîm*, and never uses the tetragrammaton.[75] The definite article appears in 32 of the 40 instances of the word. Second, Qohelet frequently uses passive constructions when discussing God's actions in instances where God is not explicitly mentioned. An emblematic instance is in the middle verse of Qohelet (6:10), which introduces the second part of the book. It reads, all in passive voice: "Whatever has come to be has already been called its name, and it is known what humans are and they are not able to understand those who are mightier than them." The second half of Qohelet is "marked by a repeated

---

72. Ibid., 253.
73. Ibid., 245.
74. Crenshaw, *Old Testament Wisdom*, 137.
75. Esther and the Song of Songs lack both the tetragrammaton and *ʾĕlōhîm*.

emphasis on what people cannot know, cannot tell, and cannot discover."[76] The use of the passive voice underscores the unknowability of the divine. Third, God is never directly addressed in the text, nor does God directly address Qohelet. This feature can be contrasted with the book of Job. Both Job and Qohelet are classified as "Protest Wisdom"—books that question the theodicy presented in Proverbs. Yet, the bulk of the book of Job consists of Job's crying out to the divine, and Job does finally have a personal audience with God out of the whirl-wind. Qohelet neither addresses God directly nor is addressed by God. Taken together, these three features indicate that whatever Qohelet's theology is, it is grounded in a healthy respect for divine distance. God may be ultimately unknowable, as Seow and Fox point out, but God's unknowability may be just as much a result of Qohelet's reticence as God's nature—a reticence not felt by Job, the other great theologian of suffering in the Bible.

By choosing either a stable theistic platform or an unrelenting atheistic position, Qohelet's book would not have generated the debates that is has. In the modern era, much of what was considered "revolutionary" reversed what had been thought of as "true." Theism becomes a-theism. Deconstructive theology, however, calls for something more than a mere reversal. It calls for an inversion that "must simultaneously be a perversion that is subversive."[77] The entire dichotomy must be de-stabilized. I look at Qohelet and find a perversion rather than an inversion; I find my own belief/disbelief reflected back at me. The book engages me because it provides a way of describing my own conflicted self. In Qohelet, with the presentation of a clear theism, but one that is sometimes com-forting and sometimes disconcerting, sometimes secure and sometimes unstable, the reader ricochets between the poles and never rests easily in either one.[78] God remains elusive and complex, Qohelet remains elusive and complex, and readers (whose selves are also elusive and complex) would do well to resist the urge to domesticate the book by embracing a definitive position on Qohelet's theology. Qohelet believes—but that belief is an empty category.

David Blumenthal draws connections between childhood abuse and the Holocaust. He does not conflate the two, but carefully traces out their similari-ties and differences in his book about the abusing God.[79] I did not live through the Holocaust. I had relatives who had remained in Eastern Europe (Warsaw and Lithuania) when my great-grandmother and great-grandfather fled their respec-tive countries, escaping pogroms and communists. These relatives are gone, murdered, but they are faceless and nameless to me.

76. Seow, *Ecclesiastes*, 240–41.
77. Mark C. Taylor, *Erring: A Postmodern A/theology* (Chicago: University of Chicago Press, 1984), 10. See also his *Nots* (Chicago: University of Chicago Press, 1993).
78. Bataille writes that a taboo and its transgression are one and the same. There is a "profound complicity" between a law and the violation of that law. This is the very way in which one approaches the holy, attracted by the erotic tension of the coming together of oppositions. See Bataille, *Eroticism*, 36.
79. David R. Blumenthal, *Facing the Abusing God: A Theology of Protest* (Louisville, Ky.: Westminster/John Knox, 1993), xvii–iii, 259–61.

But I know something about the other part of Blumenthal's equation. Experiencing suffering personally, or being open to the experiences of others can and should leave one doubting the existence of God, or at least doubting the existence of a good God. We should observe with Qohelet "all the oppressions which happen under the sun. And behold, the tears of the oppressed, and there is no one to comfort them!" (4:1), and ask the question with Qohelet, "Who knows the interpretation of a thing?" (8:1). And finally, in the end, I throw up our hands in defiance of a God who seems determined to thwart all human effort to acquire wisdom and to do good in the world. In 1550, Solomon ibn Verga wrote of a man who suffered expulsion from Spain, plague, hunger, thirst, and the death of his wife and two small sons. Upon finding his sons dead he arose and yelled up to the heavens: "Master of the Universe! You go to great lengths to force me to desert my faith. Know for a certainty that in the face of the dwellers of heaven, a Jew I am and a Jew I shall remain; all that You have brought upon me or will bring upon me shall be of no avail!"[80]

Do I believe in G-d? I unlock my door, swing in and open, kiss fingertips, touch mezuzah, step over the threshold, I am home.

---

80. Solomon ibn Verga, *Shevet Yehuda*, as quoted in David Roskies, ed. and trans., *The Literature of Destruction: Jewish Responses to Catastrophe* (Philadelphia: Jewish Publication Society of America, 1989), 98.

Chapter 8

DEPARTURES

"You see," said Reb Mendel: "at the end of an argument, there is always a decisive question unsettled."[1]

—*Edmond Jabès*

Who is Qohelet?

This question has been relentlessly pursued by all of Qohelet's readers and interpreters. This question has been relentlessly pursued by me. But, instead of offering an answer about the author or authors involved in the production of the work, I have looked at the language of selfhood and body in Qohelet. I have argued that the ways in which commentators answer the questions of authorship and integrity depend first upon their own assumptions about the nature of identity and the way in which authors' selves relate to their texts, and only secondarily on the evidence in the text itself. Because postmodern conceptions of identity—the self as a fragmented, inconsistent, and incoherent entity—inform me, I read Qohelet and do not feel the need to attribute contradictions to another hand. Yet, I have refrained from making an argument for single authorship. Both single and multiple authorship arguments are bound-up in the interpreter's own ideas about identity and texts, both are within the purview of historical-critical scholarship, and both look *through* Qohelet rather than *at* Qohelet.

So my question has been, instead: Who is Qohelet as he/she/it is right here, in my hands? In pursuit of this question I have examined the body in the book, the book as a body, and how both interact with my body as a reader. The body is embedded in the book. First, the body is part of the content of the book—Qohelet uses his eyes, speaks of and to his heart. Second, the body is part of the spatial and symbolic structure of the book. In Qohelet, this is most evident in the gardens Qohelet constructs at the beginning of his work, and the house that falls apart at the end of his work. These spaces are extensions of and metaphors for the body. Third, the body is encoded at the level of grammar, syntax, and structure—the entire book becomes a body that mirrors the body of content and symbol. Qohelet's gendered and dying bodies reflect this level most evidently. The language of the body in Qohelet has contributed to the almost palpable sense of personhood in the book.

---

1. Edmond Jabès, *The Book of Questions* (trans. Rosmarie Waldrop; Hanover, N.H.: Wesleyan University Press, 1991), 116.

The body seems to be the stable ground of coherent identity. In the words of Sidonie Smith, it "seems to be the nearest, most central home we know. . . ."[2] But, this is only an illusion of stability, of secure familiarity. As Qohelet demonstrates, houses fall apart (Qoh 12):

> the body only seems to anchor us in a finite, discrete, unified surround—a private surround, temptingly stable and impermeable. There is only apparent continuity since, paradoxically, bodies, at once so close to us as to seem indissoluble from any notion of "me" or "I," can also disrupt the too-easy stability of singular identities. . . . [T]he politics of the body can open up a space of contradiction, drift, homelessness, a gap through which a complex heterogeneity destabilizes our sense of any stable identification. . . . The body is our most material site of potential homelessness.[3]

A single body may contain multiple identities, contradictory ideas, and fragmented theologies/ideologies. Qohelet does not need to be *either* pessimistic *or* optimistic, *either* to question the justice of God *or* to commend keeping the commandments. Both impulses can co-exist within one body; both impulses can co-exist in the body of the text; both can co-exist within the body of one reader.

So Qohelet stands before its reader—a text that emphasizes some body parts over others thus fragmenting and distorting the body; a text that generates desire through the tension between pleasure and pain and through ambiguity—ambiguous words, unstable structures, and ambiguous gender identification; a text that decays in structure and in meaning. Qohelet has wandered through time and history, proliferating endlessly, changing and mutating. Who are these Qohelets? They are alterations, transmutations, transmogrifications, modifications, reformations, revisions, variations, deviations, aberrations. . . . In other words, they are all, and as readers we are all, permutations of Qohelet.

---

2. Smith, "Identity's Body," 267.
3. Ibid.

BIBLIOGRAPHY

Adam, A. K. M., ed. *Handbook of Postmodern Biblical Interpretation*. St. Louis: Chalice, 2000.

Adams, Timothy. *Telling Lies in Modern American Autobiography*. Chapel Hill: University of North Carolina Press, 1990.

Albertz, Rainer. *A History of Israelite Religion in the Old Testament Period*. Translated by John Bowden. 2 vols. OTL. Louisville, Ky.: Westminster/John Knox, 1994.

Allen, Graham. *Intertextuality*. New York: Routledge, 2000.

Alter, Robert. *The Art of Biblical Narrative*. San Francisco: HarperCollins, 1981.

Andersen, Francis I., and A. Dean Forbes. *The Vocabulary of the Old Testament*. Rome: Editrice Pontificio Istituto Biblico, 1989.

Anderson, Janice Capel, and Jeffrey L. Staley, eds. *Taking it Personally*. Semeia 72. Atlanta: Scholars Press, 1995.

Anderson, W. H. U. *Qoheleth and its Pessimistic Theology: Hermeneutical Struggles in Wisdom Literature*. Mellen Biblical Press Series. Lewiston, N.Y.: Mellen Biblical Press, 1997.

Ashley, Kathleen, Leigh Gilmore, and Gerald Peters, eds. *Autobiography and Postmodernism*. Amherst: University of Massachusetts Press, 1995.

Attridge, Derek. "Introduction: Derrida and the Question of Literature." Pages 1–29 in Derrida, *Acts of Literature*.

Austin, J. L. *How to Do Things with Words*. Cambridge, Mass.: Harvard University Press, 1962.

Bataille, Georges. *Eroticism: Death and Sensuality*. San Francisco: City Light Books, 1986.

Bal, Mieke. *Lethal Love: Feminist Literary Readings of Biblical Love Stories*. Bloomington: Indiana University Press, 1987.

Barr, James. *The Semantics of Biblical Language*. London: SCM Press, 1961.

—*The Concept of Biblical Theology*. Minneapolis: Fortress, 1999.

Barthes, Roland. *The Pleasure of the Text*. Translated by Richard Miller. New York: Hill & Wang, 1975.

—"The Death of the Author." Pages 142–48 in *Image–Music–Text*. Translated by Stephen Heath. New York: Hill & Wang, 1977.

—*Roland Barthes by Roland Barthes*. New York: Hill & Wang, 1977.

Bartholomew, Craig. *Reading Ecclesiastes: Old Testament Exegesis and Hermeneutical Theory*. Rome: Editrice Pontificio Istituto Biblico, 1998.

Barton, George A. *A Critical and Exegetical Commentary on the Book of Ecclesiastes*. ICC. New York: Scribner, 1908.

Beal, Timothy K. "C(ha)osmopolis: Qohelet's Last Words." Pages 290-304 in *God in the Fray: A Tribute to Walter Brueggemann*. Edited by Tod Linafelt and Timothy K. Beal. Minneapolis: Fortress, 1998.

Bell, Catherine. *Ritual Theory, Ritual Practice*. New York: Oxford University Press, 1992.

—*Ritual: Perspectives and Dimensions*. New York: Oxford University Press, 1997.

Bennington, Geoffrey, and Jacques Derrida. *Jacques Derrida*. Chicago: Chicago University Press, 1993.

Bertens, Hans. *The Idea of the Postmodern: A History*. New York: Routledge, 1995.

Biale, David. *Eros and the Jews: From Biblical Israel to Contemporary America*. Berkeley: University of California Press, 1997.

Bible and Culture Collective, The. *The Postmodern Bible*. New Haven: Yale University Press, 1995.

Black, Fiona C. "What is My Beloved? On Erotic Reading and the Song of Songs." Pages 35–52 in *The Labour of Reading: Desire, Alienation, and Biblical Interpretation*. Edited by Fiona C. Black, Roland Boer, and Erin Runions. Atlanta: Society of Biblical Literature, 1999.

Blenkinsopp, Joseph. "Ecclesiastes 3:1–15: Another Interpretation." *JSOT* 66 (1995): 55–64.

Blumenthal, David R. *Facing the Abusing God: A Theology of Protest*. Louisville, Ky.: Westminster/John Knox, 1993.

Boyarin, Daniel. *Reading Sex in Talmudic Culture*. Berkeley: University of California Press, 1993.

Boyle, Marjorie O'Rourke. "The Law of the Heart: The Death of a Fool (I Samuel 25)." *JBL* 120 (2001): 401–27.

Brenner, Athalya. "Some Observations of the Figurations of Woman in Wisdom Literature." Pages 59–61 in *A Feminist Companion to Wisdom Literature*. Edited by Athalya Brenner. Feminist Companion to the Bible 9. Sheffield: Sheffield Academic Press, 1995.

Brenner, Athalya, and Fokkelien van Dijk-Hemmes. *On Gendering Texts: Female and Male Voices in the Hebrew Bible*. Leiden: Brill, 1993.

Brown, William. *Character in Crisis: A Fresh Approach to the Wisdom Literature of the Old Testament*. Grand Rapids: Eerdmans, 1996.

—*Ecclesiastes*. Interpretation. Louisville, Ky.: John Knox, 2000.

—"'Whatever Your Hand Finds to Do': Qoheleth's Work Ethic." *Interpretation* 55, no. 3 (2001): 271–84.

Brownstein, Rachel M. "Interrupted Reading: Personal Criticism in the Present Time." Pages 29–39 in Veeser, ed., *Confessions of the Critics*.

Broyde, M. J. "Defilement of the Hands, Canonization of the Bible, and the Special Status of Esther, Ecclesiastes, and Song of Songs." *Judaism* 44 (1995): 66–78.

Burkes, Shannon. *Death in Qoheleth and Egyptian Biographies of the Late Period*. Atlanta: Society of Biblical Literature, 1999.

Burkitt, F. C. "Is Ecclesiastes a Translation?." *JTS* 23 (1921–22): 22–28.

Butler, Judith. *Gender Trouble: Feminism and the Subversion of Identity*. New York: Routledge, 1990.

—*Bodies that Matter: On the Discursive Limits of "Sex"*. New York: Routledge, 1993.

—"Desire." Pages 369–86 in *Critical Terms for Literary Study*. Edited by Frank Lentricchia and Thomas McLaughlin. Chicago: University of Chicago Press, 1995.

—*Excitable Speech: A Politics of the Performative*. New York: Routledge, 1997.

Byargeon, Rick W. "The Significance of Ambiguity in Ecclesiastes 2,24–26." Pages 367–72 in Schoors, ed., *Qohelet in the Context of Wisdom*.

Caputo, John, ed. *Deconstruction in a Nutshell: A Conversation with Jacques Derrida*. New York: Fordham University Press, 1997.

Cavallaro, Dani. *The Body for Beginners*. New York: Writers and Readers, 1998.

Chomsky, Noam. *Rules and Representations*. New York: Columbia University Press, 1980.

Christianson, Eric S. *A Time to Tell: Narrative Strategies in Ecclesiastes*. JSOTSup 280. Sheffield: Sheffield Academic Press, 1998.

Cixous, Hélène. "The Laugh of the Medusa." Pages 245–64 in *New French Feminisms: An Anthology*. Edited by M. Marks and I. de Courtivron. Brighton: Harvester, 1981.

—"Writing Blind: Conversation with the Donkey" (trans. Eric Prenowitz). *TriQuarterly* 97 (1996): 7-20. Repr., pages 139–52 in *Stigmata: Escaping Texts*. New York: Routledge, 1998.

—*Stigmata: Escaping Texts*. New York: Routledge, 1998.

Coakley, Sarah, ed. *Religion and the Body*. New York: Cambridge University Press, 1997.

Crenshaw, James. "The Eternal Gospel (Ecclesiastes 3:11)." Pages 548–72 in *Urgent Advice and Probing Questions*.

—*Old Testament Wisdom: An Introduction*. Atlanta: John Knox, 1981.

—"Qohelet in Current Research." *HAR* 7 (1984): 41-56.

—*Ecclesiastes*. OTL. Philadelphia: Westminster Press, 1987.

—"Popular Questioning of the Justice of God in Ancient Israel." Pages 175–90 in *Urgent Advice and Probing Questions*.

— *Urgent Advice and Probing Questions: Collected Writings on Old Testament Wisdom*. Macon, Ga.: Mercer University Press, 1995.

Dahood, M. "Canaanite-Phoenician Influence in Qoheleth." *Bib* 33 (1952): 3–52, 191–221.

de Beauvoir, Simone. *The Second Sex*. New York: Vintage, 1973.

Delitzsch, Franz. *Commentary on the Song of Songs and Ecclesiastes*. Translated by M. G. Easton. Edinburgh: T&T Clark, 1877. Repr., Grand Rapids: Eerdmans, 1982.

Derrida, Jacques. "The Law of Genre." *Glyph* 7 (1980): 202–29.

—"Positions." *Diacritics* 2 (1972): 35–43.

—"Positions." *Diacritics* 3 (1973): 33–46.

—*Speech and Phenomena and Other Essays on Husserl's Theory of Signs*. Translated by David B. Allison. Evanston, Ill.: Northwestern University Press, 1973.

—"The Purveyor of Truth." *Yale French Studies* 52 (1975): 31–113.

—*Of Grammatology*. Translated by Gayatri Chakravorty Spivak. Baltimore: The Johns Hopkins University Press, 1976.

—"Différance." Pages 1–27 in *Margins of Philosophy*. Translated by Alan Bass. Chicago: University of Chicago Press, 1982.

—*The Postcard: From Socrates to Freud and Beyond*. Translated by Alan Bass. Chicago: University of Chicago Press, 1987.

—"Signature Event Context." Pages 1–23 in *Limited Inc*. Evanston, Ill.: Northwestern University Press, 1988.

—*Mémoires: For Paul de Man*. Translated by Cecile Lindsay et al. New York: Columbia University Press, 1989.

—*Acts of Literature*. Edited by Derek Attridge. New York: Routledge, 1992

—*Given Time: I. Counterfeit Money*. Translated by Peggy Kamuf. Chicago: University of Chicago Press, 1992.

—"'There is No One Narcissism' (Autobiographies)." Pages 196–215 in *Points . . . Interviews, 1974–1994*. Edited by Elisabeth Weber. Stanford, Calif.: Stanford University Press, 1995.

—*The Gift of Death*. Translated by David Wills. Chicago: University of Chicago Press, 1996.

—*The Work of Mourning*. Edited by Pascale-Anne Brault and Michael Naas. Chicago: University of Chicago Press, 2001.

Dhorme, Edouard. *L'emploi métaphorique des noms de parties du corps en Hébreu et en Akkadien*. Paris: Librairie Orientaliste Paul Geuthnes, 1963.

Dulim, Rachel Z. "'How Sweet is the Light': Qoheleth's Age-Centered Teachings." *Interpretation* 55, no. 3 (2001): 260–70.

Edwards, Douglas R. "Heart." Pages 407–8 in *HarperCollins Bible Dictionary*. Edited by J. Achtemeier. San Francisco: HarperCollins, 1996.

Eichrodt, Walther. *Theology of the Old Testament*. Translated by John A. Baker. 2 vols. Philadelphia: Westminster, 1961.

Eilberg-Schwartz, Howard. *The Savage in Judaism: An Anthropology of Israelite Religion and Ancient Judaism*. Bloomington: Indiana University Press, 1990.

—"The Problem of the Body for the People of the Book." Pages 17–46 in *People of the Body: Jews and Judaism from an Embodied Perspective*. Edited by Howard Eilberg-Schwartz. Albany: State University of New York Press, 1992.

—*God's Phallus and Other Problems for Men in Monotheism*. Boston: Beacon, 1994.

Ellermeier, Friedrich. *Qoheleth*. Herzberg: Jungfer, 1967.

Exum, J. Cheryl. *Plotted, Shot, and Painted: Cultural Representations of Biblical Women*. JSOTSup 215. Sheffield: Sheffield Academic Press, 1996.

Farmer, Kathleen. *Who Knows What is Good? A Commentary on the Books of Proverbs and Ecclesiastes*. ITC. Grand Rapids: Eerdmans, 1991.

Feldman, Shoshana. *The Literary Speech Act: Son Juan with J. L. Austin, or Seduction in Two Languages*. Translated by Catherine Porter. Ithaca, N.Y.: Cornell University Press, 1982.

Fetterly, Judith. *The Resisting Reader: A Feminist Approach to American Fiction*. Bloomington: Indiana University Press, 1978.

Fewell, Danna Nolan, ed. *Reading Between Texts: Intertextuality and the Hebrew Bible*. Louisville, Ky.: John Knox, 1992.

Fontaine, Carol R. "Ecclesiastes." Pages 153–55 in *The Women's Bible Commentary*. Edited by Carol A. Newsom and Sharon H. Ringe. Louisville, Ky.: Westminster/John Knox, 1992.

Foucault, Michel, ed. *Herculine Barbin: Being the Recently Discovered Memoirs of a Nineteenth-Century French Hermaphrodite*. New York: Pantheon, 1980.

—*The History of Sexuality: An Introduction*. New York: Vintage, 1990.

Fox, Michael V. "Frame-Narrative and Composition in the Book of Qohelet." *HUCA* 48 (1977): 83–106.

—"Aging and Death in Qohelet 12." *JSOT* 42 (1988): 55–77.

—"The Inner Structure of Qohelet's Thought." Pages 225–38 in Schoors, ed., *Qohelet in the Context of Wisdom*.

—*Qohelet and his Contradictions*. JSOTSup 71. Sheffield: Almond Press, 1989.

—*A Time to Tear Down and a Time to Build up: A Rereading of Ecclesiastes*. Grand Rapids: Eerdmans, 1999.

Fraser, Nancy, and Linda J. Nicholson. "Social Criticism without Philosophy: An Encounter between Feminism and Postmodernism." Pages 19–38 in *Feminism/Postmodernism*. Edited by Linda J. Nicholson. New York: Routledge, 1990.

Fredericks, Daniel C. *Qoheleth's Language: Re-evaluating its Nature and its Date*. Lewiston, N.Y.: Edwin Mellen, 1988.

—"Life Storms and Structural Unity in Qoheleth 11:1–12:8." *JSOT* 52 (1991): 95–114.

—*Coping with Transience: Ecclesiastes on Brevity in Life*. The Biblical Seminar 18. Sheffield: Sheffield Academic Press, 1993.

Freud, Sigmund. *Three Essays on the Theory of Sexuality*. San Francisco: HarperCollins, 1962.

Frymer-Kensky, Tikva. *In the Wake of the Goddesses: Women, Culture and the Biblical Transformation of Pagan Myth*. New York: Ballantine, 1992.

Fuss, Diana. *Essentially Speaking: Feminism, Nature, and Difference*. New York: Routledge, 1989.

Galling, K. "Stand und Aufgabe der Kohelet-Forschung." *Theologische Rundschau* 6 (1934): 355-73.

Garber, Marjorie. *Vested Interests: Cross-Dressing and Cultural Anxiety.* New York: Routledge, 1992.

Gilbert, M. "La description de la vieillesse en Qohelet XII 1–7 est-elle allégorique?." Pages 96–109 in *Congress Volume: Vienna, 1980.* Edited by J. A. Emerton. Supplements to Vetus Testamentum 32. Leiden: Brill, 1981.

Gilmore, Leigh. "The Mark of Autobiography: Postmodernism, Autobiography, and Genre." Pages 3–20 in Ashley, Gilmore, and Peters, eds., *Autobiography and Postmodernism.*

Ginsberg, H. L. *Studies in Kohelet.* New York: Jewish Theological Seminary of America, 1950.

Ginsburg, Christian David. *Coheleth.* London: Longman, 1861. Repr., New York: Ktav, 1970.

Gliserman, Martin J. *Psychoanalysis, Language, and the Body of the Text.* Gainesville: University Press of Florida, 1996.

Good, Edwin M. *Irony in the Old Testament.* Bible and Literature Series 3. Sheffield: Almond Press, 1981.

Gordis, Robert. "Canaanite-Phoenician Influence in Qoheleth." *Bib* 33 (1952): 3–52, 191–221.

—"The Original Language of Qohelet." *JQR* 37 (1946–47): 67–84.

—"The Translation Theory of Qohelet Re-examined." *JQR* 40 (1949–50): 103–16.

—"Koheleth—Hebrew or Aramaic?" *JBL* 71 (1952): 93–109.

—*Koheleth: The Man and His World.* New York: Schocken, 1951.

—*Koheleth: The Man and His World.* New York: Schocken, 1955.

—"Was Kohelet a Phoenician? Some Observations on Methods of Research." *JBL* 74 (1955): 103–14.

Gusdorf, Georges. "Conditions et limites de l'autobiographie." Pages 105–23 in *Formen der Selbstdarstellung: Analekten zu einer Geschichte des literarishen Selbstportraits.* Edited by Günter Reichenkron. Berlin: Duncker & Humblot, 1956.

Greenstein, Edward L. "Autobiographies in Ancient Western Asia." Pages 2421–32 in Sasson, ed., *Civilizations of the Ancient Near East.*

Haraway, Donna. "The Persistence of Vision." Pages 283–95 in *Writing on the Body: Female Embodiment and Feminist Theory.* Edited by Katie Conboy, Nadia Medina, and Sarah Stanbury. New York: Columbia University Press, 1997.

Hengel, Martin. *Judaism and Hellenism: Studies in their Encounter in Palestine during the Early Hellenistic Period.* Philadelphia: Fortress, 1981.

Hofstadter, Douglas. *Godel, Escher, Bach: An Eternal Golden Braid.* New York: Norton, 1979.

Isaksson, Bo. *Studies in the Language of Qoheleth: With Special Emphasis on the Verbal System.* Stockholm: Almqvist & Wiksell, 1987.

Jabès, Edmund. *The Book of Questions.* Translated by Rosmarie Waldrop. Hanover, N.H.: Wesleyan University Press, 1991.

Jefferson, Ann. "Autobiography as Intertext: Barthes, Sarraute, Robbe-Grillet." Pages 108–29 in *Intertextuality: Theories and Practices.* Edited by Michael Worton and Judith Still. New York: Manchester University Press, 1990.

Jobling, David, Tina Pippin, and Ronald Schleifer, eds. *The Postmodern Bible Reader.* Malden, Mass.: Blackwell, 2001.

Johnston, R. K. "'Confessions of a Workaholic': A Reappraisal of Qoheleth." *CBQ* 38 (1976): 14–28, 94.

Kaplan, E. Ann. "Is the Gaze Male?" Pages 309–27 in *Powers of Desire: The Politics of Sexuality.* Edited by Ann Snitow, Christine Stansell, and Sharon Thompson. New York: Monthly Review Press, 1983.

Klopfenstein, M. A. "Die Skepsis von Qoheleth." *TZ* 28 (1972): 97–109.

Kedar-Kopfstein, B. "Semantic Aspects of the Pattern *qôtel.*" *HAR* 1 (1977): 155–76.

Kitzberger, Ingrid Rosa, ed. *The Personal Voice in Biblical Interpretation.* New York: Routledge, 1999.

—*Autobiographical Biblical Criticism: Between Text and Self.* Leiden: Deo Publishing, 2002.

Koehler, Ludwig, and Walter Baumgartner. *The Hebrew and Aramaic Lexicon of the Old Testament.* Leiden: Brill, 1995.

Knierim, Rolf P. *The Task of Old Testament Theology.* Grand Rapids: Eerdmans, 1995.

Knight, Douglas A. "The Ethics of Human Life in the Hebrew Bible." Pages 65–88 in *Justice and the Holy: Essays in Honor of Walter Harrelson.* Edited by Douglas A. Knight and Peter J. Paris. Atlanta: Scholars Press, 1989.

Kroeber, R. *Der Prediger.* Berlin: Akademie, 1963.

Lacan, Jacques. "The Signification of the Phallus," Pages 281–91 in *Ecrits: A Selection.* Translated by Alan Sheridan. New York: W. W. Norton, 1977.

Laqueur, Thomas. *Making Sex: Body and Gender form the Greeks to Freud.* Cambridge, Mass.: Harvard University Press, 1990.

Lauha, Aarre. *Kohelet.* Biblischer Kommentar Altes Testament. Neukirchen–Vluyn: Neukirchener Verlag, 1978.

Leahy, Michael. "The Meaning of Ecclesiastes (12:2–5)." *ITQ* 19 (1952): 297–300.

Leitch, Vincent. *Deconstructive Criticism: An Advanced Introduction.* New York: Columbia University Press, 1983.

—*American Literary Criticism from the 30s to the 80s.* New York: Columbia University Press, 1988.

Levinson, Jon. *The Hebrew Bible, The Old Testament, and Historical Criticism.* Louisville, Ky.: Westminster/John Knox, 1993.

Liddell, Henry George. *An Intermediate Greek-English Lexicon.* New York: American Book Company, 1888.

Loader, J. A. "Qohelet 3:2–8—A 'Sonnet' in the Old Testament." *ZAW* 81 (1969): 240–42.

—*Polar Structures in the Book of Qohelet.* New York: de Gruyter, 1979.

—*Ecclesiastes: A Practical Commentary.* Grand Rapids: Eerdmans, 1986.

Lohfink, N. "War Kohelet ein Fruenfeind? Ein Versuch, die Logik und den Gegenstand von Koh. 7:23-8:1a herauszufinden." Pages 259–87 in *La Sagesse de l'Ancien Testament.* Edited by M. Gilbert. Leuven: Leuven University Press, 1979.

Longman, Tremper, III. *Fictional Akkadian Autobiography: A Generic and Comparative Study.* Winona Lake, Ind.: Eisenbrauns, 1991.

—*The Book of Ecclesiastes.* Grand Rapids: Eerdmans, 1998.

Loretz, Oswald. *Qohelet und der alte Orient: Untersuchungen zu Stil und theologischer.* Freiburg: Herder, 1964.

Lozada, Francisco, Jr. "Identity." Pages 113–19 in Adam, ed., *Handbook of Postmodern Biblical Interpretation.*

Lyotard, Jean François. *The Postmodern Condition: A Report on Knowledge.* Minneapolis: University of Minnesota Press, 1984.

MacKendrick, Karmen. *Counterpleasures.* Albany: State University of New York Press, 1999.

Martin, Dale B. *The Corinthian Body.* New Haven: Yale University Press, 1999.

Mauss, Marcel. *Sociologie et Anthropologie.* Paris: Presses Universitaires de France, 1950.

McNeile, A. H. *An Introduction to Ecclesiastes with Notes and Appendices.* Cambridge: Cambridge University Press, 1904.

Meyenfeldt, F. H. von *Het Hart (LEB, LEBAB) in Het Oude Testament.* Leiden: Brill, 1950.

Michel, Diethelm. *Untersuchungen zur Eigenart des Buches Qohelet.* New York: de Gruyter, 1989.

Miller, Douglas B. *Symbol and Rhetoric in Ecclesiastes: The Place of Hebel in Qohelet's Work.* Atlanta: Society of Biblical Literature, 2002.

Miller, J. Hillis. "Ariadne's Thread: Repetition and the Narrative Line." *Critical Inquiry* 3 (1976): 55–77.

Miller, Nancy K. *Getting Personal: Feminist Occasions and Other Autobiographical Acts.* New York: Routledge, 1991.

Moore, Stephen. "True Confessions and Weird Obsessions: Autobiographical Interventions in Literary and Biblical Studies." Pages 19–50 in Anderson and Staley, eds., *Taking it Personally.*

—*God's Gym: Divine Male Bodies of the Bible.* New York: Routledge, 1996.

—*God's Beauty Parlor: And Other Queer Spaces in and around the Bible.* Stanford, Calif.: Stanford University Press, 2001.

Muilenberg, J. "Form Criticism and Beyond." *JBL* 88 (1969): 1–18.

Mulvey, Laura. "Visual Pleasure and Narrative Cinema." *Screen* 16, no. 3 (1975): 6–18.

Muraoka, T. *Emphatic Words and Structures in Biblical Hebrew.* Jerusalem: Magnes, 1985.

Murphy, Roland. "A Form-Critical Consideration of Ecclesiastes VII." Pages 77–85 in volume 1 of the *SBL Seminar Papers, 1974.* Edited by George MacRae. Cambridge, Mass.: Society of Biblical Literature, 1974.

—*Ecclesiastes.* WBC 23A. Dallas: Word Books, 1992.

Murphy, Roland, and Elizabeth Huwiler. *Proverbs, Ecclesiastes, Song of Songs.* Peabody, Mass.: Hendrickson, 1999.

Newsom, Carol. "Job and Ecclesiastes." Pages 177–94 in *Old Testament Interpretation: Past, Present, and Future.* Edited by James Luther Mays, David L. Petersen, and Kent Harold Richards. Nashville: Abingdon, 1995.

Nietzsche, Frederick. *The Will to Power.* Translated by Walter Kaufmann and R. J. Hollingdale. New York: Vintage, 1968.

Odell-Scott, David W. "Deconstruction." Pages 55–61 in Adam, ed., *Handbook of Postmodern Biblical Interpretation.*

Olney, James. "Autobiography and the Cultural Moment: A Thematic, Historical, and Bibliographical Introduction." Pages 3–27 in *Autobiography: Essays Theoretical and Critical.* Edited by James Olney. Princeton: Princeton University Press, 1980.

Pascal, Roy. *Design and Truth in Autobiography.* London: Routledge & Paul, 1960.

Paterson, J. "The Intimate Journal of an Old-Time Humanist." *RL* 19, no. 2 (1950): 245–54.

Perdu, Olivier. "Ancient Egyptian Autobiographies." Pages 2243–54 in Sasson, ed., *Civilizations of the Ancient Near East.*

Perdue, Leo G. *Wisdom and Creation: The Theology of Wisdom Literature.* Nashville: Abingdon, 1994.

Pippin, Tina. *Apocalyptic Bodies: The Biblical End of the World in Text and Image.* New York: Routledge, 1999.

Plumptre, E. H. "The Author of Ecclesiastes." *ExpTim* 2 (1880): 401–30.

Podechard, Emmanuel. *L'ecclésiaste.* Paris: Librairie Victor Lecoffre, 1912.

Power, A. D. *Ecclesiastes or The Preacher.* New York: Longmans, Green & Co., 1952.

Raabe, P. R. "Deliberate Ambiguity in the Psalter." *JBL* 110 (1991): 213–27.

Rad, Gerhard von. *Old Testament Theology.* Translated by D. M. G. Stalker. San Francisco: HarperCollins, 1962.

—*Wisdom in Israel.* Valley Forge, Pa.: Trinity, 1972.

Renan, E. *L'Ecclesiaste traduit de l'Hébreu avec une étude sur l'age et le caractère du livre.* Paris: Levy, 1882.

Rendtorff, Rolf. *Canon and Theology: Overtures to an Old Testament Theology.* Translated by Margaret Kohl. Minneapolis: Fortress, 1993.

Robinson, H. Wheeler. *Inspiration and Revelation in the Old Testament.* Oxford: Clarendon, 1946.

Rosaldo, Michelle Zimbalist, and Louise Lamphere, eds. *Woman, Culture, Society*. Stanford, Calif.: Stanford University Press, 1974.

Roskies, David, ed. *The Literature of Destruction: Jewish Responses to Catastrophe*. Philadelphia: Jewish Publication Society of America, 1989.

Rubenstein, Richard. *After Auschwitz: Radical Theology and Contemporary Judaism*. Indianapolis: Bobbs-Merrill, 1966.

Rudman, Dominic. "Woman as Divine Agent in Ecclesiastes." *JBL* 116, no. 3 (1997): 411–27.

Sadgrove, M. "The Song as Wisdom Literature." *Studia Biblica* 1 (1978): 245–48.

Sasson, Jack, ed. *Civilizations of the Ancient Near East*. New York: Scribner, 1995.

Sawyer, J. F. A. "The Ruined House in Ecclesiastes 12: A Reconstruction of the Original Parable." *JBL* 94 (1975): 519–31.

Scarry, Elaine. *The Body in Pain: The Making and Unmaking of the World*. New York: Oxford University Press, 1985.

—*Dreaming by the Book*. Princeton: Princeton University Press, 1999.

Schoors, Antoon. "Koheleth: A Perspective of Life After Death?" *ETL* 61 (1985): 295–303.

—*The Preacher Sought to Find Pleasing Words: A Study of the Language of Qoheleth*. Leuven: Peeters Press, 1992.

—"Words Typical of Qohelet." Pages 17–39 in Schoors, ed., *Qohelet in the Context of Wisdom*.

Schoors, Antoon, ed. *Qohelet in the Context of Wisdom*. Leuven: Leuven University Press, 1998.

Scott, Joan W. "Deconstructing Equality–Versus–Difference: Or, the Uses of Poststructuralist Theory for Feminism." Pages 134–48 in *Conflicts in Feminism*. Edited by Marianne Hirsch and Evelyn Fox Keller. New York: Routledge. 1990.

Segovia, Fernando F. "Cultural Studies and Contemporary Biblical Criticism: Ideological Criticism as Mode of Discourse." Pages 1–17 in *Reading from this Place: Social Location and Biblical Interpretation in Global Perspective*, Vol. 2. Edited by Fernando F. Segovia and Mary Ann Tolbert. Minneapolis: Fortress, 1995.

Sellers, Susan, ed. *The Hélène Cixous Reader*. New York: Routledge, 1996.

Seow, Choon-Leong. "Qohelet's Autobiography." Page 257–82 in *Fortunate the Eyes that See*. Edited by A. Beck, A. H. Bartlett, P. R. Raabe, and C. A. Franke. Grand Rapids: Eerdmans, 1995.

—"Linguistic Evidence and the Dating of Qohelet." *JBL* 115, no. 4 (1996): 643–66.

—"'Beyond Them, My Son, Be Warned': The Epilogue of Qoheleth Revisited." Pages 125–41 in *Wisdom, You Are My Sister*. Edited by Michael L. Barré, SS. Washington D.C.: The Catholic Biblical Association of America, 1997.

—"Dangerous Seductress or Elusive Lover? The Woman of Ecclesiastes 7." Pages 23–33 in *Women, Gender, and Christian Community*. Edited by Jane Dempsey Douglass and James F. Kay. Louisville, Ky.: Westminster/John Knox, 1997.

—*Ecclesiastes*. Anchor Bible Commentary 18C. New York: Doubleday, 1997.

—"Theology when Everything is Out of Control." *Interpretation* 55, no. 3 (2001): 237–49.

Sherwood, Yvonne. *The Prostitute and the Prophet: Hosea's Marriage in Literary-Theoretical Perspective*. JSOTSup 212. Sheffield: Sheffield Academic Press, 1996.

—"Derrida." Pages 69–75 in Adam, ed., *Handbook of Postmodern Biblical Interpretation*.

—"'Not with a Bang but a Whimper': Shrunken Eschatologies of the Twentieth Century—and the Bible." Pages 94–116 in *Apocalyptic in History and Tradition*. Edited by Christopher Rowland and John Barton. JSPSup 43. Sheffield: Sheffield Academic Press, 2002.

—ed. *Derrida's Bible: Reading a Page of Scripture with a Little Help from Derrida*. New York: Palgrave, 2004.

Siegfried, C. *Prediger und Hoheslied.* Göttingen: Vandenhoeck & Ruprecht, 1898.

Smith, Robert. *Derrida and Autobiography.* Cambridge: Cambridge University Press, 1995.

Smith, Sidonie. "Identity's Body" Pages 266–92 in Ashley, Gilmore, and Peters, eds., *Autobiography and Postmodernism.*

Sneed, M. "The Social Location of the Book of Qoheleth." *HS* 39 (1998): 41–51.

Spangenberg, Izak J. J. "Irony in the Book of Qoheleth." *JSOT* 72 (1996): 57–69.

—"A Century of Wrestling with Qohelet: The Research History of the Book Illustrated with a Discussion of Qoh 4,17-5,6." Pages 61-92 in Schoors, ed., *Qohelet in the Context of Wisdom.*

Staley, Jeffrey L. *Reading with a Passion: Rhetoric, Autobiography, and the American West in the Gospel of John.* New York: Continuum, 1995.

—"Autobiography." Pages 14–19 in Adam, ed., *Handbook of Postmodern Biblical Interpretation.*

Stanton, Elizabeth Cady. *The Woman's Bible.* Seattle: Coalition Task Force on Women and Religion, 1990.

Staubli, Thomas, and Silvia Schroer. *Body Symbolism in the Bible.* Translated by Linda D. Maloney. Collegeville, Minn.: The Liturgical Press, 2001.

Stone, Elizabeth. "Old Man Koheleth." *JBR* 10 (1942): 98–102.

Taylor, C. *The Dirge of Coheleth in Ecclesiastes XII.* London: Williams & Norgate, 1874.

Taylor, Mark C. *Erring: A Postmodern A/theology.* Chicago: University of Chicago Press, 1984.

—*Nots.* Chicago: University of Chicago Press, 1993.

Tompkins, Jane. "Me and My Shadow." Pages 23–40 in *The Intimate Critique: Autobiographical Literary Criticism.* Edited by Diane P. Freedman, Olivia Frey, and Frances Murphy Zauhar. Durham, N.C.: Duke University Press, 1993.

—*A Life in School: What the Teacher Learned.* Reading, Mass.: Perseus Books, 1996.

Torrey, C. C. "The Question of the Original Language of Qohelet." *JQR* 39 (1948-49): 151–60.

Trible, Phyllis. *God and the Rhetoric of Sexuality.* Philadelphia: Fortress, 1978.

Ulmer, Rivka. *The Evil Eye in the Bible and Rabbinical Literature.* Hoboken, N.J.: Ktav, 1994.

Veeser, H. Aram, ed. *Confessions of the Critics.* New York: Routledge, 1996.

Vriezen, Theodorus C. *An Outline of Old Testament Theology.* Translated by S. Neuijen. Oxford: Blackwell. 1970.

Walsh, Carey Ellen. *Exquisite Desire: Religion, the Erotic, and the Song of Songs.* Minneapolis: Fortress, 2000.

Welton, Donn, ed. *Body and Flesh: A Philosophical Reader.* Malden, Mass.: Blackwell, 1998.

Whitley, Charles F. *Koheleth: His Language and Thought.* New York: de Gruyter, 1979.

Whybray, R. N. *Two Jewish Theologies: Job and Ecclesiastes.* Hull: University of Hull, 1980.

—"Qoheleth, Preacher of Joy." *JSOT* 23 (1982): 87–98.

—"Old Testament Theology—A Non-Existent Beast?" Pages 168–80 in *Scripture: Meaning and Method.* Edited by Barry P. Thompson. Hull: Hull University Press, 1987.

—"Ecclesiastes 1:5–7 and the Wonders of Nature." *JSOT* 41 (1988): 108–10.

—*Ecclesiastes.* OTG. Sheffield: Sheffield Academic Press, 1989.

—"Qoheleth as a Theologian." Pages 239–65 in Schoors, ed., *Qohelet in the Context of Wisdom.*

—"'A Time to be Born and a Time To Die'? Some Observations of Ecclesiastes 3:2–8." Pages 469–83 in *Near Eastern Studies Dedicated to H.I.M. Prince Takahito Mikasa on the Occasion of his Seventy-fifth Birthday.* Edited by M. Mori. Wiesbaden: Harrassowitz, 1991.

Wiesel, Elie. *The Gates of the Forest.* New York: Schocken, 1966.

—*Legends of Our Time.* New York: Schocken, 1968.

Wilson, Lindsay. "Artful Ambiguity in Ecclesiastes 1,1–11." Pages 357–65 in Schoors, ed., *Qohelet in the Context of Wisdom.*

Witzenrath, Hagia H. *Süss ist das Licht . . . Eine literaturwissenschaftliche Untersuchung zu Koh 11,7–12,7.* St. Ottilien: EOS, 1979.

Wittgenstein, Ludwig. *Philosophical Investigations.* Oxford: ETG Anscombe, 1958.

Wittig, Monique. "The Mark of Gender." *Feminist Issues* 5, no. 2 (1985): 63–73.

Wolff, Hans Walter. *Anthropology of the Old Testament.* Philadelphia: Fortress, 1974.

Wright, Addison G. "The Riddle of the Sphinx: The Structure of the Book of Qoheleth." *CBQ* 30 (1968): 313–34.

—"The Riddle of the Sphinx Revisited: Numerical Patterns in the Book of Qoheleth." *CBQ* 42 (1980): 38–51.

—"For Everything there is a Season: The Structure and Meaning of the Fourteen Opposites (Ecclesiastes 3:2–8)." Pages 321–28 in *De la Torah au Messie: Mélanges Henri Cazelles.* Edited by J. Doré, M. Carrez, and P. Grelot. Paris: Gabalda, 1981.

Zimmermann, Frank. "The Aramaic Provenance of Qohelet." *JQR* 36 (1945–46): 17–45.

—"The Question of Hebrew in Qohelet." *JQR* 40 (1949–50): 79–102.

—*The Inner World of Qohelet.* New York: Ktav, 1973.

INDEXES

INDEX OF REFERENCES

INDEX OF AUTHORS